Essentials of the Laws of the Belt and Road Countries

Bangladesh, Pakistan, Sri Lanka

Edited by

Guiguo WANG

Alan Yuk-Lun LEE

Priscilla Mei-Fun LEUNG

ZHEJIANG UNIVERSITY PRESS
浙江大学出版社

图书在版编目(CIP)数据

"一带一路"沿线国法律精要 = Essentials of the Laws
of the Belt and Road Countries. 孟加拉、巴基斯坦、斯里兰
卡卷:英文/王贵国,李鋆麟,梁美芬主编. —杭州:浙江大
学出版社,2017.12(2018.9重印)
  ISBN 978-7-308-17226-4

  Ⅰ.①一… Ⅱ.①王…②李…③梁… Ⅲ.①法律 –
研究 – 孟加拉 – 英文②法律 – 研究 – 巴基斯坦 – 英文③
法律 – 研究 – 斯里兰卡 – 英文 Ⅳ.①D910.4

  中国版本图书馆 CIP 数据核字(2017)第 187279 号

"一带一路"沿线国法律精要:孟加拉、巴基斯坦、斯里兰卡卷(英文版)
Essentials of the Laws of the Belt and Road Countries:Bangladesh,Pakistan,Sri Lanka
王贵国　李鋆麟　梁美芬　主编

出 品 人	鲁东明
总 编 辑	袁亚春
丛书主持	陈佩钰　张　琛
责任编辑	陈佩钰(yukin_chen@zju.edu.cn)
文字编辑	祁　潇
责任校对	黄静芬
封面设计	城色设计
出版发行	浙江大学出版社
	(杭州市天目山路 148 号　邮政编码 310007)
	(网址:http://www.zjupress.com)
排　　版	浙江时代出版服务有限公司
印　　刷	虎彩印艺股份有限公司
开　　本	710mm×1000mm　1/16
印　　张	19.75
字　　数	475 千
版 印 次	2017 年 12 月第 1 版　2018 年 9 月第 2 次印刷
书　　号	ISBN 978-7-308-17226-4
定　　价	88.00 元

Introduction to the International Academy of the Belt and Road

Founded in January 2016, the International Academy of the Belt and Road (IABR) is the first research institution concerning the Belt and Road Initiative in Hong Kong, China, and is committed to setting up an international platform for academic and professional communication. Experts of countries along the Belt and Road from various areas, such as law, economics, finance, investment, politics and international relations, are invited to share their views and conduct research on relevant issues in the implementation of the Belt and Road Initiative. The IABR has held several international forums on the Belt and Road, and compiled Essentials of the Laws of the Belt and Road Countries series and *Dispute Resolution Mechanism for the Belt and Road Initiative*. The IABR aims at providing expert services to corporations and institutions involved in the Belt and Road Initiative.

Professor Guiguo Wang serves as the President of the Academy, while Dr Alan Yuk-Lun Lee and Dr Priscilla Mei-Fun Leung serve as Vice Presidents. The IABR has an International Advisory Board with 26 experts and scholars, 42 fellows and 7 associate fellows from all over the world. The IABR endeavours to contribute to education and training of specialists so that Hong Kong could take full advantage of its unique position to develop international economy and keep world peace.

Preface

The Belt and Road ("B & R") Initiative, since it was officially announced by the Chinese Government in 2013, has generated much excitement not only within China but also internationally. The "Belt" refers to a transnational economic cooperation initiative among the countries along the ancient Silk Road from central China to central Asia and then to Western Europe with Amsterdam as the finishing point—the "Silk Road Economic Belt"; the "Road" indicates an economic cooperation initiative among countries along a new maritime Silk Road from China, Southeast Asia, India, Sri Lanka, Yemen, Egypt, Greece, Italy to the Netherlands (Amsterdam)—the "21st-Century Maritime Silk Road". As such, the B & R Initiative mainly focuses on the connectivity and cooperation among countries in Eurasia and some African countries. The National Development and Reform Commission, Ministry of Foreign Affairs and Ministry of Commerce of China with the authorisation of the State Council of China released the official document "Vision and Actions on Jointly Building Silk Road Economic Belt and 21st-Century Maritime Silk Road" in March 2015, which outlines the direction and rough contents of the B & R Initiative. An official B & R Initiative website was launched in March 2017. Yet, none of these official documentations indicates what specific countries are covered under the B & R Initiative, which implies that the B & R Initiative is an open-ended concept. Having said that, it is clear that the B & R Initiative aims at promoting economic cooperation among the countries concerned. It is equally clear that with or without a precise coverage, the B & R Initiative includes a large number of countries with different cultures, history, traditions, religions, and political and legal systems.

By its nature, implementation of the B & R Initiative involves cross-border movement of people, goods and services, capital and technology, a process which unavoidably entails interactions among the concerned countries. What norms should be observed in transacting business in these countries? Do as the Romans do, according to Western culture. As for the traditional Chinese culture such as the *Book of Rites* (*Liji Quli I*), "When crossing the boundaries (of a state), one should ask what its prohibitory norms are; having fairly entered it, one should ask about its customs; before entering a house, one should ask about the names to be avoided whilst in it. " Knowing the prohibitory norms, customs and names to be avoided of each country along the B & R is of utmost importance for the successful implementation of the initiative. It is precisely for this reason that this book series— Essentials of the Laws of the Belt and Road Countries—has been prepared.

This book series had its origin in a workshop that was held by the International Academy of the Belt and Road in Hong Kong, where some of its authors were present. The consensus of the workshop was that mutual understanding among the B & R countries over their legal traditions, constitutional and governance frameworks, laws on trade transactions and other immediately relevant areas such as financial regulation, employment law and environmental law was crucially important for implementing the B & R Initiative. It is only through a proper understanding of commonalities and differences between these nations that we could develop a meaningful framework for carrying out the related trade, investment and other activities.

The authors were provided with terms of reference for the chapter construction. Each country study would begin with an overview of its legal system relating to cross-border commercial transactions. The substantive parts of each chapter deal with customs system, foreign trade law, law on foreign direct investment, monetary and banking law, laws relating to construction of infrastructure, labour management and treatment, environment and dispute resolution—both judicial and non-judicial (ADR).

It is also part of the terms of reference that the authors should focus not only on the black letters of the laws but also on how these laws in fact operate in the market place. The authors were given a fair amount of leeway in examining each of these aspects in order that they could highlight those areas where their own nations would have a particular interest. The result is a happy blend of not only different writing styles but also different aspects of law in action.

A distinctive feature of this highly globalised world is coexistence of multilateral and bilateral economic cooperative schemes. As a result, trade and investment barriers have been removed or reduced with the development of both multilateral and bilateral cooperative programmes. These schemes not only regulate trade, investment and finance and banking at the international level but also directly impact on law-making and law enforcement at the national level. For this reason, we decided to have chapters devoted to two such associations—the European Union (EU) and the Association of Southeast Asian Nations (ASEAN). These chapters provide support to the study of countries belonging to these associations and explain the interrelations that exist in terms of laws and legal processes between the central authorities and member states. A study of how EU and ASEAN authorities guide, coordinate and encourage a unified legal order for the promotion of trade and economic cooperation is also critical to the B & R Initiative which can learn from relative successes and lessons of the existing regional organisations.

When the B & R Initiative was first introduced, the United States and Japan were not among the B & R countries. Yet, as they are important countries for international economic cooperation, the B & R Initiative is an open concept and there are signs that the two countries may eventually take part in the B & R Initiative, we decided to include them in this book series.

We believe that, by providing an overview of the laws and legal structures that shape business relationships of the countries along the B & R, this book series will contribute in a meaningful way to the implementation of the B & R Initiative.

Guiguo WANG
Alan Yuk-Lun LEE
Priscilla Mei-Fun LEUNG

18 April 2017

About the Editors

Guiguo Wang is University Professor and Scholar of "1000 Talents", Zhejiang University, in Hangzhou, China; Eason-Weinmann Chair of International and Comparative Law, School of Law, Tulane University, in New Orleans, USA; President of the International Academy of the Belt and Road, in Hong Kong, China; Chairman of the Hong Kong WTO Research Institute; Chairman of the National Committee (Hong Kong, China) and Titular Member of the International Academy of Comparative Law; former Dean of School of Law, City University of Hong Kong, in Hong Kong, China and former Director of the Centre for Judicial Education and Research, City University of Hong Kong, in Hong Kong, China; and Vice President of the Chinese Society of International Economic Law.

Professor Wang has an arbitration experience for more than 20 years. He is now President of Hangzhou International Arbitration Court and is an arbitrator of China International Economic and Trade Arbitration Commission, Beijing Arbitration Commission, Hong Kong International Arbitration Centre, Panel of Arbitrators of Korean Commercial Arbitration Board and Chinese Arbitration Association of Taiwan, China.

Professor Wang, holder of the JSD degree from Yale Law School and LLM degree from Columbia Law School, is the first person from the Chinese mainland to obtain the JSD degree from Yale Law School since 1949. Having obtained the JSD degree from Yale, he worked in several world-renowned law firms in countries and regions such as the United States, Canada and Hong Kong of China.

Professor Wang used to be an official at the Department of Law and Treaties, Ministry of Foreign Affairs of China. At the recommendation of the Ministry of Foreign Affairs, he became the first Chinese recipient of the United Nations Institute for Training and Research fellowship which enabled him to participate in the seminars offered by the International Court of Justice and to study at The Hague Academy of International Law, the United Nations and the World Bank in 1980.

In the summer of 2010, Professor Wang served as a special lecturer at The Hague Academy of International Law and gave a series of lectures on "Radiating Impact of WTO on Its Members' Legal System: The Chinese Perspective".

Professor Wang has published more than 20 books and over 100 journal articles in established journals in China and other countries. His *Legal Order of International Trade* published by the Law Press in 1987 is one of the earliest treatises on the GATT. Professor Wang's main works include: *Sino-American Economic Exchanges: The Legal Contributions* (1984); *International Banking and Financial Law* (1988); *Contemporary Legal Prescriptions for International Investment* (1988); *China's Investment Law: The New Directions* (1988); *International Economic Law* (1992); *Wang's Business Law of China* (4th ed., 2003); *The Law of the WTO* (2003); *International Trade Law* (2004); *The Law of the WTO: China and the Future of Free Trade* (2005); *International Monetary and Financial Law* (3rd ed., 2007); *International Investment Law* (2nd ed., 2008); "Radiating Impact of WTO on Its Members' Legal System: The Chinese Perspective", *Collected Courses of The Hague Academy of International Law*, vol. 349 (2010); *International Investment Law: A Chinese Perspective* (in English) (2015); *International Law Perspective of the Belt and Road Initiative* (co-ed.) (2016); *Dispute Resolution Mechanism for the Belt and Road Initiative* (co-ed.) (2017).

Dr Yuk-Lun Lee is a Justice of the Peace. He graduated from Lincoln University, USA in 2009 with an honorary doctorate of Management, and was elected as the academician of Canadian Chartered Institute of Business Administration (CCIBA). In 2014, he obtained his Master of Business Administration at the University of Wales Newport, UK. Now, Dr Lee is studying for the collaborative PhD degree programme with Fudan University (APRU) and Stanford University.

Dr Lee is also keen on charity affairs, and is Chairman (2017/2018) of Tung Wah Group of Hospitals, Founding Chairman of Phoenix Charitable Foundation, Honorary Permanent President of Hong Kong Commerce and Industry Associations, China. He also serves as Chairman of Pico Zeman Asset Management Limited and Volk Favor Food Company Limited, Vice President of the International Academy of the Belt and Road, committee member of All-China Federation of Returned Overseas Chinese, committee member of CPPCC Beijing Committee, Director of China Overseas Friendship Association and member of Board of New Asia College of the Chinese University of Hong Kong, China.

Dr Priscilla Mei-Fun Leung has taught at the School of Law, City University of Hong Kong for 24 years and is specialised in Chinese Law, Hong Kong Basic Law and conflicts of law amongst the Chinese mainland, Hong Kong and Taiwan.

Dr Leung is the Chairman of the Judicial and Legal Affairs Committee of the Legislative Council in Hong Kong. She is Associate Professor at the School of Law, City University of Hong Kong; Barrister-at-Law; and Arbitrator (CIETAC). She received the Ten Outstanding Young Persons Award of the Year 2000.

Dr Leung has published different articles and books on the above areas both in English and Chinese, including the China Law Reports series (in English), the China International Economic and Trade Arbitration Commission Awards series (in English) and *Hong Kong Basic Law: Hybrid of Chinese Law and Common Law* (published in 2007 in English). Her publications also include *Comparative Studies of Family Law between Chinese Mainland, Taiwan and Hong Kong* published by the Joint Publishing House in June 2003 (in Chinese) and *Legal Reform of China* (co-ed.) in 1994.

Contents

Bangladesh

Writing Group led by Professor Farhana Helal Mehtab

About the Authors

Ms Farhana Helal Mehtab is an associate professor and head at the Department of Law, Daffodil International University, Bangladesh. She penned the book *An Introduction to ADR Mechanism: Bangladesh Perspective*. She received collaboration training on Arbitration, "Training of Trainers in Arbitration" (ToT) from Bangladesh International Arbitration Centre (BIAC) and International Law Institute (ILI) Washington, D. C. and was honoured as the first trainer on arbitration in June, 2013. Farhana Helal Mehtab focuses mainly on teaching and conducting research works on different legal and educational issues with social implications. Since Ms Mehtab's area of specialization is "Human Rights Law", she raises her voice in international forums so that human rights impacts are reflected in the arbitration process. In 2015, she presented her work on "Arbitration: Bangladesh Perspective" at the 7th International Conference on the New Haven School of Jurisprudence, in Hangzhou, China.

Mr Md. Abu Saleh is a lecturer at the Department of Law in Daffodil International University, Bangladesh. He is also an advocate before Dhaka Judge Court. He completed LLM in International Law from South Asian University, New Delhi, India and prior to that he pursued LLB and LLM from University of Dhaka, Bangladesh.

Mr Riad Mahmud is currently working as a lecturer at the Department of Law of Daffodil International University, Bangladesh. Previously he worked at Justice for All of USAID and also worked as a researcher at Bangladesh Institute of Labour Studies. He completed his LLB and LLM from Department of Law, University of Dhaka.

Introduction

South Asia consists of Bangladesh, India, Pakistan, Sri Lanka, Bhutan, Nepal and Maldives. Of these countries Bangladesh, Bhutan and Nepal are the least developed countries (LDCs) ,[1] the rest being developing countries. All the South Asian countries except Sri Lanka were, at one point of time, amongst the least open among the world economies.[2] South Asian countries in the post-independence period followed the policy of import-substituting industrialisation, extreme public sector planning and regulation which proved to be unsuccessful in stimulating the industrial sector and attracting foreign investment while simultaneously creating an inefficient and protected manufacturing sector, and a huge public sector.[3] Accordingly the policies of the South Asian economies towards investment were restrictive. Initially foreign direct investment was allowed only in a restrictive manner and on mutually advantageous terms with the majority stake held by the domestic firms.[4]

During 1990s, Bangladesh along with other South Asian countries reformed their economic policies leading to integration of their economies with the world economy. Such reforms were brought because of a number of reasons, growing fiscal imbalances, serious balance of payment problems, severe depletion of foreign reserves etc. Also the success of the East Asian countries under their open and export oriented regime, led to crystallisation of the belief that inward looking strategy was not yielding results and reforms were required.[5] As a part of this reform process, recognising the need of foreign capital to induce growth, Bangladesh started aggressively negotiating bilateral investment treaties and free trade agreements when

---

[1]　UN List of Least Developed Countries, http://www. un. org/en/development/desa/policy/cdp/ldc/ldc_list. pdf, accessed on 30 April 2016.

[2]　Jayatilleke S. Bandara and Marc McGillivray, "Trade Policy Reforms in South Asia" , (1998) Vol 21, Issue 7, *World Economy*, pp. 851 – 995, 851; Pravakar Sahoo, Geethanjali Nataraj and Ranjan kumar Dash, *Foreign Direct Investment in South Asia; Policy, Impact, Determinants and Challenges*, Springer, 2014, pp. 7 – 8.

[3]　Bandara and McGillivray, ibid, p. 883.

[4]　Ibid.

[5]　Ibid, pp. 884 – 885.

the country became a member of WTO as well. [1]

Bangladesh, characterised by a high population density, a low resource base and recurrent natural disasters and persistent socio-political instability, has traversed a long way since its creation in 1971. [2] Initially, after independence, Bangladesh was following a "state controlled" model of economy, which was abandoned and indeed reversed with the change in the political regime in 1975, followed by the policies of deregulation and liberalization to create an open and private sector led economy along with a liberal trade regime. [3] However, these initial reform efforts did not have either a clear direction or a broad time frame for implementation. This phase of muddling through lasted for about a decade. [4]

The period covering most of the 1980s, had several characteristics including slow and fluctuating economic growth, deteriorating macroeconomic stability with growing fiscal crisis, authoritarianism of governance including institutionalization of corruption and the rise of crony capitalism, etc. [5] In 1980, the Government enacted the Foreign Private Investment(Promotion and Protection) Act which contains provision relating to protection and equitable treatment, indemnification, expropriation and nationalization, repatriation of investment, etc. [6] And it was only in the 1980s that Bangladesh started signing IIAs and FTAs. After 1991 even more significant reforms were made which included progress on tariff reforms, reformation of import clearance procedure and movement towards a uniform tariff structure. [7] Recognizing the role of foreign investment in its comprehensive Industrial Policy of 1999, the Government of Bangladesh recognised the importance of " promoting private sector to lead the growth of industrial production and investment" and "attracting foreign direct investment in both export and domestic market oriented industries to make up for the

---

[1]   Bandara and McGillivray, ibid, pp. 884-885.

[2]   Mustafa K Mujeri, " Changes in Policy Framework and Total Factor Productivity Growth in Bangladesh" , 2004 30(3/4), *Bangladesh Development Studies*, pp. 1 – 29. http://www. bids. org. bd/bds/XXX _3&4. pdf, accessed 30 April 2016.

[3]   Ibid, p. 9.

[4]   Nurun N Rehman, " Policy Reforms and Trade Liberalization in Bangladesh" , p. 107. http://www. unctad. info/upload/TAB/docs/TechCooperation/bangladesh_study. pdf, accessed 30 April 2016.

[5]   Ibid.

[6]   Foreign Investment in Bangladesh, http://www. sdnbd. org/sdi/statisticapocketbook/Chap01/0114. htm, accessed 30 April 2016.

[7]   Bandara and McGillivray(n 2)886.

deficient domestic investment resources, and to acquire evolving technology and gain access to export markets. "①

Bangladesh, an original member of the WTO, grants at least MFN (most favored nation) treatment to all its trading partners and receives the special and differential treatment provided for in the WTO agreements. Since joining the WTO, the Government has undertaken a number of bold steps, which include liberalisation of the trade and foreign investment regime, strengthening the financial sectors and regulatory framework, closing and privatising some loss-making state-owned enterprises and taking steps to improve the governance. ② Bangladesh continued to participate actively in the work of the WTO, serving twice as the coordinator of the LDC Group in Geneva in 2007 and 2011, and advocating issues of interest to LDCs, including greater market access, increased flexibility in the development of multilateral trade rules as well as targeted assistance to trade infrastructure.

Since embracing a liberal trade policy during the 1990s, Bangladesh began reforming and enacting laws in different areas covering standards and accreditation, customs system, rules of origin, anti-dumping and countervailing measure, TBT (technical barriers to trade), SPS (sanitary and phy to sanitary), government procurement, intellectual property rights, economic zones, money laundering, insurance, tourism, telecommunications, competition, expropriation and compensation, labour management, environmental law. Moreover, to attract foreign investors and to facilitate international trade, Bangladesh has entered into many trade and investment agreements. The country provides investors or foreign traders friendly dispute settlement mechanism to resolve disputes arising out of international trade of foreign investment.

As the country embraced open and liberal trade policy to promote its economy, the Government felt it necessary to transform the temporary Law Commission into a permanent statutory body. Steps were taken and the Law Commission Act of 1996 (Act No XIX of 1996) was promulgated on 9 September 1996. ③ Under the auspices of the commission, the Government has adjusted and is continuing to adjust its laws,

---

① Foreign Investment in Bangladesh, http://www. sdnbd. org/sdi/statisticapocketbook/Chap01/0114. htm, accessed 30 April 2016.

② Nasiruddin Ahmed, *Trade Liberalization in Bangladesh: An Investigation into Trends* (2001), pp. 46 – 54; Bangladesh: Key Challenges for the Next Millennium, World Bank (1999).

③ Earlier there was a number of temporary law reform commission worked to meet specific areas of reforms. Permanent Law Commission was established by the Law Commission Act, 1996 (Act No. XIX of 1996).

regulations, and rules governing such areas as international trade, foreign investment, intellectual property protection and customs inspection, as well as arbitration and dispute resolutions as per the directions of the law commission. Although there are no specific directives to meet the international standard while drafting laws, over the years it has been observed that most of the times the law commission has given due consideration to the country's compliance with international standards while drafting any law. Section 6 (b) of the Law Commission Act may be utilised to justify reforming the law in line with international standards that promote a free market economy. Section 6(b) of the Act provides that the Commission will act

"(b) Keeping in mind the attraction of domestic and foreign investment and necessity of free market economy—

(1) to recommend amendment of relevant laws including company law or legislation of new law in appropriate cases in order to create competitive atmosphere in the field of trade and industry and to avoid monopoly;

(2) to recommend, after examination, measures with regard to relevant laws especially copyright, trademarks, patents, arbitration, contract, registration and similar other matters;

(3) to recommend necessary measures for the establishment of separate courts for disposal of cases arising out of commercial and bank loan matters. . . ".

It is clear that Law Commission has a wide mandate to recommend amendment of laws to make the legal system ready to take maximum benefit of a free economy.

Against this backdrop, this report endeavours to explain the existing institutional and legal framework of Bangladesh that addresses above mentioned issues, supporting a comparative study under the Belt and Road Initiative. This report is divided into eight chapters: Chapter 1 seeks to demonstrate the laws of Bangladesh relating to customs system; Chapter 2 deals with laws of Bangladesh relating to foreign trade system; Chapter 3 highlights laws regulating foreign direct investment in Bangladesh; Chapter 4 underlines monetary and banking laws of Bangladesh; Chapter 5 provides a brief study of laws relating to construction and infrastructure in Bangladesh; Chapter 6 offers an explanation of labour management and treatment laws in Bangladesh; Chapter 7 deals with environmental laws of Bangladesh; the last chapter looks at laws of Bangladesh relating to dispute settlement mechanism involving foreign investors before drawing a conclusion.

Chapter 1   Customs System and Laws of Bangladesh

1.1   Customs laws and procedures

The principle Act regulating customs procedure in Bangladesh is the Customs Act 1969, and the Act was amended several times after its adoption. It is pertinent to mention that Bangladesh is a founding member state of WTO and the organisation adopted Customs Valuation Agreement in 1995 as part of WTO multilateral agreements which is known as the Agreement on Implementation of Article Ⅶ of the General Agreement on Tariffs and Trade 1994.

The WTO Agreement on Customs Valuation aims for a fair, uniform and neutral system for the valuation of goods for customs purposes — a system that conforms to commercial realities, and which outlaws the use of arbitrary or fictitious customs values. The Committee on Customs Valuation of the Council for Trade in Goods (CTG) carries out work in the WTO on customs valuation.

Bangladesh adopted the WTO Agreement on Customs Valuation in February 2000, as scheduled. ① Section 25 of the Customs Act 1969 was amended to reflect this change. ② The Customs Act 1969 was also amended in 2001 in line with the Revised Kyoto Convention in order to harmonise customs procedures. Risk-based clearance has been introduced on a limited scale in customs houses through green, yellow and red channels. In particular, customs clearance of passenger baggage in airports has been simplified, and more than 95 percent of passengers pass through the green channel without any intervention and delays by customs. In addition to that, Bangladesh Customs works under the umbrella of the National Board of Revenue (NBR), the apex body for direct and indirect tax revenue in Bangladesh and is part of the Internal Resources Division(IRD) under the Ministry of Finance. The customs

---

① In May 1995, Bangladesh notified the WTO of its decision to delay application of the provisions of WTO Agreement on Customs Valuation.

② Notification No. 57-Law/2000/1821/Customs, 23 February 2000.

wing of the NBR formulates policy concerning levy and collection of customs duty and customs-related taxes/charges, and administration.

Since the beginning of the 1990s Bangladesh emphasised on the simplified process for both export and import and the current Export Policy Order 2012 – 2015 and Import Policy Order 2012 – 2015 and 2015 – 2018 endeavoured to remove all possible barriers to international trade. NBR is performing a key role in modernising customs procedures of Bangladesh mainly to introduce speedy customs clearance through automation of the process; ensure transparency in the customs clearance process as well as in revenue collection activities; and extend the maximum possible facilities to the trade communities. Significant progress in computerisation of customs procedures has been made in recent times. The latest version of ASYCUDA, i. e. ASYCUDA + + , has been put in place in Dhaka Customs House, Chittagong Customs House (CCH), Benapole Customs House, Mongla Customs House and the Export Processing Zone.

In countries like Bangladesh, regulatory issues and preparation of documents occupy most of the time for trading, while lack of infrastructure and operational inefficiency keeps the system weak. As per the World Bank Doing Business (DB) report 2016[①] a trader in Bangladesh required 35 days for import and 25 days for export costing USD 1,470 and USD 1,075 respectively whereas the East Asian average is 22 days (USD 884) and 21 days (USD 856) respectively.

Reducing the time and cost are important to ensure economic growth in Bangladesh since an extra day in the trading process can reduce exports by at least 1.0 percent (OECD & WTO) and a 10 percent reduction in export time is expected to result in 5.8 percent increase in exports for South Asian countries. According to UNCTAD, for a country's GDP (gross domestic product) to grow by 2 – 5 percent, trade needs to grow by 7 – 12 percent. If all countries reduced supply chain barriers halfway to global best practice (like Singapore), global GDP could increase by 4.7 percent or USD 2.6 trillion and world trade by 14.5 percent or USD 1.6 trillion, far outweighing the benefits from the elimination of all import tariffs (WEF).

The first ever Time Release Studies (in FY14) by the National Board of Revenue on Chittagong, the largest seaport and on Benapole, the largest land port of

---

① See http://www. doingbusiness. org/ ~ /media/GIAWB/Doing%20Business/Documents/Annual-Reports/English/DB16-Full-Report. pdf.

Bangladesh, reveals that: In Chittagong, it takes about 11 days 9 hours and 45 minutes from arrival of vessel to release of goods, i. e. import, and 4 days 22 hours and 38 minutes from arrival of cargo to release of goods, i. e. , export. In Benapole, it takes about 5 days 18 hours 24 minutes for import on an average and 4 days 5 hours 26 minutes for export. A further analysis on Chittagong port, which deals with around 92 percent of the merchandise trade in Bangladesh, reflects that customs clearance takes reasonably short time (around five days for import and less than half a day for export). The remaining time is spent for "other government agencies" including port, food safety and standards, plant quarantine and other certifying authorities. The small traders suffer the most from such bottlenecks.

Over the last decade, measures have been taken to simplify import and export procedures by reducing the number of signatures needed for clearance of consignments and frequency of inspection of the goods being traded. While 25 signatures were required for clearance of import and export consignments in 1999, in 2002 the number was reduced to five and customs is trying to further reduce the procedure and release time by automation. Since 2002, customs officials physically inspect only 10 percent of import consignments, before which date 100 percent were inspected. As a result of the introduction of automation, the average processing time for clearance of goods from customs has been reduced to one day for about 70 percent of consignments for import and three to four hours or less for export. It may be noted here that apart from a very small number of entrepreneurs, almost all the exporters and importers rely on clearing and forwarding agents (CFAs) to deal with customs clearance. The Customs Act has been modified to reduce the discretionary powers of officials and tariff rationalization, and HS code simplification at the 8-digit level, which have helped to reduce misdeclaration.

With the introduction of PSI physical inspection of consignments have been reduced from 100 percent in 1999 to around 10 percent now. Numbers of pre-clearance signatures have gone down to five from 25 and export clearance times for 95 percent of consignments have been reduced from 72 hours in 1999 to three hours now. Bangladesh has also appointed Tax Ombudsman to facilitate good governance in Tax & Tariff measures.

The Bangladesh Land Port Authority signed agreements with four private operators, awarding them rights to operate four land ports (Hilli, Sona Masjid, Banglabandha and Bibir Bazar) under build-own-operate system. Signing of four agreements was part of handing over 12 of the country's 13 land ports to private operators under the BOT system. According to the agreements, the operators will develop necessary infrastructures at the respective land ports and will provide logistic facilities for the importers, sharing a portion of the revenue earned through selling such services to the port users.

Documents generally required in Bangladesh for importation comprise: bill of lading, cargo release order, certificate of origin, commercial invoice, customs import declaration, packing list. The import process is mostly automated for the four major customs houses in the country that cover 90 percent of import cargo, with some degrees of manual processing at the rest.

Bangladesh has adopted a Strategic Development Plan (SDP) and initiated the Modernization and Automation Project (MAP) of National Board of Revenue envisaging greater transparency and accountability from both tax payers & officials. The strategies are: strengthening organisational structure, improving human resource management, strengthening the legal and regulatory framework and effectiveness of the Large Taxpayers Units (LTU), national implementation of tax administration functions/procedures, customs modernization and trade facilitation and computerisation of the NBR.

In a rapidly modernizing and globalising world, connectivity is the key to more regional trade and cooperation. Bangladesh enjoys a strategic geographical location and can be the bridge between South Asia and South East Asia. It can be the regional hub of transportation for eastern India, North East India, Nepal, Bhutan and ASEAN countries, if it can capitalise its location advantages.

1. 2   WTO Trade Facilitation Agreement and Bangladesh

On 7 December 2013 at the Bali Ministerial Conference, the 159 WTO member countries approved the Trade Facilitation Agreement (TFA), the first new WTO multilateral agreement since the establishment of the WTO in 1995. After more than nine years of negotiations, WTO members finally reached consensus on a Trade Facilitation Agreement. [1] The Trade Facilitation Agreement is a major accomplishment for the international trading community, a significant milestone for

---

[1]   Trade Facilitation, the WTO website, available at http://www. wto. org/english/tratop_e/tradfa_e/ tradfa_e. htm, accessed 8 Feb 2016.

the WTO, and stands to regulate an area of trade that until now has been largely ignored. The Trade Facilitation Agreement has addressed developing country concerns in considerable detail, using novel measures to empower developing countries in their implementation of TFA measures. Turning to the text of the TFA, Section II of the two-part Agreement contains the special and differential treatment provisions. Over the various drafts, the TFA has evolved from only perfunctorily addressing the genuine concerns of developing country members to recognizing the need to provide structured and mandated support in relation to capacity building and implementation of trade facilitation rules by means of conditional obligations which will only become mandatory when or if certain conditions are met. Developed country members, acting as donors, agree to help developing and least developed country members by providing assistance and support for capacity building, including promotion of regional and sub-regional integration. [1] With regards to least developed countries, targeted assistance and support is to be provided by the donors. [2] In addition, many of the amended provisions involve lengthening the time available to developing and least developed member countries to implement various provisions relating to trade facilitation. The implementation of the TFA has the potential to increase global merchandise exports by up to USD 1 trillion a year, according to WTO's flagship World Trade Report (WTR) released on October 26 in Geneva. The report said developing countries will benefit significantly from the TFA, capturing more than half of the available gains.

If the TFA is implemented properly, export from the developing countries is estimated to increase between USD 170 billion and USD 730 billion, and developed economies' exports to increase between USD 310 billion and USD 580 billion in a year, according to the WTR. Fuller and faster implementation of the TFA will also increase overall world export growth by up to 2.7 percent and global GDP growth by 0.5 percent, the report added. The TFA is expected to help developing countries diversify their exports, the WTR said.

Bangladesh will soon ratify the Trade Facilitation Agreement of the World Trade Organisation as more than 50 nations have already approved the deal to simplify their

---

① TFA, Section II, Article 21.1, Article 21.3.
② TFA, Section II, Article 21.2.

trade rules. ① National Board of Revenue has formed a 19 members committee under the chairmanship of Member (Customs) comprising officials/representatives of relevant ministries/ departments / trade bodies. In order to achieve the goal of TFA, the committee was given responsibility to lead the implementation of the TFA and also to undertake appropriate means to improve trading environment in Bangladesh. This committee is working as a forum for the concerned stakeholders to develop new ideas and to raise issues regarding trade facilitation.

Bangladesh has already undertaken step to reform the existing customs laws of the country to comply with WTO standard under TFA 2013. The draft of new Customs Act 2014 has been approved by the Cabinet and will soon be placed in National Parliament for approval.

With assistance from development partners, a number of reform initiatives have been undertaken such as SASEC Trade and Transport facilitation.

The government of Bangladesh and development partners have already initiated a number of significant reforms which are consistent with TFA objectives. Some key initiatives include: introduction of ASYCUDA World in a number of customs stations, electronic data exchange between Chittagong port and Customs, initial approval of the Cabinet on the draft new Customs Act 2014 setting the legal foundation for border modernisation and related TFA reforms, proposed connectivity between customs and banks, introduction of an electronic payment of customs duties and taxes and rolling out of a National Trade Portal initiative by the Ministry of Commerce. Apart from customs reforms, Bangladesh Standards and Testing Institute (BSTI) and Plant Quarantine Wing have taken up initiatives for automation, capacity building and business process reengineering to simplify clearance process.

These are important steps to establish the modernised and facilitative border environment intended by the Trade Facilitation Agreement. As customs and other border agencies reform their policies, procedures and operations to implement the TFA, the needs and priorities of the private sector—the main beneficiaries of these efforts—must be taken into account. To that end, NBR is hosting a trade facilitation committee comprising all key public and private sector stakeholders, which meets periodically to exchange views. However, the collaboration has to be ramped up to

---

① Refayet Ullah Mirdha,"Bangladesh to ratify TFA soon to ease trade", *The Daily Star* (28 Oct 2015) available at http://www. thedailystar. net/business/bangladesh-ratify-tfa-soon-ease-trade-163291.

undertake reform initiatives not just through improvement in infrastructure but also through changes in policies, procedures and day-to-day operations. ①

---

①   Nusrat Nahid and M Masrur Reaz, "WTO Trade Facilitation Agreement and Bangladesh", *The Financial Express*. available at http://print. thefinancialexpress-bd. com/2014/10/18/61590, accessed 5 May 2016.

Chapter 2   Foreign Trade System in Bangladesh

The foreign trading system of Bangladesh is primarily regulated by three Acts; the Imports and Exports (Control) Act 1950, the Foreign Exchange (Regulation) Act 1947, and the Customs Act 1969. These three Acts are complementary and infringement of one may also involve infringement of another and be punishable under more than one Act. The principal responsibility for making trade policy is shared between the Ministry of Commerce and the Ministry of Finance, although a large number of other ministries and agencies are involved in the formulation and implementation of trade and investment policies. The Imports and Exports (Control) Act has empowered the Government to control, restrict and even prohibit the export or import of any product. Section 3 of the Act provides as follows:

"(1) The Government may, by order published in the official Gazette and subject to such conditions and exceptions as may be made by or under the order, prohibit, restrict or otherwise control the import or export of goods of any specified description, or regulate generally all practices (including trade practices) and procedure connected with the import or export of such goods, and such order may provide for applications for licences under this Act, the evidences to be attached to such applications, the grant, use, transfer, sale or cancellation of such licences, and the form and manner in which and the periods within which appeals and applications for review or revision may be preferred and disposed of, and the charging of fees in respect of any such matter as may be provided in such order.

(2) No goods of the specified description shall be imported or exported except in accordance with the conditions of a licence to be issued by the Chief Controller or any other officer authorised in this behalf by the Government.

(3) All goods to which any order under Subsection (1) applies shall be deemed to be goods of which the import or export has been prohibited or restricted under Section 16 of the Customs Act, 1969 (IV of 1969), and all the provisions of that Act shall have effect accordingly.

(4) Notwithstanding anything contained in the aforesaid Act the Government

may, by order published in the *Official Gazette*, prohibit, restrict or impose conditions on the clearance whether for home consumption or warehousing or shipment abroad of any imported goods or class of goods. "

The Import Policy Order (IPO) 2012 – 2015 formulated under the authority of 1950 Act obligates all importers, exporters and "indenters" (e. g. firms, institutions, bodies, organisations, persons or group of persons) to be member of a recognised Chamber of Commerce and Industry and a Bangladeshi "organisation" representing their own trade. ①

The Government has introduced new export policy for three years (2015 – 2018) prioritising 12 sectors as the "most potential" while 14 other sectors as "special development". The 12 highest priority sectors in the new export policy are high value added RMG accessories, software and IT-enabled services and ICT products, pharmaceutical products, shipbuilding, shoe and leather products, jute and jute-based products, plastic products, agro products and agro-processed products, furniture, home textile and terry towel, home furnishing and luggage.

The 14 special development sectors are multifarious jute-based products, electronic and electric products, ceramic products, light engineering, value added frozen fish, printing and packaging, crude diamond and jewellery, paper and paper products, rubber, silk products, handicraft and cottage products, lungi and tent industry products and coconut coir.

The 17 export prohibited products that have been identified in the new export policy are edible oil, wheat, onion, garlic, all sorts of pulses except processed one, general rice except the fragrant rice, jute seed, arms and ammunition-related products, etc. ②

The 1950 Act has criminalised the violation of its provision with the imposition of penalty or fine or with both. Section 5 provides as follows: " If any person contravenes any provision of this Act or any order made or deemed to have been made under this Act or the rules made thereunder, or makes use of an import or

---

① Rule 29 of the Import Policy Order 2012 – 2015 provides that " All importers, exporters and indentors shall obtain membership from a recognised Chamber of Commerce and Industry or membership from the concerned trade organisation formed on all Bangladesh basis representing his own trade, provided that, Government may exempt any importer, exporter or indentor from the aforesaid provision in the public interest. "

② Export Policy 2015 – 2018 available at https://ogrlegal. files. wordpress. com/2015/11/export-policy-2015 – 18 – bn. pdf.

export licence otherwise than in accordance with any condition in that behalf imposed under this Act,he shall without prejudice to any confiscation or penalty to which he may be liable under the provisions of the Customs Act 1969(Ⅳ of 1969),as applied by Sub-section(3)of Section 3 of this Act be punishable with imprisonment for a term which may extend to one year,or with fine,or with both. "

2.1   Licence system and rules of origin

All industrial consumers, except enterprises located in export processing zones (EPZs) and commercial importers, must register with the Chief Controller of Imports and Exports(CCIE) in the Ministry of Commerce, who issues an import registration certificate(IRC).[1] Registration with IRC is required only for private importers exempting the public entities. An IRC is generally issued within 10 (previously 15)days of receipt of the application.

After fulfilling the initial two requirements,importers are allowed to import with a letter of credit authorisation(LCA)form.[2] Along with the LCA form,importers must submit a number of documents to the executing bank, including an L/C application form,an invoice,and an insurance cover note. In addition,private sector importers must submit a membership certificate from the registered Chamber of Commerce and Industry or any trade association;proof of IRC renewal payment;a declaration of income-tax; Tax Identification Number; and any other documents required by the Import Policy Order or other Public Notice. Public sector importers are required to submit an attested photocopy of the allocation letter issued by the administrative ministry,division or authority.

Some other documents required for imports in Bangladesh include a bill of lading or airway bill,commercial invoice or packing list,and a certificate of origin. In case of importing restricted list products or controlled list products, some other documentation may be required in accordance with the notification issued by the government. The restricted or controlled list is given in Annexure 1 of the Import

---

[1]   Importers remain classified into private and public sectors, private sector importers have been further divided into industrial importers and commercial importers.

[2]   LCA form is required for opening Letter of Credit(L/C).

Policy Order 2012 – 2015. [1]

Import against an LCA form may be allowed without opening an L/C for: (i) import of books, journals, magazines, and periodicals; (ii) any permissible item for an amount not exceeding USD 25,000 during each financial year against remittance made from Bangladesh; (iii) import under commodity aid, grant or such other loans for which there are specific procurement procedures for imports of goods without opening an L/C; and (iv) import of "international chemical references" through bank drafts by recognised pharmaceutical (allopathic) firms on approval of the Director, Drug Administration, for the purpose of quality control of their products. Moreover, an L/C is not required for imports of perishable goods valued between USD 10,000 and USD 15,000(Tecknaf Customs Station) or between USD 5,000 and USD 7,500 (other land routes) per consignment, or for capital machinery and raw materials for industrial use.

Rules of origin(RO) are the criteria that are used to define where a product was made. The origin of a product is important because it will determine how it is treated at the border of an importing country and the origin may impact the import duty payable and admissibility into the country. These are the criteria needed to determine the source of origin of a product for the purpose of determining what tariff, if any, applies to it. If the rules of origin are relaxed, it might erode competitiveness of the backward linkage industries of Bangladesh.

Although a note on RO as prepared by GATT (General Agreement on Tariffs and Trade) Secretariat in 1981 and ministers of member countries agreed to study the RO used by GATT contracting parties in November 1982, not much work was done on RO until well into the Uruguay Round negotiations. After transforming GATT into World Trade Organisation in 1995, the RO have been frequently used in the trade arena. These rules have been playing a critical role in the export of many countries, especially LDCs like Bangladesh. The trade structure of Bangladesh is unique in nature. The export bundle of the country is mainly composed of garments items. Moreover the export destination is mostly the European Union (EU). Nearly 79 percent of the total exports of the country comprise of ready-made garments(RMG) of which about 58. 73 percent were exported to EU in FY 2010 – 2011. Therefore,

---

[1]   See details at http://pflanzengesundheit. jki. bund. de/dokumente/upload/98e82_bd3-import_policy_ order_12-15. pdf.

apparel exporters need to know what requirement of RO the EU has fixed for accessing Bangladesh RMG into their apparel market.

Bangladesh has called for a relaxation of stringent rules of origin so that more products from least developed countries can enjoy duty benefits. Rules of origin are used at the port of entry to determine the national source of a product for duty purposes and easing them has been a longstanding demand of less developed countries.

Due to strict rules, many products originating from less developed countries are subject to entry barriers or high duty. Bangladesh became a victim of rigid rules on exports of clothing items to Japan. The apparel items were manufactured from imported cotton or yarn, so they were not considered products originating from Bangladesh. But in April 2016, Japan relaxed its rules of origin, as of result of which Bangladesh is now enjoying duty benefits on export of knitwear items.

2.2   Technical barriers to trade in goods

Bangladesh has notified the WTO of its acceptance of the Code of Good Practice of the WTO Agreement on Technical Barriers to Trade (TBT); no further notification has been received. [1]

The Ministry of Industries is responsible for leading and facilitating the legal and technical institutional framework for national standards, quality and conformity assessment. The main institutions are the Bangladesh Standards and Testing Institution (BSTI) and the Bangladesh Accreditation Board (BAB) along with a planned new regulatory body to enforce mandatory technical regulations. BSTI works on the implementation of the TBT Agreement.

BSTI has been Bangladesh's WTO TBT national enquiry point since 2002. It has an internal committee on WTO affairs and participates in the working groups on WTO agreements in the Ministry of Industries and Ministry of Agriculture. BSTI is working on the implementation of the TBT and SPS Agreements.

BSTI, the national standardisation body, formulates national standards for all products except pharmaceutical products, enforces compliance with standards, and certifies the quality of products for local consumption, export or import. The BSTI

[1]   See WTO document G/TBT/CS/N/92, 18 January 1998.

Council, the highest decision-making organ of the institution, consists of representatives from different ministries, business chambers, scientific organisations, and universities. As of 2012, there were 3,498 standards in Bangladesh, of which 155 compulsory standards are in force. Testing and certification procedures for compulsory standards are the same for domestic and imported products. In exercising the power conferred by the Bangladesh Standards and Testing Institution Ordinance 1985, BSTI develops national standards for products and services.

The main policy objectives in the area of standards and technical regulations are the harmonization of national standards with international standards and the adoption of international standards. As of today, international standards adopted by BSTI include 1368 International Standardisation Organisation (ISO) standards and 163 International Electrotechnical Commission (IEC) standards. Bangladesh is a member of the ISO 1974 and in 2001 became an affiliate member of IEC. According to the Government, the standards and quality of manufactured products and exports will be maintained and further improved by enhancing TBT assurance capacities. To that end, the BSTI is being strengthened in the areas of quality assurance, accreditation and certification.

There are many national and international organisations working to maintain quality and safety of a product by issuing certificate in that regard. The International Standard Organisation is such an organisation working globally whereas Bangladesh Standard Testing Institute is working domestically.

The product safety and quality is ensured in Bangladesh through various laws.

The preamble of BSTI Ordinance 1985 declares that it is "an Ordinance to provide for the establishment of an Institution for standardisation, testing, metrology, quality control, grading and marking of goods". The institution is authorised to grant or revoke licences. Section 20 (2) of the Ordinance provides as follows: "The Institution may grant a licence if, after such enquiry as it deems necessary, it is satisfied that: (a) the article or process in respect of which the Standard Mark is to be used conforms to the related Bangladesh Standard; and (b) there is arrangement for routine inspection and testing to ensure that the article or process concerned conforms to the related Bangladesh Standard".

Bangladesh is upgrading its quality infrastructure to an international level by collaborative efforts with the newly operational Bangladesh Accreditation Board. Under the Bangladesh Accreditation Act 2006, Bangladesh Accreditation Board

(BAB) was established as an autonomous organisation and now functions under the administrative control of the Ministry of Industries with the task of developing an accreditation process in Bangladesh.

2.3　Sanitary and phytosanitary measures

The legal framework of sanitary standards in Bangladesh is found in the Pure Food Ordinance 1959, as revised by Food Safety Ordinance 1994, and the Pure Food Rules. Phytosanitary standards in Bangladesh are governed by the Destructive Insects and Pest Rules 1966 and the Plant Quarantine Act 2011. Formulation of rules under the Plant Quarantine Act 2011 is under way. Sanitary and phytosanitary standards are also governed by other legal instruments, notably: Bangladesh Diseases of Animal Act 2005, Bangladesh Diseases of Animal Rules 2008, Bangladesh Animal and Animal Product Act 2005, Bangladesh Fish and Animal Feed Act 2010, and Bangladesh Animal Slaughter and Meat Quality Control Act 2011.

The following acts and rules regulate SPS measures in the fisheries sector for both the export market and for domestic consumption: Fish and Fish Products (Inspection & Quality Control) Ordinance 1983; Fish and Fish Products (Inspection & Quality Control) Rules 1997 (amended in 2008); Fish Feed and Animal Feed Act 2010; Fish Feed Rules 2011; Fish Hatchery Act 2010; Fish Hatchery Rules 2011.

SPS matters are handled by the Ministries of Agriculture, Health, and Fisheries and Livestock. Sanitary certificates and radioactivity test certificates are required for imports of food and edible products. A sanitary certificate issued by the competent authority of the exporting country must indicate that the product is free of injurious insects, pests, and diseases. Foreign certifications of radioactivity tests are also accepted in Bangladesh. In addition, a purity test is conducted by the Bangladesh Council of Scientific and Industrial Research for imports of palm oil, olein, and refined bleached and deodorised (RBD) palm stearin. All expenses incurred for the tests are borne by importers.

According to a 2005 World Bank survey, the infrastructure that deals with sanitary, hygiene and standards-related issues (including environmental issues) is extremely weak. [1] This weakness includes the absence of adequate human resources

---

[1]　See World Bank (2005b).

and technical capacity to address increasingly stringent global demands in standardisation.

In the light of requirements in the WTO Agreements on TBT and SPS measures, a product labelling policy was introduced in 2004, to ensure that no barriers are created for import (and export) of goods and that imported products have proper labels. The policy refers explicitly to international labelling standards to be observed in 13 sectors. ①

All imports are required to carry a label indicating the country of origin. The label must also indicate quantity, weight, measurements, trade description, component materials, and date of manufacture/expiry. Bangla or English is permissible for labelling. Imported goods, including their containers, must not bear any words or inscription of a religious connotation. ②

2.4   Anti-dumping and countervailing duties laws

The Finance Act of 1995 introduced regulations and procedures for examining dumping and subsidy complaints, by amending Section 18 of the Customs Act,1969. The legislation was passed to bring the provisions on anti-dumping and countervailing actions into conformity with the WTO Agreements on Implementation of Article VI of the GATT 1994 and on Subsidies and Countervailing Measures. The Bangladesh Tariff Commission(BTC) conducts dumping and subsidies investigations.

An application for an investigation, whether for an anti-dumping or countervailing measure, must be made in writing to the BTC by or on behalf of a domestic industry. The BTC must terminate the investigation within one year of issuing public notice, and submit its findings and recommendations to the Government. Provisional anti-dumping or countervailing duties, no greater than the margin of dumping or of the subsidy rates, may be imposed within 60 days of initiation and applied for a period of six months, extendable by three months.

The final findings must be available within one year of the date of initiation. Imposition of the final duty is made by notification in the *Official Gazette*. Final measures may be taken for a period of five years from the date of imposition; however, the Government may renew the duty for a further five years, upon review, if

---

① See Ministry of Industries(2004).

② See UNESCAP(2004).

it is believed that there would be continued injury. If the initial five-year period expires while a review is in progress, the anti-dumping duty can be extended for a maximum of one year.

Appeals against an anti-dumping or countervailing duty can be made to the Customs, Excise and Appellate Tribunal, under Section 196 of the Customs Act 1969, and must be filed within 90 days of the imposition of the duty.

No investigations have been initiated on anti-dumping or countervailing measures during the review period. The previous TPR report noted that lack of technical expertise and financial resources both by the administration and industries, as well as lack of authenticated data essential for submission of an application, made it difficult to initiate investigations. The authorities note that this is still the case. ①

The budget for the fiscal year 2015 – 2016 provided some protection to the domestic industries of Bangladesh. Although most of the local manufacturers and producers are not happy enough as they find that the protection measures mostly through tariffs are limited or inadequate.

It is undoubtedly difficult for the government to continue with such direct protection of the domestic industries for long during a time when the country has significantly liberalised its trade regime and is committed to do more in near future. An analysis prepared by the Policy research Institute reveals that in the fiscal year 2016 budget average nominal protection rate has declined to 25.8 percent from 26.7 percent in fiscal year 2015.

There is a safeguard mechanism since June 2010 when the government of Bangladesh appointed the chairman of the Bangladesh Tariff Commission as the designated safeguard authority. The function of the safeguard authority is to investigate whether a surge in import of a particular product is hurting similar local products and recommend necessary remedial measures through imposition of safeguard duty.

Bangladesh has interesting experience with anti-dumping procedure following the imposition of anti-dumping duty by India on export of lead-acid batteries by the Bangladeshi company, Rahimafrooz, the company took up the matter with the Government. After a long delay of several years, Bangladesh Government finally

---

① WTO, Trade Policy Reuiew, Report by the Secretariat-Bangladesh, WT/TPR/G/270 – 10 September 2012.

moved in January 2004 to the Dispute Settlement Body (DSB) of WTO to challenge the Indian anti-dumping measure. WTO took the matter into cognizance and as part of WTO procedure DSB called India and Bangladesh for consultation. This is the first dispute involving an LDC member as a principal party to a dispute. On 28 January 2004, Bangladesh requested consultations with India concerning a certain anti-dumping measure imposed by India on imports of lead acid batteries from Bangladesh. After the consultation stage, India unilaterally withdrew the anti-dumping duty in January 2005.

Bangladesh textile manufacturers had long been complaining about dumping of Indian textile and fabric in Bangladesh. More than a decade ago, they had taken the initiative and formally lodged a complaint with the tariff commission, but the failure to provide adequate supporting information and documentation left the procedure incomplete.

There is a huge concern regarding information secrecy in spite of the fact that the Bangladesh Tariff Commission assures that no data or information would be disclosed to third parties or any government authority; however, a certain legal complications still do exist. So far, there is no legal protection against the disclosure of information gathered from investigation which could potentially be a big concern for the stakeholders. Without legal provision for keeping business information confidential, the safeguard authority cannot be expected to be functional.

2.5　Regulatory Guidelines for Mobile Financial Services (MFS) in Bangladesh

Bangladesh Bank (BB) has decided in principle to licence new banking companies in the private sector pursuant to Section 31 of the Bangladesh Banking Companies Act, 1991 after considering the need and overall strategy congenial to effective monetary and financial sector policy for the country. Terms and conditions for establishment of the new bank are given in the website of Bangladesh Bank. [1]

The financial sector in Bangladesh has undergone tremendous growth in volume and complexity over the recent years. However, despite impressive growth gains in

---

[1]　See details at http://www. bu. edu/bucflp/files/2012/01/Guidelines-on-Mobile-Financial-Services-for-the-Banks-consumer-protection-related. pdf and also at http://www. bb. org. bd/aboutus/regulationguideline/guidelist. php.

capital base, income, return on equity and other areas, the financial sector remains lagging in reaching out with adequate financial services to large swathes of farm and non-farm economic activities of low income rural and urban population in Bangladesh. Rapid country-wide expansion of mobile phone networks and Bangladesh Bank led modernisation of the country's payments system and financial sector IT infrastructure have opened up opportunities for innovating mobile phone based cost efficient modes of off-branch financial service delivery to the underserved population segments. Bangladesh Bank is issuing these regulatory guidelines for mobilephone-based financial service platforms in Bangladesh with a view to providing an orderly, enabling and competitive environment for utilising this new window of opportunity of innovatively extending the outreach of financial services.

In Bangladesh about 25 million customers use mobile banking, of whom not all are registered customers. It is important to mention that the number of customers and agents has been growing exponentially. Despite the rapid development of mobile finance services, around 60 percent of the population, especially in rural areas, are yet to subscribe to mobile banking services.

The first revolution that happened in MFS was back in 2011 when Bangladesh Bank issued MFS guidelines and later updated this in December 2011 that works mostly as the basis of the whole system. These guidelines gave two ownership structure related model. MFS could work as a wing of the bank and the guideline also allowed the MFS to act as a subsidiary to bank where at least 51 percent is owned by a single bank. And the most predominant model here today is bKash.

Bangladesh Bank is issuing these guidelines in terms of Article 7A (e) of Bangladesh Bank Order 1972, and Section 5 of Bangladesh Payment and Settlement Systems Regulations, 2014. These guidelines shall apply to provision of MFS in Bangladesh by scheduled commercial bank-led MFS platforms.

BB shall permit delivery of the following broad categories of financial services by scheduled commercial bank-led MFS platforms in Bangladesh: disbursement of inward foreign remittances; cash in/cash out into Mobile Accounts through agents/ bank branches/ATMs/Mobile Network Operator (MNO) outlets; person to business payments, e. g. utility bill payments, merchant payments, deposits into savings accounts/schemes with banks, loan repayments to banks/nonbank financial institutions(NBFIs)/micro-finance institutions(MFIs), insurance premium payments to insurance companies, and so forth; business to person payments, e. g. salary disbursements, dividend/refund warrant payments; loan disbursements to borrowers, vendor payments, etc; government to person payments, e. g. pension payments, old age allowances, freedom-fighter allowances, input subsidy payments to farmers, and so forth; person to government payments, e. g. tax, fee, levy payments etc; person to person payments(from one mobile account to another mobile account).

MFS platforms in Bangladesh will be sponsored and led only by the payments system member scheduled commercial banks, with prior BB approval. The scheduled commercial bank-led MFS platforms may have both banks and non-bank entities including mobile network operators(MNOs) as equity holders, subject to: (i) banks holding majority beneficial ownership in total equity, (ii) no bank or non-bank entity holding more than fifteen percent beneficial ownership in equity, and (iii) beneficial ownership of MNOs in an MFS platform not exceeding thirty percent of its total equity. MFS platforms will be expected to choose non-bank equity partner entities with promise of bringing in innovative dimensions in business model and technology base. Acceptance of an MNO as equity partner in an MFS platform will be conditional on its extending reliable telecommunication access to all licensed MFS platforms at the same effective standard of ease of access and pricing. Before approving equity ownership of an MNO in an MFS, BB will verify the satisfaction level of all operating MFS platforms about the quality of services extended to them by the MNO.

BB reserves the discretion of withholding, suspending or cancelling its approval for operation of an MFS platform if its actions are deemed by BB to be detrimental to public interest; alongside appropriate steps towards protecting legitimate interests of the Mobile Account holders and other stakeholders in the MFS platform concerned. [1]

2. 6   Regional and bilateral trade laws

Over the past decade, Bangladesh has successfully negotiated several regional trade and economic agreements, including the South Asian Free Trade Agreement (SAFTA), the Asia-Pacific Trade Agreement (APTA), and the Bay of Bengal Initiative for Multi-Sectoral, Technical and Economic Cooperation (BIMSTEC).

---

[1]   For details see Regulatory Guidelines for Mobile Financial Services(MFS)in Bangladesh(Revised version, July 2015) available at https://www. bb. org. bd/aboutus/draftguinotification/guideline/mfs_final_v9. pdf; also Bangladesh bank website https://www. bb. org. bd/aboutus/regulationguideline/guidelist. php.

Bangladesh has taken steps to strengthen bilateral economic relations with China. As a founding member of the WTO and as an LDC, Bangladesh has been an active advocate for LDC interests in WTO negotiations. Exports to SAFTA and BIMSTEC partner countries have remained limited during the review period, accounting for only three percent of total exports in each case.

The 1975 Bangkok Agreement, the oldest preferential trade agreement in the region aimed at boosting intra-regional trade, was revised in 2005 and renamed the Asia-Pacific Trade Agreement. The Framework Agreement on Trade Preferential System among the Members States of the Organisation of the Islamic Conference (TPS – OIC) was adopted in 1990, but entered into force only in 2002.

Bangladesh is one of the 43 member states of the GSTP. The third round of GSTP negotiations concluded in December 2010, after six years of negotiations, launched at UNCTAD XI in Sao Paulo in 2004.

2.6.1   Bilateral agreements

Bangladesh has bilateral trade agreements with the following countries, namely: Albania, Algeria, Belarus, Bhutan, Brazil, Bulgaria, Cambodia, China, Czech Republic, Egypt, Germany, Hungary, India, Indonesia, Iran, Iraq, Kenya, Democratic People's Republic of Korea, Kuwait, Libya, Malaysia, Mali, Morocco, Myanmar, Nepal, Pakistan, the Philippines, Poland, Romania, Senegal, Sri Lanka, Sudan, Thailand, Turkey, Uganda, Ukraine, the United Arab Emirates, Uzbekistan, Vietnam, Zambia and Zimbabwe. All the agreements are general in nature and aimed at promoting bilateral trade.

2.6.2   Other preferential arrangements

Under the Generalised System of Preferences (GSP), Bangladeshi products currently receive preferential market access from almost all developed members of the WTO. In addition, Bangladesh is eligible for LDC preferential schemes adopted by emerging countries, including China and India.

Bangladesh could benefit from China's duty-free and quota-free programme (DFQF) for LDC products which was launched on 1 July 2010. Currently, the programme covers products of 4,788 tariff lines (8-digit level), accounting for 60 percent of all China's tariff lines. China has reiterated its commitment to further open its market to LDCs by expanding the programme's coverage to 97 percent of all tariff lines. The programme was notified to the WTO in 2011. While the rules of origin requirements are not laid out in that notification, the Bangladeshi authorities indicated that the rules of origin criteria associated with China's DFQF programme stipulate a value addition of 40 percent or a change of tariff heading (CTH). At present, the LDC DFQF programme covers around 92 percent of Bangladesh's current exports to China.

Chapter 3 FDI System in Bangladesh

Bangladesh is considered as one of the most open economies to foreign investment in the South Asian region in line with international benchmarks. The country has already presented itself as being fully open to FDI and offering high standards of treatment to foreign entities. Bangladesh has significantly liberalised its foreign direct investment policies since late 1970s. The government took a major initiative by enacting different legislation at different points of time; furthermore the open attitude of the country has been expressed in various governmental instruments and strategies. [1] The consistent inclination of the country to sign and ratify many bilateral and multilateral investment treaties provides evidence that Bangladesh is open to foreign entities and protects foreign investment in accordance with international standards. [2]

3.1 Investment laws of Bangladesh

Bangladesh is a signatory to the International Convention for Settlement of Investment Dispute (ICSID) and the Multilateral Investment Guarantee Agency (MIGA). It is a member of World Intellectual Property Organisation(WIPO)and the World Association of Investment Promotion Agencies(WAIPA). Hence, property and other rights of foreign investors are safeguarded according to international standards. Trade has been liberalised and duties reduced. However, in absence of any multilateral investment agreement at the international level, there is no single encompassing national investment law that regulate the entry or admission of foreign investment, establishment, treatment, protection, expropriation and compensation of FDI rather these issues are being regulated by a number of laws and most importantly:

• The Foreign Private Investment Promotion and Protection Act(FPIPPA)1980;

---

[1] The speech of Prime minister, Outline Perspective Plan of Bangladesh 2010 – 2021, Sixth Five-Year Plan FY2015 and National Industrial Policy 2010.

[2] Signing of BITs and ICSID.

- The Investment Board Act 1989;
- The Bangladesh Export Processing Zones Authority Act 1980;
- The Small and Cottage Industries Corporation Act 1957;
- The Companies Act 1994;
- The Acquisition and Requisition of Immoveable Property Ordinance 1982.

The Foreign Private Investment Act was enacted to ensure legal protection to foreign investment in Bangladesh against nationalization and expropriation. It guarantees repatriation of profit, capital and dividend and equitable treatment with local investors. Intellectual property rights, such as patents, designs and trademarks and copyrights, are protected. Bilateral Investment Guarantee Agreements have been signed with a number of countries.

Customs and bonded warehouses assist exporters. Free repatriation of profits is allowed, and the Taka is almost fully convertible on the current account. No prior approval is required for FDI except registration with the Board of Investment(BOI). Despite such policy reforms, Bangladesh could not attract handsome flow of FDI as yet. Bangladesh is also a signatory of MIGA, OPIC (Overseas Private Investment Corporation) of America, ICSID and WIPO. Bilateral agreements to avoid double taxation have been signed with negotiation. Several Government agencies like Board of Investment and Bangladesh Export Processing Zones Authority (BEPZA) have been formed to facilitate both foreign and local investment. ①

Bangladesh has significantly liberalized its foreign direct investment policies since late 1970s. The government took a major initiative by providing national treatment to them in 1980. This has helped the economy move towards a market economy. Recently more flexible rules and policies have been implemented to attract foreign investment. Many procedures and institutional processes for setting up businesses have been simplified or deregulated. A privatization commission was set up to facilitate governmental procedures and documentation.

3.2   Admission of foreign direct investment

The principal law regulating foreign investment in Bangladesh is Foreign Private

---

①   Investing in Bangladesh, Handbook and Guideline, 2011 by BOI. http://boi. portal. gov. bd/sites/default/files/files/boi. portal. gov. bd/publications/c2a7a276 _ c4dd _ 4f98 _ 9921 _ 6cf36df09add/Handbook%202011%20(1). pdf.

Investment Act 1980, and this Act does not clarify the admission procedure of FDI in the country. Instead of enumerating steps of entry, the Act confers it upon the discretions of the government. ①The Investment Board Act(1989) provides additional guidance on entry and establishment procedures for foreign investors. The Act establishes the Board of Investment and defines its functions. ② It also puts in place regulatory requirements and mechanisms for the registration and approval (the "sanction") of national and foreign investments in industrial undertakings. While the Foreign Private Investment (Promotion and Protection) Act 1980 does not explicitly require foreign investors to obtain regulatory approval prior to investing, the Investment Board Act stipulates that all industrial undertakings must be registered with the BOI, which is also authorised to grant industrial licences if eligibility conditions are met. ③

Registration and licensing of industrial undertakings with the BOI is not limited to foreign investors only rather it equally applies to national investors as well. The conditioning of different incentives with the registration process with BOI makes it indispensable.

Projects or industrial undertakings in EPZs are regulated and registered separately by the Bangladesh Export Processing Zones Authority, which was established under the BEPZA Act of 1980. This registration process is to enable the investors to avail themselves of the necessary government policy support and receive certification to relieve the difficulties often experienced in dealing with the various public enterprises.

Apparently FDI is welcome in all sectors, except five reserve sectors, namely: (a) arms, ammunition and other defence equipment and machinery, (b) production of nuclear energy, (c) forest plantation and mechanized extraction within the bounds of reserved forests, (d) security printing (currency notes) and (e) mining. ④ This reservation is for the purposes of national security. Moreover, the Industrial Policy of 2010 establishes a list of 17 "controlled industries" in which the Government sets

① Section 3(2) of FPIPPA 1980 provides that "Sanction of the establishment with foreign capital of an industrial undertaking under sub-section(1) may be subject to such conditions as the Government may deem fit to impose".

② BOI Act, Section B.4.

③ Section 3 of the Foreign Private Investment Act 1980.

④ Bangladesh Foreign Investment Guide, 2014 at 2. DDFL.

maximum shares of foreign ownership and for which approval from the line ministry is required before registration with the BOI, BEPZA or BSCIC. This list includes important sectors of the economy, such as banking and finance, insurance, power, natural gas and coal, large-scale infrastructure projects, telecommunications and ports. [1]

Bangladesh offers generous opportunities for investment under its relaxed industrial policy and export-oriented, private sector-led growth strategy. Foreign entities are permitted to establish wholly owned subsidiaries that can be as a private limited or public limited company to be registered under the Company Act 1994. Foreign investors are allowed to own up to 100 percent of the equity in Bangladeshi companies except for certain regulated entities and there are also no restrictions on ownership of land by 100 percent foreign-owned companies.

As with wholly owned subsidiaries, foreign companies may incorporate joint venture companies with Bangladeshi partners. Foreign companies may also carry out their business activities in Bangladesh through branches/liaison/representative offices. These offices are expected to confine their activities to the boundaries set by the National Board of Investment.

Branches/liaison/representative offices will be required to submit documents to BOI including a filled, signed, and stamped application form, the memorandum of association (MOA) and the articles of assocition (AOA) of the head company, and the nationalities of the directors along with accounts of the immediately preceding financial year.

Prospective international investors may apply for visas for periods ranging from one month to five years. Branches/liaison/representative offices must obtain a work permit from the BOI. Such offices however are free and encouraged to hire employees locally. The number of expatriate employees in an industrial enterprise cannot exceed the ratio of 1:20 (foreign: local) for industrial settings and 1:5 (foreign: local) for commercial establishments. In addition, Bangladesh offers citizenship, permanent resident and multiple entry visas for the foreign investors.

3.3 Investment promotion agencies

The Board of Investment and the Bangladesh Export Processing Zones Authority

---

[1] Investment Policy Review, UNCTAD 2013 at 32.

are the primary investment promotion agencies in Bangladesh. Companies must register with the BOI to obtain benefits such as tax incentives or preferential duties for imported equipment. The BOI also administers the approval of some foreign loans and payments on behalf of the Bangladesh Bank. Though the BOI is frequently touted as a one-stop shop for all investors, authority for managing foreign investment remains fragmented. The BOI can register investors in industrial projects outside the export processing zones and assist them with tax inquiries, land acquisition, utility hook-ups, and incorporation. The BEPZA performs the same functions for companies investing in the EPZs. Investors in infrastructure and natural resource sectors, including power, mineral resources and telecommunications must seek approval from the corresponding government ministries. Although the BOI is housed organisationally in the Prime Minister's Office, regulatory and administrative powers remain vested in the line ministries. Companies often complain that ministries require unnecessary licences and permissions. ①

3.4   Currency convertibility

Free repatriation of profits is allowed and profits are almost fully convertible on the current account; however, companies report that the procedures for repatriation of foreign currency are lengthy and cumbersome. When rising fuel imports helped swing balance of payments from surplus to deficit in 2010 – 2011, scarcity of foreign exchange and currency depreciation temporarily increased convertibility risks. Since 2011, the balance of payments has swung back into surplus, foreign reserves reached an all-time high at the end of 2012, and convertibility risks have declined. ②

3.5   Privatisation

The Government of Bangladesh privatised some state-owned enterprises(SOEs) during the past twenty years, but many SOEs retain an important role in the economy, particularly in the financial and energy sectors. The current government has taken steps to restructure several SOEs to improve their competitiveness. Biman Bangladesh Airline was converted into a public limited company that initiated a

---

① Investment Climate Statement, Bureau of Economic and Business Affairs, February 2013 Report, available at http://www. state. gov/e/eb/rls/othr/ics/2013/204599. htm.

② Ibid.

rebranding and fleet renewal program, including the purchase of 10 aircraft from Boeing. Three nationalised commercial banks(NCBs)—Sonali, Janata and Agrani—have been converted to public limited companies. Bangladesh allows private investment in power generation and natural gas exploration, but efforts to allow full foreign participation in petroleum marketing and gas distribution have stalled.

The telecommunications sector was liberalised during the last decade, leading to the development of a competitive cellular phone market. The Government has been slow to allow greater competition for international connectivity and internet telephony. In 2007, the Caretaker Government revised the International Long Distance Telecommunication Services Policy of 2007 to legalise VoIP, but the government has not yet implemented this policy. ①

3.6   Preferential treatment and protection of foreign investment

The Government of Bangladesh actively seeks foreign investment, particularly in energy, power and infrastructure projects. It offers a range of investment incentives under its industrial policy and export-oriented growth strategy, with few formal distinctions between foreign and domestic private investors. ② The policy eases the process of setting up a business by simplifying the process of leasing and buying private land, incorporating an entity, allowing corporate tax holiday for seven years (15 years in the power sector) and implementing an exemption of income tax of foreign employees for up to three years in some respects.

In 2014, BOI approved 5,694 work permits. Among these, 43.05 percent were in the commercial offices and the rest 56.95 percent were in the industrial projects. Besides, 41.08 percent were new and 58.92 percent were extension of the existing permits. ③

Bangladesh has been committed to providing non-discriminatory treatment to foreign investors over the past decades on a post-establishment basis. The existing legal framework of the country guarantees fair and equitable treatment for foreign

---

① For details see http://www.state.gov/e/eb/rls/othr/ics/2013/204599.htm.

② Ibid.

③ See BOI, Annual Report 2014. http://www.boi.gov.bd/site/publications/1be68621 – 076f – 499f – 96ae – 362ad94185c7/Annual-Report-2014.

investment. ① The FPIPPA provides some indications as to the meaning of this concept by stipulating that foreign investment shall not be accorded less favourable treatment than what is accorded to similar private investment by nationals in the application of relevant laws and regulations. ②

Broadly, the various generations of the Industrial Policy repeat this stance. Version 2010 for example mentions that foreign investors are entitled to the same conditions as national investors in terms of tax holidays, royalty and technical fees and others. Access to courts is provided on a non-discriminatory basis.

Bangladesh has signed almost 30 BITs, all of which guarantee MFN and National Treatment(post establishment). These two principles systematically ensure non-discrimination as the standard of treatment accorded to foreign investors. None of the treaties has conditioned these two principles to the protection of public policy by the country.

Most of the BITs which Bangladesh has signed contain provision on the avoidance of double taxation. Having accorded statutory protection to foreign investments and ensured equal treatment for local and foreign investors, Bangladesh welcomes foreign investments and guarantees equal, and in many respects, favourable treatment to foreign investors. The government assures protection against nationalisation and expropriation through the Foreign Private Investment Act of 1980 which inclusively assures the repatriation of capital and dividend for foreign investors. The FPIPPA stipulates that foreign investments may be expropriated or nationalized only for a public purpose and against adequate compensation paid "expeditiously" and freely transferable. The law, however, does not refer to non-discrimination of expropriation. Adequate compensation is defined as the market value immediately prior to the announcement of expropriation or nationalisation. Bangladesh has also made adequate legislative provisions to protect intellectual property rights.

3.7   Relationship between IIAs-BITs-FTAs and local laws

All BITs, IIAs and FTAs, to which Bangladesh is a contracting State, are part of

---

①   Article 4 of FPIPPA 1980 provides that "The Government shall accord fair and equitable treatment to foreign private investment which shall enjoy full protection and security in Bangladesh".

②   Ibid, Article 5.

international law and the approach of the judiciary towards implementation of international law would be analysed in the present section of the report.

Bangladesh adheres to the theory of dualism or incorporation in relation to international treaties according to which no international treaty will become part of Bangladeshi law, unless it is incorporated into its domestic law by legislation. While this represents the strictly technical position an examination of the relevant provisions of the constitution and the case law clearly establishes that the Bangladeshi judiciary has been receptive to the indirect incorporation of international law into domestic law, that is, in the absence of express incorporation of international law by local legislation.

Part II of the Bangladesh Constitution sets out fundamental principles of state policy to guide the State, which however do not have binding effect. Article 8(2) sets out the position: "The principles set out in this Part shall be fundamental to the governance of Bangladesh, shall be applied by the State in the making of laws, shall be a guide to the interpretation of the Constitution and of the other laws of Bangladesh, and shall form the basis of the work of the State and of its citizens, but shall not be judicially enforceable." The last of the principles set out in Part II of the Constitution is found in Article 25, which states as follows: "The State shall base its international relations on the principles of respect for national sovereignty and equality, non-interference in the internal affairs of other countries, peaceful settlement of international disputes, and respect for international law and the principles enunciated in the United Nations Charter, and on the basis of those principles shall: a. strive for the renunciation of the use of force in international relations and for general and complete disarmament; b. uphold the right of every people freely to determine and build up its own social, economic and political system by ways and means of its own free choice; and c. support oppressed peoples throughout the world waging a just struggle against imperialism, colonialism or racialism. "

Fundamental principles of state policy, while not judicially enforceable, are not to be easily disregarded. In fact, interpretation of the Constitution and national laws must be in conformity with the basic principles of international law. [1] The approach of the Court is reflected in the case of *BNWLA v. Government of Bangladesh and*

---

[1]   *Pro Nurul islam and ors v Bangladesh and ors*, Writ petition, 52 DLR(2000), 7 February 2000.

others[1], where the Court declared:"Our courts will not enforce those Covenants as Treaties and Conventions even if ratified by the State, as they are not part of the corpus juris of the State unless those are incorporated in the municipal legislation. "

The application of international instruments including the Universal Declaration of Human Rights(UDHR)in the domestic arena has been reaffirmed by the Supreme Court in *BNWLA v. Government of Bangladesh and others*[2] where the Court observed as follows:"It has now been settled by several decisions of this subcontinent that when there is a gap in the municipal law in addressing any issue, the courts may take recourse to international conventions and protocols on that issue for the purpose of formulating effective directives and guidelines to be followed by all concerned until the national legislature enacts laws in this regard. "

The High Court Division of the Supreme Court of Bangladesh has held that: "Where there is a gap in the municipal law in addressing any issue, the courts may take recourse to international conventions and protocols on that issue for the purpose of formulating effective directives and guidelines to be followed by all concerned until national legislature enacts laws in this regard. "[3]

The judicial approach has clearly been that if there is no provision in national legislation regarding a particular matter, relevant international conventions and protocols may be taken into consideration which implies that there is no bar to directly applying international law to resolve a question of law or principle, although such international instrument has not been expressly incorporated in the domestic law.

Moreover, guidelines provided by the Court on the basis of provisions of UDHR have significant value and importance. The Court in *BNWLA v. Government of Bangladesh and others*, 2001, 40 *CLC(HCD)*, *para* 23, declared as follows:"We hold that the definition and directive guidelines given, and/or to be given by this Court in this case, are law of this country, and in view of Article 111 of the Constitution [which states that Supreme Court decisions are binding on all subordinate courts], they are binding on all concerned and are to be implemented everywhere until an effective legal measure is evolved and/or enacted by our

---

[1]   14 BLC(2009)703.

[2]   2001,40 CLC(HCD),para 20.

[3]   *BNWLA v Government of Bangladesh* 31 BLD,(HCD)2011,324.

legislature. ”

Bangladeshi legal system is a common law system and is not significantly different from other common law countries. Bangladeshi position in relation to domestic application of international law is characterized by paucity of case laws, ambiguity of constitutional and statutory provisions and reluctance of our judges as well as the lawyers to refer to international instruments. These characteristics are largely the results of traditional and stereotype thinking of our legal community, lack of willingness to know more of international legal developments, lack of sufficient emphasis on international law in law school curriculum, and finally rigid adherence to common law principles with little or no interest in taking anything from the civil law system, or even with little interest to learn from other common law jurisdictions which are now devoting more time and effort to accommodate international law within domestic law. So far as international treaties are concerned, member states cannot defend any national law which violates international law. The judicial practice of Bangladesh hints that where trade and investment treaties are concerned the country is keen to comply with its international obligations.

Chapter 4　Monetary and Banking System and Law

Nationalism, socialism, democracy and secularism that inspired the people of Bangladesh in their heroic struggle of liberation war are the four fundamental principles of the Constitution. The post-independence planners were so influential in convincing the founder father "Bangabandhu" that Bangladesh would turn into a paragon of progress by simply following a full-scale model of massive nationalization. A bureaucracy-led business plan did not work in other parts of the world, nor did it function in Bangladesh. The theoretical utopia soon nosedived soon after its launching, sending growth prospects down and making Bangladesh a developmental guinea pig. Over the 1970s, Bangladesh's average GDP growth was 1. 5 percent. Coming out from the womb of socialist planning, a rapid march for privatization and market economy has been difficult for the beleaguered nation. Bangladeshi leadership took a risk in unleashing the potential of private enterprises. Steering Bangladesh's policy in a diametrically opposite direction had truly been challenging. The liberalisation policy graduated in three steps in the mid-1980s, early 1990s and mid-1990s, marking a wonderful journey to the pro-market move. Since the 1980s, Bangladesh's decade-wise average growth shifted roughly one percentage point higher, starting from 3. 5 percent to reach 6. 5 percent in the 2010s. [1] The country is different in projecting 7 percent growth for the financial year 2016.

The financial system of Bangladesh is made up of three broad fragmented sectors, namely: formal sector, semi-formal sector and informal sector. The formal sector includes all regulated institutions like banks, non-bank financial institutions (FIs), insurance companies, capital market intermediaries like brokerage houses, merchant banks etc. , and micro finance institutions (MFIs). The semi-formal sector includes those institutions which are regulated otherwise but do not fall under the jurisdiction of central bank, Insurance Authority, Securities and Exchange

---

[1]　Biru Paksha Paul, "Why is the Bangladesh economy different?" *The Daily Star*, 2016, http://www. thedailystar. net/op-ed/economics/why-the-bangladesh-economy-different-511861.

Commission or any other enacted financial regulator. This sector is mainly represented by specialised financial institutions like House Building Finance Corporation (HBFC), Palli Karma Sahayak Foundation(PKSF), Samabay Bank, Grameen Bank and non-government organisations. The informal sector includes private intermediaries which are completely unregulated. ①

Bangladesh Bank is the central bank of Bangladesh and is designed to regulate and monitor these sectors with the help of legal instruments passed by the House of Nation time to time. In this report the legal instruments that control the monetary and banking system of Bangladesh will be discussed. Especially the laws relating to foreign exchange system, movements of funds, banking system and restriction of foreign banks and financial institutions will be scrutinised.

4.1   Laws relating to the monetary and banking system

According to the manual of the Bangladesh Bank legal instruments those controlling the financial system of Bangladesh are follows:
- Bangladesh Bank Order 1972;
- Bank Companies Act 1991;
- Bank Company(amendment)Act 2013;
- The Negotiable Instruments Act 1881;
- The Bankers' Book Evidence Act 1891;
- Foreign Exchange Regulations(Amendment)Act 2015;
- Foreign Exchange Regulations Act 1947;
- Financial Institutions Act 1993;
- Financial Reporting Act 2015;
- Bank Deposit Insurance Act 2000;
- Money Loan Court Act 2003;
- Micro Credit Regulatory Authority Act 2006;
- Money Laundering Prevention(Amendment)Act 2015;
- Money Laundering Prevention Act 2012;
- Anti-terrorism(Amendment)Act 2013;
- Anti-terrorism Act 2009.

---

① "Financial System", Bangladesh Bank; Central Bank of Bangladesh. https://www. bb. org. bd/fnansys/ index. php.

4. 2   The Bangladesh Bank Order 1972

Bangladesh Bank acts as the central bank of Bangladesh, which was established on 16 December 1971 through the enactment of Bangladesh Bank Order 1972— President's Order No. 127 of 1972 (Amended in 2003). The general superintendence and direction of the affairs and business of the Bangladesh Bank have been entrusted to a nine member Board of Directors which is headed by the Governor who is the Chief Executive Officer of this institution as well. BB has 40 departments and 9 branch offices. In Strategic Plan (2010 – 2014), the vision of BB is " to develop continually as a forward looking central bank with competent and committed professionals of high ethical standards, conducting monetary management and financial sector supervision to maintain price stability and financial system robustness, supporting rapid broad based inclusive economic growth, employment generation and poverty eradication in Bangladesh".

The main functions of BB are(Section 7A of BB Order 1972) :

• to formulate and implement monetary policy;

• to formulate and implement intervention policies in the foreign exchange market;

• to give advice to the Government on the interaction of monetary policy with fiscal and exchange rate policy, on the impact of various policy measures on the economy and to propose legislative measures it considers necessary or appropriate to attain its objectives and perform its functions;

• to hold and manage the official foreign reserves of Bangladesh;

• to promote, regulate and ensure a secure and efficient payment system, including the issue of bank notes;

• to regulate and supervise banking companies and financial institutions.

4. 3   Foreign Exchange Regulations Act 1947 and Foreign Exchange Regulations(Amendment) Act 2015

4. 3. 1   Foreign Exchange Regulation Act 1947

Foreign Exchange Regulation Act 1947 (FERA) was adopted in Bangladesh immediately after independence. This Act empowered BB to regulate certain payments, dealings in foreign exchange and securities and the import and export of currency and bullion. The Act has 27 sections and a number of subsections.

The main objectives of the Act are to conserve the limited foreign exchange resources and to ensure that the available foreign exchange is utilised only for priority requirements in the economic and financial interests of Bangladesh and the maintenance of the proper accounting of foreign exchange receipts and payments. BB is responsible for administration to regulation. Under the Act BB reviews the exchange control measure from time to time and revises the instruction on policy and measures, whenever necessary through different foreign exchange circulars. Authorised dealers in foreign exchange are required to bring the foreign exchange regulations to the notice of their customers in their day to day dealings. Actually all the regulatory amendments or changes are implemented by the authorised dealers at the levels where transactions with the customers take place. And so authorised dealers are to ensure compliance with the regulations by the customers.

Bangladesh has very strict foreign exchange control laws. Transaction of foreign exchange is highly regulated. Remittance of money outside Bangladesh is allowed only for specific circumstances and is required to be supported by appropriate documentation. BB, the central bank of Bangladesh, is responsible for administering foreign exchange transactions in Bangladesh. BB time to time issues directives regarding foreign exchange transaction and summaries of the main directives are published by BB and named as Guideline for Foreign Exchange Transactions (the "Guidelines"). All foreign exchange should be transacted pursuant to the Guidelines and FERA, otherwise criminal charges could be brought in.

Some basic features of the FERA 1947 are as follows:

a. *Authorised dealer and the money changers:* BB issue licences to deal in foreign exchange empowered by the FERA, 1947. Central bank may issue general licences or licences with authority to perform limited functions only. The authorised dealers (AD) must maintain adequate and proper records of all foreign exchange transactions and furnish such particulars in the prescribed returns for submission to the BB. In addition to AD, there are registered moneychangers to buy foreign currencies from tourists and sell them to outgoing Bangladeshi travellers as per entitlement. ①

---

① "Foreign Exchange Laws", OGR LEGAL, Resource Portal, 2016. https://resource. ogrlegal. com/ foreign-exchange-laws/.

b. *Bringing in cash from abroad by a foreign investor or any person*: A foreigner can bring in foreign exchange in any form including cash without limit, provided that for amounts in excess of USD 5,000 a declaration on prescribed form must be made and submitted to the Customs Authorities at the time of entry. Amounts brought in may also be taken out freely, subject to production of the declaration where applicable. [1]

c. *Repatriation of capital and profits*: Foreign investors are free to repatriate their invested capital, profits, capital gains, post-tax dividends, and approved royalties and fees through AD provided the appropriate documentation is in order. Foreigners employed in Bangladesh with the approval of the Government may remit 50 percent of salary/net income, actual savings and admissible retirement benefits through an AD. Net salary of foreign nationals' payable for the period of leave admissible to them as per their service contract duly approved by the Government may be remitted. [2]

4.3.2   Foreign Exchange Regulation(Amendment)Act 2015

The Foreign Exchange Regulation Act 1947 was amended on 9 September 2015 by Foreign Exchange Regulation (Amendment) Act 2015. The amendment brought changes in the following areas:

Applicable to all residents in Bangladesh: This Act will be applicable to virtually all persons living in Bangladesh irrespective of their nationality except foreign diplomatic representations or accredited officials of such representations located within Bangladesh and offices of organisations established by international treaty located within Bangladesh. [3]

The definition of securities expanded[4]: The current definition includes deposit receipts in respect of deposits of securities, units of mutual fund or collective investment scheme, as defined in Securities and Exchange Commission (Mutual Fund) Rules 2001 as well as other instruments defined as security in the Securities and Exchange Ordinance 1969.

---

[1]   "Foreign Exchange Laws", OGR LEGAL, Resource Portal, 2016. https://resource. ogrlegal. com/foreign-exchange-laws/.

[2]   Ibid.

[3]   Ibid.

[4]   Ibid.

New definition introduced: The amendment introduces some new definitions such as export, import, capital account transaction, current account transaction, goods, person resident in Bangladesh, service, etc. [1]

Export of service will be covered: The Government will be able to prohibit the export of any goods or classes of goods or services or classes of services from Bangladesh unless a declaration supported by such evidence that the amount representing the full export value of the goods or services has been or will be received in a prescribed manner within the prescribed time. [2]

Section 18A and 18B got repealed: The Branch Office or Liaison Office or Representative Office will have to report to BB within 30 (thirty) days of obtaining permission from Board of Investment or similar competent authority in Bangladesh to establish their presence in Bangladesh. [3]

More information can be sought: The Government or the BB will be able to ask any person resident in Bangladesh to make a return of their holdings of foreign exchange, foreign securities, any immovable property or industrial or commercial undertaking or company outside Bangladesh, held, owned, established or controlled by that person. [4]

Punishment for breaching any provision of the FERA: Punishment for breaching any provision of this Act is now maximum seven years.

Provisions Regarding Permission: No person is required to take any permission from BB to act as a technical or management advise or as an agent in trading or commercial transactions of a person resident (but not citizen) in Bangladesh or of a company (other than a banking company) not incorporated under any law in force in Bangladesh.

4. 4   The Banking Companies Act 1991

The Banking Companies Act 1991 was enacted in February 1991 in order to make the role of BB authoritative in dealing with licensing, monitoring, regulating

---

① "Foreign Exchange Laws", OGR LEGAL, Resource Portal, 2016. https://resource. ogrlegal. com/foreign-exchange-laws/.

② Ibid.

③ Ibid.

④ Ibid.

and supervising the banking sectors.

The Act deals mainly with the operations and permitted activities of the banking companies. BB exercises the powers given it by the Act in order to re-establish the discipline in the sanctioning and rescheduling of loans and advances. Direct or indirect relationship between the borrower and bank authority which is known as the "connected lending" was identified as the most critical problem in the banking sector. In order to prevent this sort of lending, some restrictions were imposed on loans and advances as set out in Section 27 of the Act. Rescheduling of defaulted loans is now critically monitored by BB. A banking institution is not allowed to reschedule its outstanding loans more than twice. [1]

4. 4. 1 Licensing of banking companies

Bank Company Act 1991 empowers BB to issue licences to carry out banking business in Bangladesh. [2] Before granting a licence the BB may require any of the following conditions to be fulfilled: that the company is or will be in a position to pay the claims of its present or future depositors in full; the affairs of the company are not being or are not likely to be conducted in a manner detrimental to the interests of its present or future depositors; in the case of a banking company incorporated outside Bangladesh, the Government or law of the country in which it is incorporated provides the same facilities to the company as the Government or law of Bangladesh grants to companies incorporated in Bangladesh, and that the company complies with all the provisions of this Act applicable to companies incorporated outside Bangladesh.

The Bangladesh Bank may cancel a licence granted to a banking company under this section on account of the following reasons, namely:

(a) if the company ceases to carry on banking business in Bangladesh;

(b) if the company at any time fails to comply with any of the conditions imposed upon it under the law.

Any banking company aggrieved by a decision cancelling a licence under this

---

① Muhammad Mustafizur Rahman, "Banking Sector Reforms in Bangladesh and Its Impact" (2012), a thesis delivered at Asian Institute of Technology School of Management, pp. 13 – 14.

② Salahuddin Ahmad & Dilli Raj Khanal, "Services Trade in Developing Asia: A case study of the Banking and Insurance Sector in Bangladesh" (2007), Asia-Pacific Research and Training Network on Trade Working Paper Series, p. 38.

section may, within thirty days from the date on which the decision of the Bangladesh Bank is communicated to it, appeal to the Government. The decision of the Government where an appeal has been preferred to shall be final.

4.4.2   Other important features of the Bank Companies Act of 1991

A summary of the important sections of the Bank Companies Act of 1991 may be given here:

Disposal of non-banking assets: No banking company shall hold any immovable property for any period exceeding seven years. BB may extend another five years (s. 10).

Minimum capital requirements: Requirement as to minimum paid-up capital and reserve capital is one hundred million takas or the amount of risk based assets. BB may alter the conditions in consultation with the government (s. 13).

Regulation of shareholder rights: Regulation of paid-up capital, subscribed capital and authorised capital and voting rights of shareholders. Restriction on buying shares of banks. Not more than 10 percent share of a bank to be centralised (s. 14).

Appointment of directors: BB may require any banking company (other than BB may require any banking company (other than new or specialised) to call a general meeting of the new or specialised) to call a general meeting of the share holders. The election shall not be called in question in any court (s. 15). The post of CEO shall not be kept vacant for a consecutive period of more than three months. BB may appoint an Administrator and the company shall bear the expenses. Tenure of office director shall not be more than six years consecutively in two terms (except CEO). In special cases a director can hold this office.

Vacancy of the office of a director: If any director of a banking company fails to

a) pay advances or loans accepted by him or instalments or interest on that advances or loans, or

b) pay the money he is bound to for any security, or

c) accomplish any duty to be accomplished by him and the responsibility for which he has taken on in writing (s. 17(1)).

Benefits of directors: Where any director of a banking company execute any business transaction other than banking business with any business establishment where he is associated or he has at least 10 percent shares, the banking company shall submit a report on that in its general meeting (s. 18).

Prohibition of common directors: A director of any other banking company or financial institution, an external auditor, legal adviser or otherwise engaged in any responsibility of profit of the banking company, a director of companies having voting rights in excess of 20 percent of the banking company can never become a common director (s. 23).

Restrictions on loans and advances to directors : No banking company can grant loans or advances against the security of its own share, to any of its Directors/ family members, any firm in which the banking company itself or its directors are involved. Bank companies shall send list of defaulted borrowers to the BB. BB shall send the list to all banking companies. No banking company shall provide any credit facility to any defaulting borrower. The lending banking company shall file suit against the defaulting borrower (s. 27).

Restriction as to payment of dividend : No banking company except new and special banks shall pay any dividend on its shares, unless all capitalised expenses are not in writing, shortfall in required paid-up capital and reserve and some other exceptions (s. 22).

Advances by banking companies : BB may determine the lending policy to be followed by the banking companies. BB may give directions to banking companies in the following matters :

- credit ceilings to be maintained ;
- the minimum ratio of small loans to the total advances ;
- the purpose of loan ;
- the rate of interest to be charged on advances (s. 29).

Audits : Balance Sheet and Profit and Loss account shall be audited by a person duly qualified under the Bangladesh Chartered Accounting Order, 1973 (s. 39).

Miscellaneous controls : The BB has power to inspect, provide directions and remove directors from the office of any bank (ss. 44, 45, 46).

Criminal sanctions : The powers of supervision and control are backed by the imposition of criminal sanctions. Section 57 provides as follows :

(1) No person shall

a) Obstruct any person from lawfully entering or leaving any office or place of business of a banking company or from carrying on any business there ; or

b) Hold, within the office or place of business of any banking company, any demonstration which is violent or do anything which obstructs, or is calculated to obstruct, the usual activities and transactions of the banking company ; or c) Act in any manner calculated to undermine the confidence of the depositors in the banking company.

(2) Whoever violates any provision of Subsection (1) without any reasonable excuse shall be punishable with imprisonment of no more than two years or a fine of no more than twenty thousand takas or both.

(3) For the purpose of this section, " banking company " shall include Bangladesh Bank.

4. 5　Bank Company Amendment Act 2013

The latest amendment has fixed the maximum number of directors at 20, including three independent directors, in each bank, whereas previously there was no limit to the number of directors, and has empowered the BB to remove the errant managing directors (MDs) of the state-owned banks. It also limits a bank's capital market exposure to 25 percent of its regulatory capital (the sum total of paid-up capital and reserves). Other important amendments relate to: the lowering of job experience of aspirants for the posts of MDs of banks from 15 years to 10 years; entrusting the central bank with the authority to visit and inspect cooperative societies who allegedly enter into banking transactions with non-members; and enabling it to impose heavy fines on banks that fail to meet capital adequacy within a specific period of time. The amendments are particularly important in view of the prevailing situation in the country's banking sector, more so in the case of public sector banks. From now on, the banks will not be allowed to invest more than 25 per cent of their regulatory capital in stocks. ①

4. 6　Money Loan Court (Artha Rin Adalat) Act 1990 & Amendment Act 2003

Artha Rin Adalat Act was enacted in 1990 in order to recover loans in default. The word "Adalat" means court in Bangla. In the Bangladeshi legal system, money lent by financial institutions/banks to individuals, private limited companies, public limited companies, corporations, partnership firms, societies, co-operatives,

---

① "Latest Amendment to Bank Company Act", *The Financial Express*, (2013). http://print. thefinancialexpress-bd. com/old/index. php? ref = MjBfMDdfMTdfMTNfMV82XzE3NjcyMg.

proprietorship firms, etc. when due for default, is realised through money suits, suits for foreclosure, mortgage by instituting the same to competent civil courts. The civil courts were heavily burdened with litigation: the addition of banking litigation added to laws delays. Court delays caused much loss to banks, who could not recover loan repayments in a timely fashion. To remove this difficulty, the government enacted "the Artha Rin Adalat Ain, 1990" which had undergone some amendments since its inception. The law brought changes to a great extent in the administration of justice for regulating those suits but failed to fulfil the expectation of the legislators/bankers to recover the dues expeditiously from the defaulters. The result was a new law, "The Artha Rin Adalat Ain, 2003" (hereinafter Adalat) which repealed and replaced the previous Act. ①

The law came into force on 1 May 2003 except Sections 46 and 47 which came into operation on 1 May 2004. The purpose of the law is to amend and consolidate the existing laws relating to recovery of loans of financial institutions/banks. The contents of the law have been divided into six chapters and 60 sections. Chapter 1 deals with preliminary matters (Sections 1 – 3); Chapter 2 deals with establishment of Adalat (Section 4); Chapter 3 deals with power and jurisdiction of Adalat (section 5); Chapter 4 deals with institution of suit, practice and procedure of Adalat (Sections 6 – 20); Chapter 5 deals with alternative dispute resolution (Sections 21 – 25); Chapter 6 deals with execution (Sections 26 – 39); Chapter 7 deals with appeal & revision (Sections 40 – 44); and Chapter 8 deals with miscellaneous matters (Sections 45 – 60). ②

Chapter 3 confers an exclusive jurisdiction upon the Adalat to try Artha Rin suits which are registered under Section 5(8) of the law. It has no other civil or criminal jurisdiction. ③ Chapter 5 contains provisions for settling disputes through Settlement Conference or Mediation (Sections 21 and 22). This system has been introduced with the aim of resolving a dispute at an early stage and helping parties to reach a mutually beneficial solution. Sections 38 – 46 of the law allow more instalments and time for the payment of money due, whereas Section 49 allows the defaulter to pay the money by four instalments in a year or twelve instalments in a three year period of time. If a defaulter fails to pay an instalment, the whole outstanding amount will

① Syed Jahed Monsur, "The Artha Rin Adalat Ain/2003: A Review", Law & Our Rights, *The Daily Star*, 2006. http://archive.thedailystar.net/law/2006/07/01/analysis.htm.
② Ibid.
③ Ibid.

fall due and no further time for settlement is permitted under of the law. ①

Chapter 6 of the law authorises financial institution (s)/bank (s) to sell defaulters' property by public auction. The institution can have the possession of the defaulter's property under Section 33(5) if the property remains unsold by auction. Moreover a financial institution can apply to court to obtain certification of title to the property if the institution wishes to retain the property. ②

Chapter 7 provides for appeal and revision of any decision taken by the Artha Rin Adalat (Money Loan Court). The court in this situation will follow the procedures recommended by the Code of Civil Procedure 1908(CPC) but the Act is silent about the process of review under Section 114 and Order 47 of the CPC.

In Section 46, Chapter 8, the law has set a time limit for instituting suit and provided consequence for non-filing the suit within the given time. Each suit shall be instituted within one year of violation of repayment schedule. If any institute files a suit out of time, the court will inform the administrative head of the organisation and the authority will take disciplinary action against the officer of the bank (s) responsible for such late filing and inform the court within 90 days of such notice.

Apart from the aforementioned barriers, the law has been playing a very vital role in recovery of loans in default. Its achievement in loan recovery has been so immense that the scenario of loan defaulting has improved significantly with the number of pending Artha Rin suits falling below the expected level of litigation. ③

4. 7   The Financial Institutions Act 1993

The Financial Institutions Act 1993 was enacted to deal with the affairs of Non-banking Financial Institutions (NBFIs). For the purposes of the Act, financial institutions mean such non-banking financial institutions, which (ⅰ) make loans and advances for industries, commerce, agriculture or building construction; or (ⅱ) carry out the business of underwriting, receiving, investing and reinvesting shares, stocks, bonds, debentures issued by the Government or any statutory organisation or stocks or securities or other marketable securities; or (ⅲ) carry out instalment transactions

---

① Syed Jahed Monsur, "The Artha Rin Adalat Ain/2003; A Review", Law & Our Rights, *The Daily Star*, 2006. http://archive. thedailystar. net/law/2006/07/01/analysis. htm.

② Ibid.

③ Ibid.

including the lease of machinery and equipment;or (iv) finance venture capital;and shall include merchant banks, investment companies, mutual associations, mutual companies,leasing companies or building societies. ①

The Act takes a cautious approach to issuing of licences to new NBFIs and provides a monitoring and supervision scheme for the existing NBFIs. ②

Some important sections of the Act are:

Restrictions on the opening of branches: "(1) No financial institution may, without the prior consent in writing of the BB,open at any place in or outside of Bangladesh a branch or office, nor change the location of an existing branch or office. (2) The BB shall approve of or reject an application of a financial institution for the opening of a branch or office under Subsection (1) on consideration of the matters mentioned in Section 4(3) and the decision of the BB in this matter shall be final" (s.7(1) and(2)).

Restriction on the payment of dividends: No financial institution shall pay any dividend on its shares, unless all its capitalised expenses including preliminary expenses,organisation expenses,commission for share selling and brokerage, losses and other items have been completely written off(s.10).

Restrictions regarding credit facilities,etc. : Section 14 provides as follows:

No financial institution shall

(a) accept any such deposit as is repayable on demand through cheque,draft or order of the depositor;(b) deal in gold or any foreign coins;(c) grant credit facilities in excess of thirty percent or,subject to the consent of the BB,of hundred percent of its capital to any particular person, firm, corporation or company or any such company,person or group as controls or exerts influence on such person, firm, corporation or company; (d) grant credits in excess of 50 percent of its credit facilities or in excess of such percentage of its credit facilities as the BB may determine from time to time; (e) grant any unsecured advance, credit or credit facilities to any firm in which any of its directors,individually or jointly,is interested directors unless the total amount of such facilities does not exceed 10 percent of its paid-up share capital and reserves;and(f) grant, in the manner mentioned in clause

① Mohammad Ashrafuzzaman and Md. Tanim-Ul-Islam,"Statement of Cash Flows Disclosures:A Study on Listed Financial Institutions in Bangladesh" ,(2015)5(3), *World Journal of Social Sciences*,p.177.

② Abdur Raquib,"Financial Sector Reform in Bangladesh – An Evaluation" , Bank Porikroma,p.8.

(e) , advances, credits or credit facilities in excess of BDT 500,000 to any person or group of persons other than those stated in the said clause. Explanation: In this sub-section, "director" includes also the wife, husband, father, mother, son, daughter, son-in-law, daughter-in-law, father-in-law and mother-in-law of a director.

(2) "Unsecured advance", "unsecured credit" or "unsecured credit facilities" as mentioned in Subsection(1) (e) mean any advance, credit or credit facilities granted without security or surety, and shall include, in the case of advances, credits or credit facilities granted against securities or sureties, that part of the credit which exceeds the market value of the securities or sureties and, in the case that, in the opinion of the BB, securities or sureties have no market value, the amount settled by the said Bank.

(3) No financial institution shall grant any advance or credit allowing its own shares as securities or grant credits or advances to any other institution for the purpose of buying and selling its own shares.

(4) Where there arises any loss as a result of the granting of any unsecured advance, credit or credit facilities in contravention of the provisions of Subsection (1), all the directors of the financial institution shall, jointly and individually, be responsible for the compensation.

Restrictions regarding the business of financial institutions: Section 15 provides as follows:

(a) No financial institution shall, alone or in a body, be engaged in any wholesale or retail business including export and import trade otherwise than for the purpose of carrying on its financing business.

(b) No financial institution shall carry on any business other than the business of financing and such business as has been mentioned in this Act.

Restrictions on investments: No financial institution shall expend or use more than 25 percent of its paid-up capital and reserves for the acquisition or holding of any kind of shares of financial, commercial, agricultural or industrial institutions or of any similar institution and shall, as fast as possible, sell to the institutions concerned the shares acquired in the interest of realising the credits granted by it: Provided that any financial institution may, subject to its application and on consent of the Bank, expend or use up to 50 percent of its paid-up capital and reserves for the acquisition and holding of the abovementioned kind of shares(s. 16).

Restriction on the possession of immovable property: No financial institution may acquire or possess immovable properties exceeding in value 25 percent of its paid-up capital and reserves, provided that nothing contained in this section shall be applicable in the case of immovable property required for the granting of facilities to employees of the financial institution and in the case of property acquired in the interest of realising unrealised credits granted by it(s. 17).

Power to issue guidelines: BB can issue guidelines under this section. The instructions described in the guidelines are supplementary to the standards set by the legislative requirements which will not replace or supersede them(s. 18). [1]

Financial information: the directors of every financial institution shall submit to the BB a copy of the profit and loss account and balance sheet prepared in accordance with the Companies Act(s. 23). [2]

Criminal Punishment for contravention of the statute: If any financial institution carries on the business of financing in its branches in contravention of the provisions of Section 7, it shall be punishable with a fine amounting to BDT for every day during which the offence continues(s. 34). If any financial institution grants credit facilities in contravention of the provisions of Section 14, it shall be punishable with a fine which may extend to BDT 2,000,000.

4.8   The Negotiable Instruments Act 1881

The Negotiable Instruments Act 1881 (NI Act) was enacted to regulate matters relating to negotiable instruments in Indian subcontinent during the colonial era. According to Section 13 of the Act, "Negotiable instrument means promissory note, bill of exchange and cheque payable either to order or to bearer." However, instruments not recognised by the Act, are known as Quasi-Negotiable Instruments", e. g. Bill of Lading, Railway Receipt, etc.

Dishonouring a cheque is an offence under the Negotiable Instruments Act (Section 138). The law has been designed to punish and not to recover the amount due. The section, however, keeps the possibility of recovery as the holder of the cheque may be paid by the court an amount up to the cheque amount from any fine that is recovered. If someone wishes to recover unrealised money then he or she can

---

① Department of Financial Institutions & Markets Bangladesh Bank, Guidelines on Products & Services of Financial Institutions in Bangladesh, (2013)2.

② Mohammad Ashrafuzzaman and Md Tanim-Ul-Islam, supra note 64, at 181.

file a civil suit for recovery of money. However, in reality it has been found that filing a criminal proceeding under Section 138 has been the most effective form of recovery of money. Most of the time, the drawers pay the amounts due when cases under NI Act are commenced in the anticipation of conviction. ①

A cheque is valid for six months. If a cheque is not honoured, the person presenting the cheque to the bank will receive a bank memo stating the reason for return of the cheque. A cheque may be dishonoured for several reasons but the NI Act mainly protects the rights of a cheque holder if the cheque is dishonoured for lack of funds. To start the process under the NI Act the person must send a notice to the drawer within 30 days from the date receiving such information from the bank. Notice shall be served by personal delivery or by registered post with Acknowledgement Due or Acknowledgement of Delivery or may be by publication in the widely circulated newspapers. If the drawer fails to pay within these 30 days, then a cause of action will accrue against him. In such a case, the aggrieved person must file a case before the Court of Judicial Magistrate of First Class within the next 30 days from the date when such cause of action arose. Maintaining the timeframe state above is the key to file action under the NI Act. ②

4.9   The Bankruptcy Act 1997

The Bankruptcy Act 1997 was enacted in March 1997. According to the Bankruptcy Act, all the District Judges are deemed as bankruptcy courts and they are empowered to authorise an Additional District Judge to deal with and dispose of bankruptcy issues. Apart from these, two exclusive Bankruptcy Courts have been set up in Dhaka and Chittagong. All these courts are additional to the financial loan courts. ③

The economy of Bangladesh is growing rapidly and maintaining a six percent growth rate for more than a decade and has earned a reputation in the global market for low-cost, high-quality manufacturing. The impact of this reputation was demonstrated by the fact that the exports of readymade garments from Bangladesh

---

① Barrister Omar Khan Joy, Cheque Dishonour, Your Advocate, *The Daily Star*, (2015), http://www. thedailystar. net/law-our-rights/cheque-dishonour-72010.

② Ibid.

③ Muhammad Mustafizur Rahman, supra, at 13 – 14.

rose by a sharp 19. 95 percent year-on-year during the first half of financial year 2013 – 2014, defying odds. [1] The investment-friendly laws and strict governance of the central bank played a vital role in promoting this growth. Bangladesh has a huge population. This advantage may accelerate expansion and growth of Bangladeshi banking sector and already there are 10 foreign banks active in Bangladesh. [2] Such a stable economic growth depends on refined and flexible economic vision of successive administrations. Such vision of legislation is also prominent in the laws that are regulating the economic sectors of Bangladesh. Therefore it can surely be said that investors in Bangladesh are highly protected by the law.

---

[1]   Syed A. Al-Muti, "Bangladesh's Development Surprise: A Model for Developing Countries", 2014. http://asiafoundation. org/2014/06/25/bangladeshs-development-surprise-a-model-for-developing-countries/.

[2]   Mansur Ahamed, "A Report on Banking Sector of Bangladesh", Research Department, Japan Bangladesh Business Center Corporation, (2014)12.

Chapter 5　Laws Relating to Construction of Infrastructure

In its Vision 2021 the Government of Bangladesh (GoB) has set the goal of becoming a middle income country by 2021. To sustain high growth rates against weakening external demand, increase productivity, and allow Bangladesh to take full advantage of its young population and low labour costs, private investment (including foreign) needs to increase and exports should be diversified into new, higher value-added goods and services. This requires better public infrastructure. Efforts should focus on increased public investment on high priority and cost-effective projects in power and transport infrastructure and fostering private participation through public-private partnerships (PPPs). [1]

Participation of the private sector through PPP is considered an important route to reduce the investment deficit. The GoB has taken a number of measures to create an enabling environment for attracting private investments on a sustainable basis. In 2004, the Bangladesh Private Sector Infrastructure Guidelines (PSIG) was issued to facilitate projects in line with PPP concepts. Since then, there has been some success in attracting private investment in some sectors such as power, gas, and telecommunications. However, much more investment is required in these sectors and several other priority sectors in order to accommodate economic growth. These priority sectors include ports, roads, railway, water supply, waste management, tourism, e-service delivery, etc. [2] In 2015 the government commenced additional initiatives to improve the PPP environment in Bangladesh. A new PPP law was approved by the Parliament and enacted on 16 September 2015.

---

[1]　International Monetary Fund, 2015 Article IV Consultation—Press Release; Staff Report; and Statement by the Executive Director for Bangladesh, IMF Country Report No. 16/27, January 2016.

[2]　The Asia Foundation, Promoting Public-Private Partnership in Bangladesh, A Brief Guide for Partners, (2010)5.

5. 1   Background of PPP in Bangladesh

Bangladesh has been facing many development challenges since gaining independence in 1971. To overcome some of these challenges, the country requires significant investment in energy, transport, and water supply infrastructure and several other sectors. [1] A policy framework for PPPs was introduced in Bangladesh as early as the mid-1990s with the Private Sector Power Generation Policy (PSPGP) 1996. This marked the launch of PPP projects in the power sector, with the 450 MW Meghnaghat and 360 MW Haripur Power Projects; two early success stories. The policy for encouraging partnerships with the private sector continued throughout the 2000s with the introduction of PSIG 2004 (Private Sector Infrastructure Guidelines 2004). [2]

The GoB first introduced the concept of PPP through its Financial Year 2009 – 10 national budget and made a significant allocation of funds for PPP projects, demonstrating a strong commitment from the GoB to the implementation of PPPs in the country. The government also issued a position paper on PPPs entitled, "Invigorating Investment Initiative through Public Private Partnership", in June 2009. In spite of all these commitments, the PPP initiative did not achieve significant results in terms of project work on the ground. This was mainly due to the absence of clear policy and strategic guidelines. [3]

Due to the absence of clear guidelines, most of the budget allocated for partnerships by the government was not utilised and the intended public-private engagement did not take place. Informal conversations with business leaders and government officials revealed a need for dialogue between the government and business representatives to identify and resolve obstacles in the implementation of Public-Private Partnerships (PPPs). The GoB has agreed to address the limitations of the initiative taken in 2009. The Policy and Strategy for Public-Private Partnership (PPP), 2010 (PPP Policy 2010) has been introduced (replacing the PSIG 2004) to update the policy framework and incorporate best international practice to further boost the use of the PPPs across multiple sectors and to provide a clear and

---

[1]   The Asia Foundation, Promoting Public-Private Partnership in Bangladesh, A Brief Guide for Partners, (2010)5.

[2]   Public Private Partnership Office, Your Guide to Public Private Partnership in Bangladesh, (2013), 2.

[3]   Ibid. at 5.

transparent regulatory and procedural framework. ① The PPP policy was administered under the Prime Minister's Office (PMO), indicating high level support for its effective implementation. ②

Regulation of PPPs has improved since the introduction of the 2010 Policy and Strategy for PPP and the creation of a PPP Office(PPPO)under the Prime Minister's Office in Dhaka. ③Among other responsibilities, the PPPO is tasked with advice and oversight of PPP projects. For this purpose, the PPPO has been publishing PPP process related and sector specific guidance documents. ④Another PPP unit based in the Ministry of Finance assesses the financial viability of projects and determines the level of government support.

In 2013, PPP Office published a draft law for public consultation. Bangladesh had its first PPP law. On 16 September 2015 GoB published the Act through gazette. Previously, "Policy and Strategy for Public Private Partnership(PPP)2010" was the only relevant policy. That Policy is now repealed by the new Act. The law will provide public-private partnership a firm legal basis and hopefully will promote economic development.

5. 2   Bangladesh Private Sector Infrastructure Guidelines(PSIG)

The Bangladesh Private Sector Infrastructure Guidelines (PSIG) was issued by the Cabinet Division in 2004. This has not been issued under any law passed by the national parliament. As a result, there were doubts and lack of clarity regarding the consistency between Public Procurement Regulation(PPR)2003 and the private sector project development, approval and financing that are to be implemented under the jurisdiction of PSIG 2004.

5. 3   The Public Procurement Act(PPA)2006

The Public Procurement Act(PPA)2006 was enacted by the national parliament. Section 66, which incorporated concessions agreement related provision, extended the

---

① Public Private Partnership Office, Your Guide to Public Private Partnership in Bangladesh, (2013), 2.

② The Asia Foundation, supra, at 1 −2.

③ Public Private Partnership Authority Bangladesh.

④ SYED AFSOR H UDDIN, Making a real difference in delivering public services in Bangladesh, World Bank Group, 2015.

government's legal jurisdiction to formulate independent PPP guidelines.

5.4   The Public Procurement Rules(PPR)

The Public Procurement Rules(PPR) promulgated by the government in 2008, rule 129 incorporated various PPP related models.

5.5   Policy and Strategy for Public Private Partnership(PPP)2010

The GoB's Policy and Strategy for Public Private Partnership (PPP) 2010 provides a detailed definition along with some key characteristics of PPP:

"Public-private partnership(PPP) projects normally cover public good provisions characterised by indivisibility and non-excludability, natural monopoly characterised by declining marginal cost (and associated average cost), and lumpy investment characterised by long gestation period. PPP is a win-win relationship between the government and various private sector players for the purpose of delivering a service by sharing the risks and rewards of the venture under a contractual obligation."

According to this Policy, public-private partnership also means, a cooperative venture between public and private sectors through contract; where the private sectors supplies assets and/or services of a public nature traditionally which are usually provided for by the Government.

Under the agreement, the private partner is obliged to undertake the investment. The GoB defines its requirements by way of output and result. Private sector assumes the associated risks in exchange for the right to earn an adequate return.

Objectives of Policy and Strategy for PPP 2010:
- spell out the principles of partnership with the private sector;
- define an institutional framework;
- ensure balance between risk and reward for both the Government and private partners.

Different contractual models for PPPs applied in Bangladesh

The PPP contractual model is determined on a case-by-case basis following the conclusion of the feasibility and market engagement study that will determine the optimum option to deliver the public sector objectives through a viable, bankable and sustainable project for the private sector. ①

There are different models and approaches for PPPs:②

Build-Own-Operate (*BOO*): In this model, the private sector manages the infrastructure on a build-own-operate basis. The Government usually does not manage the infrastructure developed under this model. The Independent Power Producer(IPP) is an example of the BOO model.

Build-Operate-Transfer (*BOT*): Here the private sector manages the infrastructure on a build-operate-transfer basis. The private sector manages the infrastructure until a specified time, after which the Government is responsible for its management.

Build-Own-Operate-Transfer(*BOOT*): This is an extended version of the BOT model. Under this model the ownership and management belongs to the private sector until a specified time. After expiry of the term, ownership and management is transferred to the government.

Applicability of PPP under the Policy and Strategy for Public Private Partnership (PPP) 2010

Projects through PPP can be conducted where at least one of the following circumstances exists:

- financial resources constraint or absence of expertise with the Government alone;
- private investment would increase the quality or level of service or reduce the time to implement;
- opportunity for competition, among prospective private investors;
- private investment in public service provides an opportunity for innovation; and
- no regulatory or legislative restrictions in taking private investment in the delivery of public service.

The following action/activities will not fall under the PPP purview:

- outsourcing of a simple function of a public service;
- creating a Government-owned enterprise(state-owned company) ; and
- borrowing by government from the private sector.

Time Period for PPP procurement process

---

① Public Private Partnership Office, supra, at 4.
② The Asia Foundation, supra, at 3.

The PPP procurement timescales differ from project to project depending on the project size, complexity, market interest and other linked issues (e. g. environmental and social). Generally PPP projects using the two-stage procurement process are targeted to be completed within 16 – 20 months of the RFQ being issued. The completion target for single stage procurements is about 10 – 12 months. [1]

The Government's incentives to encourage investment in PPP projects

The Government of Bangladesh has provided for a number of incentives and benefits for PPP investors in its PPP policy framework. These include:

Viability Gap Financing: A budgetary fund to provide financial subsidy for PPP projects that have high socio-economic value but are not sufficiently commercially viable to be delivered on a PPP basis. Up to 30 percent of the total project cost can be subsidised either as part of a capital contribution during construction or in the form of annuity payments during operation.

Fiscal Incentives: There are provisions permitting PPP investors to benefit from various fiscal incentives (for e. g. reduced import tax on capital goods, various tax holidays) to reduce the cost of implementing the project and to enhance viability of project.

Special Incentives (Non-Fiscal) : Any specific project may get special incentives or other non-fiscal incentives to support the implementation of policy objectives or to enhance the ease and efficiency of delivering the project. These may include exemption from specific provisions relating to insurance regulations, banking regulations, foreign exchange regulations, etc.

Unsolicited Proposal: To encourage private investor participation and innovation in PPP projects, government has permitted the submission of unsolicited proposals for the delivery of PPP projects. However, to ensure openness and transparency, unsolicited proposals are also subject to an open and competitive procurement process. The unsolicited bidder is incentivised through the application of either the Swiss Challenge System (where the unsolicited bidder is given the right to resubmit and enhance his bid) or Bonus System (where the unsolicited bidder is given a pre-agreed bonus to be applied during the evaluation). [2]

The Government's long term financing facilities for PPP projects

---

[1]   Public Private Partnership Office, supra, at 6.

[2]   Ibid.

The government recognises the importance of availability of long term finance to enable private investors to finance the implementation of PPP projects. To facilitate access to longterm finance the GoB has established two non-bank financial institutions, IDCOL and BIFFL with the remit to provide funds to private investors for the financing of infrastructure and PPP projects. IDCOL is capitalised mainly through the contribution of multilateral donors; while BIFFL is capitalised through the provision of ring fenced budgetary funds from Government of Bangladesh. ①

5.6   The Public Private Partnership (PPP) Act 2015

In 2013, PPP Office published a draft laws for public consultation. Bangladesh got its first public private partnership law. On 16 September 2015 the Government published the Act through gazette. The law will provide public private partnership a firm legal basis and hopefully will promote economic development.

Earlier, the only legal basis for procurement existed for goods and services, which proved insufficient for developing infrastructure using private capital. The new PPP law is intended at streamlining the formulation and execution of PPP projects. It has also expanded the definition and process of government procurement to include concessions. The PPP law also provides for the establishment of a PPP Authority overseen by a Board of Governors. The PPP Authority will, among other tasks, develop policy, guidelines and standard documents, appoint consultants and advisors, provide approvals, and develop capacity within ministries and agencies through provision of training. ②

Key Provisions of the Public Private Partnership PPP Act 2015, Establishment of PPP Authority

The Government will set up the Public Private Partnership Authority. The PPP Authority can take any project apart from the Annual Development Programmes and implement that project through PPP. The PPP Authority will operate under the Prime Minister's Office. It will be governed by a Board of Governors. The Prime Minister will be the Chairman and the Finance Minister will be the vice Chairman of the Board of Governors. At least six meetings of the Board must be held in a year. The

① Public Private Partnership Office, supra, at 6.
② Jenn Stanley, "Bangladesh Turns to Public-Private Partnerships to Fix Infrastructure", https://nextcity.org/daily/entry/bangladesh-public-private-partnerships-infrastructure-investment.

PPP Authority will have a CEO. The head office of the PPP Authority will be in Dhaka. The Authority will be able to set up branch offices anywhere in the country and abroad. Policies and guidelines of the body will be formulated by its authority.

Key Responsibility of the PPP Authority

The Authority has responsibility for developing PPP related policy, regulations and guidelines; developing standard documentation for PPP Project; developing standard for TOR and salary of consultants and experts; providing consents and opinions in relation to PPP projects; and organising seminars and training sessions, etc.

Identification and approval of PPP projects

The relevant government agency or the PPP Authority will take initiative for PPP projects. The Cabinet Committee on Economic Affairs (CCEA) is mandated to provide the final approval for PPP projects.

Subsidy by government

Under the Act, the government will be able to provide the following subsidy in any PPP project: technical assistance financing; viability gap financing; financing against equity and loan; and financing against linked component.

Selecting a private partner to develop and execute PPP projects

The Act does not provide detail guideline on selecting private partner for PPP roject. There will be subsequent regulations in this regard.

Unsolicited proposal

Any private party may submit unsolicited Proposal to the Contacting Authority or the PPP Authority. There will separate subsequent guidelines in this regard.

Project company

All PPP projects with be contracted with a separate project company other than the sponsors. The project company will be limited by shares and incorporated in Bangladesh. All liability should be borne by this project company.

Corruption and conflict of interest

The Act set out provisions for corruption and conflict of interest which are similar to Public Procurement Act 2006 and Public Procurement Rules 2008.

Project agreement

The Act does not provide much restriction or detail guideline about the project agreements including the governing law of the agreements. For dispute resolution, the Act requires arbitration before going to the court. Following the enactment of the new

PPP law, the PPPO is planning a program to further strengthen support for the structured operationalization of PPPs in Bangladesh. The program will be based on several components including the development of a policy framework, strengthening of institutional capacity, building a project pipeline and improving the investment climate. ①

5.7   Full list of sectoral coverage for PPP in Bangladesh

According to the Policy and Strategy for PPP, 2010, any project fulfilling one or more of the PPP applicability criteria in any economic sector, according to the International Standard Industrial Classification (ISIC) of all Economic Activities, Revision 4, specified by the United Nations, is eligible for PPP.

With this coverage in perspective, the GoB has identified the following priority sectors:

(a) exploration, production, transmission and distribution of oil, gas, coal, and other mineral resources (ISIC 05 –09);

(b) oil refinery and production of LPG (ISIC 19);

(c) production of fertilizer (ISIC 20);

(d) power generation, transmission, distribution and services (ISIC 35);

(e) airports, terminals and related aviation facilities (ISIC 42 and 51);

(f) water supply and distribution, sewerage and drainage, effluent treatment plans (ISIC 36 –39);

(g) land reclamation, dredging of rivers, canals, wetlands, lakes, and other related facilities (ISIC 42);

(h) highways and expressways including mass-transit, bridges, tunnels, flyovers, interchanges, city roads, bus terminals, commercial car parking, etc. (ISIC 42 and 49);

(i) port development (sea, river and land) including inland container terminals, inland container depot, and other services (ISIC 52);

(j) deep sea port development (ISIC 52);

(k) telecommunication systems, networks and services including information and communication technology (ICT) (ISIC 60 –63);

---

①   PPP Knowledge Lab, Bangladesh, https://pppknowledgelab. org/countries/bangladesh.

(l) environmental,industrial,and solid waste management projects(ISIC 38 –39);

(m) railway systems,rolling stock,equipment and facilities(ISIC 49);

(n) tourism industry(ISIC 79);

(o) economic zone,industrial estates and parks,city and property development, including services to support commercial and non-commercial activities(ISIC 81 – 82);

(p) social infrastructure e. g. health,education,human resource development, research and development,and cultural facilities(ISIC 85 –88);

(q) e-service delivery to citizens(ISIC 85);

(r) poverty Alleviation Projects(ISIC 84);

- Pourashava and village water supply(ISIC 36);
- Remote Area Power Supply Systems(RAPSS),rural gas supply(ISIC 35);
- rural Internet projects(ISIC 61);
- river passenger terminals/landing stations(ISIC 52);
- rural health services and hospital(ISIC 86);
- irrigation and other agricultural services(ISIC 36);

(s) other urban,municipal,and rural projects that the Government views as priority areas for development so as to support economic development activities.

To boost private investment and potential growth over the medium term and make the growth processes more inclusive,Bangladesh needs wide-ranging structural reforms. These include reducing the deficit in public infrastructure and improving the business climate. The PPP Act passed in September 2015 should enable private participation in public infrastructure projects,particularly in the power and transport sectors.

Chapter 6   Laws Relating to Labour Management and Treatment

Bangladesh has a population of over 160 million people and a labour force of 57 million people. Approximately 40 – 50 percent of the labour force work in the agricultural sector, roughly 10 – 20 percent in industry, and the remaining in the services sector. Low official unemployment statistics obscure a huge and growing under-employment problem in Bangladesh. Bangladesh's comparative advantage in cheap labour for manufacturing is partially offset by low productivity due to low skills, poor management, pervasive corruption, and inefficient infrastructure and machinery, as well as an increase in minimum wage rates in 2013, particularly in the garment sector. [1]

6. 1   A brief history of the labour laws of Bangladesh

The labour law system is more than a century old in Bangladesh. The first labour law was enacted in the Indian sub-continent during the British period, in 1881. Subsequently, the British Government introduced several laws concerning different labour issues, e. g. working hour, employment of children, maternity benefit, trade union activities, wage, etc. The Factories Act (1881), Workmen's Compensation Act (1923), Trade Unions Act (1926), Trade Disputes Act (1929), Payment of Wages Act (1936), Maternity Benefit Act (1939) and the Employment of Children Act (1938) were remarkable labour laws enacted during the British period. [2]

After the separation of the Indian sub-continent in 1947, almost all the laws during the repartition period were kept in force with some modifications and amendments, in the form of administrative rules, by the Pakistan Government. After the independence in 1971, the Bangladesh Government retained the previous laws

---

[1]   Bureau of Economic and Business Affairs, US Department of State, "Investment Climate Statement-Bangladesh" 2015, http://www. state. gov/e/eb/rls/othr/ics/2015/241475. htm.

[2]   Jakir Hossain, Mostafiz Ahmed and Afroza Akter, "Bangladesh Labour Law: Reform and Directions", 2010 *Bangladesh Institute of Labour Studies* 5.

through the Bangladesh Laws Order (President's Order No. 48). It also enacted additional laws in response to the changing circumstances and needs of the working class and the country. In 2006, the country adopted the revised Bangladesh Labour Law of 2006 or BLL.

The BLL is fairly comprehensive and progressive. The law is a consolidation and updating of the 25 separate acts. The comprehensive nature of the law can immediately be gleaned from its coverage conditions of service and employment, youth employment, maternity benefit, health and hygiene, safety, welfare, working hours and leave, wages and payment, workers' compensation for injury, trade unions and industrial relations, disputes, labour court, workers' participation in company's profits, regulation of employment and safety of dock workers, provident funds, apprenticeship, penalty and procedure, administration, inspection, etc.

The BLL is also considered an advanced law because it removes certain ambiguities in the old and diverse labour acts and aligns the labour law system with the ILO core conventions. On the removal of ambiguities, the definition of a "worker" is now very specific. Another example is the exclusion under the term "wages" of the following items: expense for housing facilities like lighting and water supply, employers' contribution to the provident fund, travelling allowances and other sums paid to worker that are needed to cover work-related expenses.

The BLL is also an advanced law because of its wider coverage, for example, workers and staff of hospitals, nursing homes and even non-governmental organisations are now covered by the law. Also, certain welfare and social benefits have been improved or instituted, e. g. , death benefit (financial support to family of deceased worker), application of provident fund benefit to all workers in the private sector, expansion of maternity benefit from 12 to 16 weeks, adoption of group insurance for establishments with 200 or more workers, and increased employee compensation for work-related injury, disability and death.

The amendment of the Bangladesh Labour Act 2006, adopted on 15 July 2013, was the first step towards fulfilling the Government's obligation to respectfully the fundamental rights to freedom of association and collective bargaining and to address the critical need to bolster occupational safety and health. The amendment makes a large number of amendments to the 2006 Act. In particular the Act amends the 2006

Labour Act with respect to: adding a new section concerning the status of workers[1]; compensation due to death[2]; termination of employment[3]; adding a new section 28A entitled "Employers-Workers relations due to any disaster beyond control or damage thereby"; resolving dispute over a child's age[4]; dangerous work for children[5]; emergency exits[6]; access to gangways, stairs, etc., for workers[7]; adding a new section 78a concerning mandatory use of personal safety equipment; notification of competent authority in case of incident[8]; establishment of a health centre in companies employing more than 5000 workers[9] adding a new section on formation of a safety committee[10]; adding a new section 94a entitled "Residential Facility for Physically Challenged Workers' compulsory group insurance"[11]; adding a new section 124a entitled "Payment of dues including wages through conciliation;" adding a new section 140a entitled "Special Power of the Government;" prohibition on deducting money to survivors of a worker who has died[12]; provisions on social dialogue, trade unions and dispute resolution[13]; employers and companies responsibilities[14].

On the ILO core conventions, Bangladesh has ratified the following International Labour Conventions (ILCs):

- ILC 29 (Forced Labour),
- ILC 87 (Freedom of Association and Protection of the Right to Organise),
- ILC 98 (Right to Organise and Collective Bargaining),
- ILC 100 (Equal Remuneration),

---

[1] Bangladesh Labour Act, 42 B. C. S 4, 2006.

[2] Ibid. ,42 B. C. S 19.

[3] Ibid. ,42 B. C. S 23, 24 and 27.

[4] Ibid. ,42 B. C. S 36.

[5] Ibid. ,42 B. C. S 39.

[6] Ibid. ,42 B. C. S 62.

[7] Ibid. ,42 B. C. S 72.

[8] Ibid. ,42 B. C. S 80.

[9] Ibid. ,42 B. C. S 89.

[10] Ibid. ,42 B. C. S 90.

[11] Ibid. ,42 B. C. S 99.

[12] Ibid. ,42 B. C. S 155.

[13] Ibid. ,42 B. C. S 168, 176, 177, 178, 179, 180, 183, 187, 200, 202, 202a, 205, 211, 213, 214 and 215, (2006).

[14] Ibid. ,42 B. C. S 232, 233, 234, 235 and 236 2006.

- ILC 105(Abolition of Forced Labour),
- ILC 111(Discrimination in Employment and Occupation),and
- ILC 182(Elimination of the Worst Forms of Child Labour).

The only core convention not ratified by Bangladesh is ILC 138(Minimum Age Convention). However, the BLA provides that the minimum age to work is 14 (although a special clause states that children between the ages of 12 and 14 may be employed to do "light work" that does not endanger their health, development and education).

6. 2   Laws relating to labour management and treatment

Bangladesh has labour laws that specify employment conditions, working hours, minimum wage levels, leave policies, health and sanitary conditions, and compensation for injured workers.

A worker is defined as any person, including a trainee/probationer, whether the terms and conditions of his/her employment are expressly written or not, who is employed directly or through a contractor/agency, for any skilled, unskilled, physical, technical, business development or clerical job in any establishment or industry. "Worker" does not include a person employed mainly in a managerial, administrative [or supervisory] capacity. Forced labour is prohibited. ①

Workers are classified into six categories:

Apprentice: A worker who is employed in an establishment as a trainee and during the period of training he is paid an allowance is called an apprentice.

Badli: A worker who is employed in an establishment for the period of temporary absence of a permanent or probationer worker.

Casual worker: A worker employed on a casual basis.

Temporary worker: A temporary worker in an establishment for work that is basically temporary in nature and is likely to be finished within a limited period.

Probationer: A worker provisionally employed in any establishment to fill up a post of permanent vacancy and his probationer period has not to be completed.

Permanent worker: A worker employed with a view to fill up a permanent post or if he completes satisfactorily his probation period in the establishment.

---

① Jakir Hossain, Mostafiz Ahmed and Afroza Akter, "Bangladesh Labour Law: Reform and Directions", (2010) *Bangladesh Institute of Labour Studies* 6.

Appointment letters and ID cards

Appointment letters, ID cards and service books are made mandatory. The law specifies what information should be included in the appointment letter and in the service book, and requires the latter to be signed by both the employer and the worker. [1]

The law defines who is responsible for payment of wages

Employer/owner; CEO; manager/person assigned responsible by the company; and the contractor, in case of worker appointed by the contractor. In case of the failure of the contractor to pay the wages to the worker, the principal owner shall pay the same and subsequently it can be adjusted with the accounts of the contractor.

Provisions relating to termination

On job terminations, the employer is required in the case of

Retrenchment: To give one month's notice and the equivalent 30-day wages or gratuity for every year of service if the worker is employed on continuous service for not less than one year;

Discharge: To give financial benefit equivalent to 30-day wages for every completed year of service by an employee found to have physical or mental incapacity.

Termination simpliciter: To terminate services of worker without explaining any reason by giving a written notice of 120 days for permanent workers employed in a monthly basis and 60 days to other workers.

Misconduct: To dismiss workers without serving prior notice due to worker's conviction for any criminal offence, or if the worker is proved guilty of misconduct, which may be any of the following—wilful insubordination (alone or in combination with others) to any lawful or reasonable order, theft or fraud or dishonesty, taking or giving bribes, habitual absence without leave for more than 10 days, habitual late attendance, habitual breach of any rule or law applicable to the establishment, riotous or disorderly behaviour, habitual negligence or neglect of work, frequent repetition of work on which fine can be imposed, resorting to illegal strike or to go slow or instigating others to do so, and falsifying, tampering the official document of the

---

[1]   Jakir Hossain, Mostafiz Ahmed and Afroza Akter, "Bangladesh Labour Law: Reform and Directions", (2010) *Bangladesh Institute of Labour Studies* 6.

employer.

Retirement: Retirement age for workers employed in any establishment is 57.

Working Hours: Work hours are set at eight hours a day, 48 hours a week, with a weekly rest day. Overtime (OT) work is maximum of two hours a day. OT pay is twice the hourly remuneration. No young worker is permitted to work in any establishment between the hours of 7 pm and 7 am. Workers are entitled to rest and meal in a day as follows:

A. one hour interval for over six hours' work a day;

B. half an hour interval for more than five hours' work; and

C. one hour interval once or half an hour interval twice for more than eight hours' work a day.

Leave: Workers are entitled to holidays, casual leave, festival leave, annual leave and sick leave.

Wages: A "Minimum Wage Board" is established to determine the minimum rates of wages in different private sectors, taking into consideration varied criteria— cost of living, standard of living, cost of production, productivity, price of products, business capability, and economic and social conditions of the country. Every worker has the right to participate in company's profits/benefits. Employers are mandated to observe equal wages for male and female workers for work of equal nature or value. [1]

Occupational safety and health

Establishments are required to put up for every 150 workers one first aid box and one trained person per first aid box, and an equipped dispensary with a patient-room, doctor and nursing staff. Employers are required to take appropriate measures to protect workers from danger and damage due to fire. Every establishment is required to be kept clean and free from effluvia arising out of any drain, privy or other nuisance. The work room should not be overcrowded and injurious to the health of the workers. Every establishment should provide pure drinking water, sufficient light and air, and separate toilets for its male and female workers. [2]

The ILO also launched in October 2013 a USD 24.2 million, three-and-a-half

---

[1] Jakir Hossain, Mostafiz Ahmed and Afroza Akter, "Bangladesh Labour Law: Reform and Directions", (2010) *Bangladesh Institute of Labour Studies* 6.

[2] Ibid.

year programme to support implementation of Bangladesh's National Tripartite Plan of action on fire safety and structural integrity in the ready-made garment(RMG) sector. Key elements are already being implemented, including building and fire safety assessments; labour inspection reforms; and occupational safety and health, rehabilitation and skills training. The ILO, in partnership with the International Finance Corporation (IFC), also initiated the Better Work program in Bangladesh which will provide assessments of factory compliance with national law and core international labour standards, provide transparent public reporting on findings, advisory services to factories, and build worker-management dialogue. ①

The Accord on Fire and Building Safety in Bangladesh(the Accord) is a five-year independent, legally binding agreement between 190 apparel brands and retailers and trade unions designed to build a safe and healthy Bangladeshi Ready Made Garment(RMG) Industry. The Accord covers over 1600 factories. The Alliance for Bangladesh Worker Safety(Alliance) was founded by a group of 26 North American companies and brands who have joined together to improve safety in Bangladeshi ready-made garment(RMG) factories. The Alliance covers more than 580 factories. Both initiatives began in 2013 and are five-year commitments. Both initiatives have conducted safety inspections and are assisting with the implementation of Corrective Action Plans at members' factories. ②

Welfare and social protection

Gratuity is defined under the law as separation payment, at least 30 days, for workers discharged from work and yet have worked not less than 6 months.

Factories are required to have an in-house canteen for every 100 workers.

Every establishment/employer is required to form a Provident Fund if three-fourths of its workers demand it by written application, and a Workers' Participation Fund and a Workers' Welfare Fund for its workers.

Establishments with 200 or more workers should institute a group insurance.

Every employer should provide compensation to its workers for work-related injury, disability and death.

Various women's issues are also covered: maternity leave of 16 weeks(8 weeks

---

① Bureau of Economic and Business Affairs, US Department of State, "Investment Climate Statement-Bangladesh" (2015), http://www. state. gov/e/eb/rls/othr/ics/2015/241475. htm.

② Ibid.

before and eight weeks after child birth), no gender-segregated wage structure, prohibition of any form of discrimination against women, prohibition of women working between 10:00 pm and 6:00 am without consent, prohibition for women handling running or dangerous machines (unless they are sufficiently trained to operate such machinery), prohibition for women working under water or underground.

6.3   Labour relations and social dialogue

Every worker employed in any establishment has the right to form and join a trade union of their own choice. Trade unions have the right to draw up their own constitution and rules and to elect their representatives. Also, trade unions have the right to form and join in a federation and such unions and federations have the right to affiliate with any international organisation and confederation of trade unions.

The trade union is allowed to serve as a collective bargaining agent in any establishment. In case of industrial disputes, the two sides can seek resolution through negotiation followed by conciliation and eventually arbitration if negotiation fails. The collective bargaining agent is entitled to file a notice of strike(or lockout in the case of the employer) with a 15-day cooling-off period. Employers cannot recruit new workers during the period of a strike. Employers are also prohibited in terminating workers in the course of trade union organizing in the work place.

Freedom of association and the right to join unions are guaranteed in the constitution. In practice, compliance and enforcement of labour laws are inconsistent, and companies frequently discourage the formation of active labour unions. Historically, unions are heavily politicized, and labour-management relations are often contentious, particularly in the ready-made garment sectors. The Joint Directorate of Labour(JDL) is the body responsible for approving union applications and has broad authority in this regard. [1]

In July 2004, parliament enacted a law for export processing zones. The law allows the formation of worker welfare associations that elect leaders and can collectively bargain, although there are no collective bargaining agreements in the EPZs in practice. The implementation of worker welfare councils in the export

---

[1]   Bureau of Economic and Business Affairs, US Department of State, "Investment Climate Statement-Bangladesh" (2015), http://www.state.gov/e/eb/rls/othr/ics/2015/241475.htm.

processing zones is uneven with many larger factories ignoring the provision altogether. ①

Enforcement

Government shall appoint the Director of Labour and " such number " of additional Director of Labour, Joint Directors of Labour, Deputy Directors of Labour and Assistant Directors of Labour as necessary for monitoring workplace activities.

The Government shall appoint a Chief Inspector and requisite number of Deputy Chief Inspectors, Assistant Chief Inspectors or Inspectors. These officers have the power to enter, inspect and examine any workplace premises and ascertain the observance of labour laws.

The Government has the power to establish as many Labour Courts as it considers necessary. A Labour Court shall consist of a chairman and two members (one representing employers and the other, the workers).

6.4   Child labour

No children(under 14 years of age) are allowed to work in any occupation or establishment. However, a child who is 12 years of age is permitted to do light work not harmful to his health, development and education. Section 34 of the 2006 Labour Act, prohibit child labour in certain sectors, ranging from transport workers to tea plantation labour, but these have not been consistently applied to informal sectors, such as agriculture and domestic work, where the majority of children are employed. As a result, child labour in Bangladesh has historically been a problem.

On 4 July 1995, Bangladesh's garment exporters association signed a memorandum of understanding (MOU) with the United Nations Children's Fund (UNICEF) and the ILO under which child labourers were removed from EPZ textile factories and enrolled in education programs. ILO-assisted monitoring teams, which found child labourers in 43 percent of EPZ factories in 1996, found them in fewer than five percent in 2001. The MOU program has been phased out, and the US embassy considers the project a success, with most child labour now eradicated from the EPZs and from the formal garment sector in general. Child labour laws are not

---

① Bureau of Economic and Business Affairs, US Department of State, "Investment Climate Statement-Bangladesh" (2015), http://www. state. gov/e/eb/rls/othr/ics/2015/241475. htm.

effectively enforced outside of the EPZs, particularly in the informal sector that employs roughly 80 percent of the workforce. Bangladesh, however, is working to improve compliance with ILO conventions on child labour. ①

6.5 Bangladesh Labour Rules 2015

After much delay, Bangladesh Government has introduced the Bangladesh Labour Rules 2015 on 15 September 2015 through a gazette. The Government was under pressure from various sources to promulgate the Labour Rules for a long time.

Some key points are described below:

Employment policy/Service rules: If any establishment wants to have its own Employment Policy/Service Rules, it must obtain approval from the Chief Inspector of Labour. All existing Employment Policy/Service Rules must be submitted to the Chief Inspector of Labour within 15 November 2015 for approval.

Registration of manpower supply agency: The Rules prescribed the process and forms for the registration of manpower supply agencies under the Labour Act. Some new conditions are also imposed on the manpower supply agencies.

Organogram: Every owner of an establishment must prepare an organogram for the establishment and must obtain the approval of Chief Inspector of Labour for such organogram.

Appointment letter: Under the Labour Act, an appointment letter must be issued for hiring any labour. The Labour Rules makes it mandatory that the appointment letter must contain certain information such as salary, other financial benefits, applicable rules, etc.

Various registers: The Labour Rules prescribe certain forms for various register such as service book, labour register, leave register, etc.

Misconduct and punishment: The Rules prescribe the process for investigation of misconduct.

Festival bonuses: The Rules make it mandatory that a labour, who continuously works for a year, must receive two festival bonuses in every year. Each bonus shall not be more than a basic salary.

Provident fund elaborated: The Rules provide detailed guidelines regarding

---

① Bureau of Economic and Business Affairs, US Department of State, "Investment Climate Statement-Bangladesh" (2015), http://www. state. gov/e/eb/rls/othr/ics/2015/241475. htm.

provident fund. New additions includes provisions relating to selection of nominee, management of the fund, activities of the trust for managing provident fund.

Holidays: The Rules give the provisions relating to holidays. in detail They also clarify the provisions relating to compensatory weekly holiday.

Health and fire safely: The Rules provide a detail guideline on health and fire safety.

Wages: The Rules give the provisions relating to wages in detail. Clarification is provided for the mechanism of calculating wages for fraction of month and deduction from wages.

Prescribed from for filling case in Labour Court: The Rules introduced some prescribed forms for filling cases in the Labour Court.

Approval of factory plan and any extension: The Rules put an end to the Factories Rules and provide detail guideline how approval of factory plan and any extension thereof should be obtained.

The labour related laws of Bangladesh attempted to cover almost all the labour related situations through a single legal instrument. Moreover, the law tried to cover all the possible labour related sectors. As a result the provisions may seem comforting for one sector and harsh for other sectors at the same time. In short, the law and its rules are investment friendly and labour friendly also.

Chapter 7   Environmental Law

As human beings, we exploit the environment in our endeavour for better living. Such exploitations, over the centuries, have resulted in serious threat to the environment itself. Industrialisation, exponential population growth, increased dependence on use of automobiles, indiscriminate felling of trees and such other activities have been the root causes to the present-day vulnerability of the global environment resulting in global warming with consequent gradual disappearance of polar ice-caps and rise in sea-levels.

Conventionally economic growth implies growth of goods and services produced in an economy. Economic growth has been considered as the precondition of human welfare and development. But the traditional system of estimating economic growth on the basis of goods and services do not consider environmental effect. Recently the emergence of the concept of sustainable development made it clear that alternative method is needed for estimating physical and economic development appropriately to measure standard of living of human beings. In this method, the depletion of natural resources and environmental issues that have impact on sustainable development are taken into account.

7.1   Environmental laws and policies in Bangladesh

At present, there are about 210 laws relating to environment. This however, does not suggest a long tradition of environmental law making nor were the objectives "conservation oriented" or "environment oriented".

There are about 60 policies, strategies and action plans pertinent to environmental administration. Policies being recent documents contain more progressive notions. Policies, however, are mere administrative documents, *ad hoc* and are not enforceable.

7. 2   Bangladeshi environmental laws

The first major law that has been promulgated for the specific purpose of protection of environment and conservation of nature is the Environmental Conservation Act (ECA) of 1995, which was followed by the Environmental Conservation Rules(ECR) of 1997. [1]

The majority of environmental laws in Bangladesh were passed under substantially different population and development conditions. For example, the Factories Act of 1965 and some other health protection laws were designed before industrial pollution and hazardous substances became serious concerns. The Environmental policy of 1992 of Bangladesh has recognised the need for a better and comprehensive approach to address environmental issues. Very few of the elements of the Environmental policy, however, are yet to be translated into laws. The only legislation which specifically deals with environment issues is the Bangladesh Environment Conservation Act(ECA) 1995. The Act was passed for conservation and improvement of environmental standards and for controlling and mitigating environmental pollution. It however, provides very few substantive obligations relating to environmental management of industries. Industries and projects would require environmental clearance from the Department of the Environment, and any person affected or likely to be affected by such activities can apply to the Director General seeking remedy for environmental pollution or degradation. The major limitations of the Act are its silences on the standards, parameters, emission levels and management elements based on which the environmental clearance should have been applied and obtained.

The Environmental Conservation Rules 1997 were promulgated in furtherance of the objectives of the ECA 1995. Regarding management of toxic and hazardous substances, the Rules have broadly defined guidelines for disposal of waste from different categories of industries. But unlike the Environmental Protection Rules of India, The Environmental Conservation Rules 1997 have not specified the permissible extent of emissions or the obligations of corrective actions(IUCN 2000).

Among Bangladeshi scrotal laws, environmental issues are seldom referred to,

---

[1]   Asian Development Bank, Country Environmental Analysis: Bangladesh(2004) ,19.

and when they are there, those are of no real substance. For example, Article 6 of The Bangladesh Petroleum Act 1975 provides that it shall be the duty of any person engaged in any petroleum operation to ensure that the operation is carried out (i) in proper and workmanlike manner and in accordance with good oil-field practice, (ii) in a manner that does not interfere with navigation, fishing, and conservation of resources of the sea and sea-bed, and to consider factors connected with the ecology and environment. The Act has not defined what the factors "connected with the ecology and environment" are and what management elements a company should establish and maintain to discharge its obligations under the Act.

Laws having relevance to natural resources management in Bangladesh can be broadly divided into the following categories:

• Laws having non-sectoral approach—Environmental Conservation Act (ECA) of 1995 and Environmental Conservation Rules (ECR) of 1997.

The following table provides a list of available laws that have bearing on environment.

Table 1. **Laws Related to Environment**

Law	Sectors
The Environmental Conservation Act of 1995	Major laws and regulations in the environment sector. Laws and relevant Regulation Major components Environmental Conservation Act of 1995 empowered the MOEF to formulate rules and guidelines for the management. It also designates DOE responsible for enforcing the 1997 EIA procedures air pollution, water pollution, noise.
Environmental Conservation Rules of 1997	Air pollution, water pollution, noise EIA Guidelines of Industries of 1997. The EIA process is categorised into four classes, that is, green, amber A, amber B, and red, according to the degree of impacts.
Environment Court Act 2010	The Act is passed to establish Environment Court for speedy disposal of cases concerning environmental offences as defined in the Environmental Law.
Environmental Pollution Control Ordinance 1997	Including national water quality standards according to the WHO guidelines, air quality standards, noise, solid waste management.

(Continued)

Law	Sectors
Factories Act 1965	Air pollution, occupational health .
Motor Vehicles Act 1939	Air pollution, noise.
Non Agricultural Tenancy Act 1947	Land use .
State Acquisition and Tenancy Act 1950	Land use .
Acquisition of Waste Land Act 1950	Land use .
Town Improvement Act 1950	Land use.
Municipality Ordinance 1977	Land use .
Local Government Ordinance 1982	Land use.
Land Reforms Ordinance 1984	Land use.
Land Reform Board Act 1989	Land use.
Chittagong Hill Tract Regulation Act 1990	Land use.
Pesticide Ordinance 1971(Amended in 1980)	Toxic and hazardous substance.
Agricultural Pest Ordinance 1962	Toxic and hazardous substance.
Dangerous Drug Act 1930	Toxic and hazardous substance.
Dangerous Drug Control Order 1982	Toxic and hazardous substance.
Agriculture and Sanitary Improvement Act 1920	Land use.
Toxic and Hazardous Substance Poison Act 1930	Toxic and hazardous substance.
Explosive Substances Act 1908 (Modified in 1983)	Toxic and hazardous substance.
Explosive Act 1884	Toxic and hazardous substance.
Municipality Ordinance 1977	Solid waste management laws and relevant Regulation Description.
Private Forest Ordinance 1950, Forest Act 1927(Modified in 1973)	Forest conservation, biodiversity conservation, soil conservation.
Wildlife(Preservation) Act 1973 (Amended in 1974)	Wildlife conservation, wetland management, biodiversity conservation.
Private Fisheries Protection Act 1889	Biodiversity conservation.
Conservation and Protection of Fisheries Act 1950	Coastal resources management, biodiversity conservation.

(Continued)

Law	Sectors
Marine Fisheries Ordinance 1983	Coastal resources management, biodiversity conservation marine pollution.
Territorial Water and Marine Zone Act 1974	Coastal resources management, marine pollution.
Mines Act 1927	Mineral resources development and management.
Petroleum Act 1934	Mineral resources development and management.
Antiquities Act 1986	Cultural heritage.
Antiquities Ordinance 1986	Cultural heritage.
Policy for management of closed waterbody (Jalmahal) 1990	Water resources management.
Water Supply and Sewerage Authority Ordinance 1963 (Amended in 1989)	Water resources management.
Inland Shipping Ordinance 1976	Water resources management.
Embankment and Drainage Act 1952	Water resources management.
Water Hyacinth Act 1939	Water resources management.
IWTA Ordinance 1958	Water resources management.
Canals Act 1864	Water resources management.
Irrigation Act 1876	Water resources management.
EPC Ordinance 1977	Marine pollution.

7.3   The Bangladesh Environment Conservation Act 1995

The Bangladesh Environment Conservation Act (BECA) of 1995 was enacted for fulfilling three major objectives namely: conservation of environment, improvement of environmental standards and the control and mitigation of environmental pollution. The Act was formulated on the basis of the policy framework provided by the Environmental policy of 1992 and the National Environment Management Action Plan (NEMAP) of 1995. The BECA also defines certain environmental offences and prescribes for their punishments. Moreover, to supplement and fulfil the objectives of the Act, the Bangladesh Environment Conservation Rules (BECR) 1997 was adopted in accordance with Section 20 of the BECA 1995. However, the Bangladesh Environment Conservation Act 1995 and Rules

1997 are not free from a number of loopholes or shortcomings. There is a maxim that "prevention is better than cure", but the BECA of 1995 by the terms "improvement of environmental standards" and "mitigation of environmental pollution" in its preamble indicates that it is cure-oriented and it only copes with the curative measures rather than the preventive measures. The BECA 1995, in a true sense, deals with the post-harm situations.

In Section 3, the term "Government" is a vague one. It creates the question in our minds; who is the Government under the BECA 1995? There is no reference to any specific criteria for determining the "Government" who would set up the Department of Environment (DoE) headed by the Director General (DG).

Section 3(2) of the BECA 1995 speaks about the appointment of the Director General in the Department of Environment, but it does not state any definite qualifications upon which the DG will be appointed. The appointment process is totally dependent upon the satisfaction of the Government.

Section 4 of the Act gives unfettered and unlimited powers to the Director General (DG) of the Department of Environment (DoE). The wording "may" in Section 4 denotes that the DG is not bound to take necessary measures in order to conserve the environment and the DG can do anything at his sweet will. It is noteworthy that under Section 4 the DG is empowered to take immediate action against any industry and to close the industry without giving any "prior notice" to the industry, if he "considers" that the industry is likely to endanger public life. Taking any action against any person or any industry or corporation without giving any prior notice absolutely goes against the principles of natural justice. Also, such a closure of the industries is totally dependent on the DG's satisfaction. This most often creates room for DG to resort to corruption.

Section 5 of the Act requires the Government to declare the "ecologically critical areas". It is palpable that the environment experts can play a vital role in declaring the ecologically critical areas. Section 5 has no reference to the matter.

According to Section 6B, the hill or hillock may be cut for "inevitable national interest". The term "inevitable national interest" is a vague one. There are no specific objective criteria to determine "inevitable national interest".

Though the Section 6C speaks about production, import, stock, transportation of hazardous waste, it does not speak about reuse, recycling and reduction of waste.

Section 12 of the Act speaks about "Environment Clearance Certificate". It is yet unclear what will happen if the Department of Environment is unable to meet the timetable to grant the Environment Clearance Certificate(ECC). Section 12 is silent about the standards and parameters upon which the ECC should be obtained. Section 12 also speaks about the formulation of Environment Impact Assessment (EIA) report, but it does not prescribe the role of environment experts in preparing the EIA report. However, it provides for EIA report only of the industrial projects not of the non-industrial projects. As per Rule 7 of the Bangladesh Environment Conservation Rules(BECR)1997, the industries belonging to highly polluting Red categories must obtain "No Objection Certificate(NOC)" of the local government authority. But the Conservation Act or Rules does not provide any procedures to be followed by the local government authority in issuing such a "No Objection Certificate (NOC)". However, India and some other countries prescribe "public hearing" which means that before establishing any industry, the people of the locality will be convened by the concerned government local authority in order to know whether they have any objection to the erection of the industry and what are the harms and risks which they think, will occur to the environment. On the other hand, Principle 10 of the Rio Declaration 1992 provides for the participation of all concerned citizens in environmental issues as well as an opportunity for all concerned citizens to participate in decision making processes. Unfortunately, any single provision concerning such a public hearing and public participation has not yet been incorporated in BECA 1995 and BECR 1997.

Section 14 of the Act ousts the court's jurisdiction in terms of entertaining appeal from an order or direction issued under the Act. Only the Appellate Authority constituted by the Government has the jurisdiction to entertain appeal under the Act. The decision of such Appellate Authority shall be final. No review and revision against the orders of such an Appellate Authority will be allowed.

7. 4   The Environment Courts Act 2010

The environment court, as portrayed in ECA 2010, has, at least twofold limitations in terms of jurisdiction namely, lack of integrated jurisdictions over the laws *pari materia* and insufficient penal policy. Apparently, the court can exercise jurisdiction only in the matters arising out of the Environment Conservation Act 1995, disregarding a bulk of environmental laws. An integrated jurisdiction over all environmental laws is required for the coherent dispensation of justice. A harmonious reading of Section 2 (c) of the ECA 2010 read with section 15 of the Environment Conservation Act 1995 , substantiates that the court can impose the maximum penalty of taka ten lac both for natural and juristic persons irrespective of the gravity of offence or torts.

As per Section 4 of the ECA 2010 the joint-district judges are persona designate in the environmental courts as judges. Remarkably , their role as part-time judges in environment courts ipso facto proves the " window dressing approach " of the government towards environmental governance regime. Given the deadlock of cases in civil courts , a joint-district judge cannot perform functions of both offices , i. e. as a civil court judge and a judge of environment court unless he is Dworkin's "Hercules".

Section 17 of the ECA 1995 read with Sections 6 (3) and 7 (4) of the Environment Court Act 2010 transpires that a court cannot take cognisance of a cause on the basis of averments made by an aggrieved person without previous authorisation of an executive , i. e. the inspector of the DoE. This is a clear legislative hegemony to executive over the judiciary , necessarily resulting in bar to access to justice.

In this era of epistolary jurisdiction in environmental governance , procedural requirements to access to justice , e. g. rule of standing have undergone epoch-making liberalization.

7. 5   International Environmental Agreements

Policy regime is also very much influenced by the international policy regimes , i. e. International Conventions , Treaties and Protocols (ICTPs) that Bangladesh chose to become signatory. Recently promulgated Environment Policy , National Conservation Strategy , National Biodiversity Strategy and Action Plan (underdevelopment) are examples of offshoots that developed under the influence of obligations entailed due to signing of ICTPs. Not much significant work has been done so far to implement the obligations with regard to the ICTPs signed. Participation in the negotiations and subsequent adoption and implementation stages are handled mostly on an ad hoc basis. No attempt is made for maintaining the continuity of documentation. Little attempt is made to develop the right kind of expertise in the concerned agencies (Islam , 1996). Following are some of the important ICTPs signed and ratified by Bangladesh which are likely to initiate changes in the policy or commence new projects/activities towards that.

Convention on Biological Diversity(CBD) : Bangladesh signed the Convention at Rio in 1992 and ratified the same in 1994. All signatories were expected to develop their own Biodiversity Strategy and Action Plan(BSAP). Bangladesh has just started to develop its own BSAP.

Framework Convention on Climate Change and the Montreal Protocol on Ozone Depleting Substances : Bangladesh signed the Framework Convention on the Climate Change at the Earth Summit in Rio de Janeiro, Brazil in June 1992 and ratified it in 1994. The participation of Government of Bangladesh in the negotiation through the Intergovernmental Negotiating Committee (INC) has been minimal. In terms of institutionalization, a National Steering Committee was formed to oversee the activities under the Climate Convention.

The Ramsar Convention : In view of the fundamental ecological functions of wetlands as regulators of water regimes and as habitats supporting characteristic fauna, especially waterfowl, the broad objectives of the Ramsar Convention are to reduce the loss of wetlands and to ensure their conservation.

Basel Convention on the Control of Transboundary Movement of Hazardous Wastes and Their Disposal : Bangladesh has ratified the Basel Convention and has begun enforcing it since 30 June 1993 and also attended in the voluntary information exchange of the amended London Guidelines, 1989.

7. 6 Landmark decisions of the Supreme Court

In Bangladesh, the Supreme Court has interpreted the right to life to include the protection and preservation of the environment and ecological balance free from pollution of air and water. [1]

Cases filed by the Secretary General of the Bangladesh Environmental Lawyers Association similarly led the Supreme Court to hold that any person other than an officious intervener or a wayfarer without any interest in the cause may have sufficient interest in environmental matters to qualify as a person aggrieved. [2]

In *Bangladesh Environmental Lawyers Association v The Election Commission and Others*, SC of Bangladesh, High Court Div. , Writ Petition No. 186 of 1994, Dr

---

[1] *Dr Mohiuddin Farooque v Bangladesh*, represented by the Secretary, Ministry of Irrigation, Water Resources and Flood Control and Others, 48 DLR(1996) , p. 438.

[2] Ibid.

Mohiuddin Farooque, Secretary-General of the Bangladesh Environmental Lawyers Association (BELA), alleged that political candidates were flouting election laws and causing environmental pollution in the city with noise from loudspeakers and unscheduled processions. The Supreme Court noted that "it is desirable to mitigate the environmental pollution as alleged by the Petitioner", but found that the Election Commission and the Dhaka City Corporation had taken clear steps to stop the alleged pollution. In view of those facts and with the assurance of the Attorney General that the government would take all necessary steps to implement the directions of the Election Commission, the Supreme Court held that further direction was unnecessary. ①

Environment court, as a tool of environmental governance in the context of Bangladesh, must be designed in such a way which can overcome the traditional procedural drawbacks of civil or criminal courts and play an innovative role as a means to reach the end of transcendent environmental justice.

7.7   The Environment Policy of the Government

The latest draft environment policy, which has not yet been passed, provides guidelines for the following sectors:

Agriculture: Environmentally sound agricultural practices are to be encouraged and ensured for attainment of self-sufficiency in food. Among the various specific measures, use of natural fertilizers and insecticides is encouraged as opposed to the application of agro-chemicals and artificial materials exerting adverse impact on the environment.

Industry: Environmental Impact Assessment(EIA) for new industries, corrective measures for polluting industries, ban on establishment of polluting industries and development of environmentally sound and appropriate technology is required for sustainable and efficient utilization of natural resources.

Health and sanitation: Healthy environment for rural and urban area, prevention of activities, which are harmful to public health and healthy workplaces for workers are to be ensured.

Energy and fuel: Reduction of the use of fuel-wood and agricultural residues,

---

① Dinah Shelton and Alexandre Kiss, *Judicial Handbook on Environmental Law*, United Nations Environment Programme, 2005, pp. 116 – 117.

exploring alternative energy resources, precautionary measures against potentially harmful use of nuclear energy and nuclear radiation, conservation of forest fuel and development of improved energy saving technology are recommended options for the sector. Apart from these, EIA has been made mandatory before implementing projects for exploration and extraction of fuel and mineral resources.

Water: Environmentally sound water resource management is suggested in utilization and development of water resources, construction of irrigation network and embankments, dredging of watercourses and in taking measures against river pollution. EIA is required before undertaking projects related to water resource development and flood control measures.

Land: Activities that cause or result in land erosion, salinity and alkalinity, and loss of soil fertility are prohibited. Compatible land use systems for different ecosystems and environmentally sound management of newly accreted land are recommended.

Forest, wildlife and bio-diversity: Conservation and expansion of forest zones, conservation of wildlife and biodiversity and conservation of wetlands are recognised as priority areas for action.

Fisheries and livestock: Conservation of fisheries and livestock, mangrove forest and others ecosystems and prevention of activities that diminish the wetlands and natural habitats for fishes are the basic objectives in this sector. The need for an inter-ministerial co-ordination is indicated by requiring evaluation by the concerned agencies, of the existing projects on water development, flood control and irrigation, in order to minimize their adverse impact on fish growth and their habitat.

Food: Hygienic and environmentally sound method of production, preservation, processing and distribution of food and measures to ensure prohibition of import of harmful food items are recommended.

Coastal and marine environment: Coastal and marine eco-systems are identified as potential areas for intervention, where all internal and external polluting activities should be stopped. Fishing in coastal and marine environment within regeneration limits is recommended.

Transport and communication: Road, rail, air and water transport systems should be operated without polluting the environment. EIA is required before undertaking any projects in these sectors.

Housing and urbanisation: Environmentally sound planning and development of housing and urban centres is required. Existence of water bodies in the cities is recommended for maintaining environmental and ecosystem balance in the urban areas.

Population: Planned and proper utilisation of manpower including ensuring the participation and mainstreaming of women in all spheres is targeted for environmentally sound development activities.

Education and public awareness: Eradication of illiteracy through formal and non-formal education, building and raising public awareness of the environmental issues, dissemination of environmental knowledge and information are the policy guidelines for the conservation, improvement and sustainable use of natural resources.

Science, technology and research: Research and development institutes are required to consider the incorporation of the environmental issues in their research programs. For the implementation and leadership, the Ministry of Environment and Forest (MoEF) was assigned to play the role of lead agency. A National Environmental Committee was created with the Prime Minister as the Chairperson to give overall direction for implementation of this policy. The policy emphasised that the MoEF would take timely steps for appropriate amendment and modification of this policy on the backdrop of changes in the state of environment and socioeconomic and other needs of the country.

Therefore, it can be said that the laws and policies relating to the environment of Bangladesh are investment-friendly. These laws are improving day by day. As a developing country the government of Bangladesh is investment-friendly. Therefore the laws relating to environment impose less challenge to the foreign investment in Bangladesh.

Chapter 8   Laws Relating to Dispute Resolution Concerning Foreign Entities

8. 1   The court structure of Bangladesh

8. 1. 1   The Supreme Court of Bangladesh

The Supreme Court established under the Constitution of Bangladesh is the highest Court of the Republic. It has two Divisions, namely, Appellate Division and the High Court Division. High Court Division has original, appellate and other jurisdictions, powers and functions conferred on it by the Constitution or by any other law. On the other hand, Appellate Division hears and disposes of appeals from judgments, decrees, orders or sentences of the High Court Division. The Appellate Division has power to issue such directions, orders, decrees or writs as may be necessary for doing complete justice in any cause or matter pending before it, including orders for the purpose of securing the attendance of any person or the discovery or production of any document. The Supreme Court is headed by the Chief Justice of Bangladesh. [1]

8. 1. 1. 1   History of higher judiciary in the territory of Bangladesh

The territorial area of Bangladesh originally being part and parcel of the then Indian sub-continent, the history of its legal system may be traced back to 1726, when King George I issued a Charter changing the judicial administration of the Presidency towns of Calcutta, Bombay and Madras, which established the Civil and Criminal Courts, deriving their authority from the King. During the Mughal Empire the East India Company which took the settlement from the Emperor created the three presidency towns, Madras, Bombay and Calcutta, and introduced the English legal system for administration of the presidency towns. This is how the English judicial system entered the Sub-continent. The filing of the appeals from India (as it was then) to the Privy-Council in England was introduced by the Charter of 1726.

---

[1]   Annual Report 2014, the Supreme Court of Bangladesh, 2014, p. 64.

Thereafter, the East India Company Regulating Act 1773 was introduced to place the East India Company under the control of the British Government and provision was made for the establishment of a Supreme Court of Judicature at Fort William, Calcutta. The Supreme Court of Judicature at Fort William in Bengal was established by Letters Patent issued on 26 March 1774, which as a Court of Record had power and authority to dispose of all complaints against the Majesty's subjects in respect of any crime, suit or action within the territory of Bengal, Bihar and Orissa. By an Act passed in 1833 the Privy Council was transformed into an Imperial Court of unimpeachable authority, which played a great role as a unifying force for establishment of rule of law in the Indian Sub-continent.

The judicial system of the then India was re-organised by introducing the Indian High Courts Act 1861 by which High Courts were established, abolishing the Supreme Courts at Fort William Calcutta, Madras and Bombay. The High Courts were given civil, criminal, admiralty, testamentary and matrimonial jurisdictions, both original and appellate. With the transfer of power from the British Parliament to the people on division of India, the High Court of Bengal (Order) 1947 was promulgated under the Indian Independence Act 1947. The High Court of Judicature for East Bengal at Dhaka was established as a separate High Court for the then East Pakistan. It was commonly known as the Dhaka High Court and was vested with all appellate (both civil and criminal) and some original civil jurisdictions.

With the promulgation of the Constitution of the Islamic Republic of Pakistan in 1956, the Supreme Court of Pakistan was established as the apex Court of the country, consisting of East Pakistan and West Pakistan, in place of Federal Court, with the appellate jurisdiction in respect of decisions of the High Courts established in the provinces of Pakistan. The Dhaka High Court had the jurisdiction to issue writs in the nature of *Habeas Corpus*, *Mandamus*, Prohibition, *Quo-Warranto* and *Certiorari*, with further authority to declare void any law infringing any provision of the Constitution. ①

8. 1. 1. 2   Jurisdiction of the Supreme Court

The Supreme Court of Bangladesh derives its authority from the Constitution of the People's Republic of Bangladesh. Article 94 (1) of the Constitution provides that

---

① Annual Report 2014, the Supreme Court of Bangladesh, 2014, p. 64.

there shall be Supreme Court for Bangladesh comprising the Appellate Division and the High Court Division. These two Divisions of the Supreme Court have separate jurisdictions. The sources of this jurisdiction, apart from the Constitution, are general laws (Acts of Parliament) of the country. [1]

(A) Jurisdiction of the Appellate Division

The Constitution has conferred on the Appellate Division the following jurisdictions:

a. Appellate Jurisdiction: Article 103 of the Constitution provides that the Appellate Division shall have jurisdiction to hear and determine appeals from judgments, decrees, orders or sentences of the High Court Division. An appeal to the Appellate Division shall lie as of right where the High Court Division: (a) certifies that the case involves a substantial question of law as to the interpretation of the Constitution; or (b) has sentenced or confirmed the sentence of a person to death or to imprisonment for life; or (c) has imposed punishment on a person for contempt of that division; and in other cases if the Appellate Division grants leave to appeal and also pursuant to an Act of Parliament. [2]

b. Issue and execution of processes of Appellate Division: Under Article 104, the Appellate Division shall have power to issue such directions, orders, decrees or writs as may be necessary for doing complete justice in any cause or matter pending before it, including orders for the purpose of securing the attendance of any person or the discovery or production of any document. [3]

c. Power of review: Article 105 provides that the Appellate Division shall have power, subject to the provisions of any Act of Parliament and of any rules made by the Division, to review any judgment pronounced or any order made by it. Part IV, Order XXVI of the Supreme Court of Bangladesh (Appellate Division) Rules, 1988, deals with the power and procedural matters of review of the Appellate Division. [4]

d. Advisory jurisdiction: Article 106 of the Constitution provides that if at any time it appears to the President that a question of law has arisen, or is likely to arise, which is of such a nature and of such public importance that it is expedient to obtain the opinion of the Supreme Court upon it, he may refer the question to the Appellate

---

[1]   Annual Report 2014, the Supreme Court of Bangladesh, p. 66.

[2]   Ibid.

[3]   Ibid.

[4]   Ibid.

Division for consideration and the Division may, after such hearing as it thinks fit, report its opinion thereon to the President. ①

e. Rule-making power of the Supreme Court: Subject to any law made by Parliament, the Supreme Court may with the approval of the President make rules for regulating the practice and procedure of each Division of the Supreme Court and of any Court subordinate to it. ②

(B) Jurisdiction of the High Court Division

Article 101 of the Constitution provides that the High Court Division shall have such original, appellate and other jurisdictions, powers and functions as are or may be conferred on it by the Constitution or any other law.

a. Original jurisdiction: Original jurisdiction of the High Court Division refers to its jurisdiction to hear a case or suit as a court of first instance. The Constitution has conferred on the High Court Division special original jurisdiction under Article 102 of the Constitution to enforce fundamental rights guaranteed in Part III of the Constitution and to exercise its power of judicial review. There are some other ordinary laws (Acts of Parliament) namely, the Companies Act 1994; the Admiralty Court Act 2000; the Bank Companies Act 1991; Will and Probate under Succession Act 1925; the Divorce Act 1869; the Representation of the People Order 1972; Bangladesh Merchant Shipping Ordinance 1983; the Contempt of Courts Act 1926 etc. , which fall under the ordinary/original jurisdiction of the High Court Division. Further jurisdiction of the High Court Division is guided by the Code of Civil Procedure 1908 and the Supreme Court (High Court Division) Rules 1973. ③

b. Appellate jurisdiction: Any law may confer on the High Court Division appellate jurisdiction on any matter. The Code of Criminal Procedure 1898, the Code of Civil Procedure 1908, Section 42 of Value Added Tax Act 1991, Section 196D of the Customs Act 1969, etc. and the High Court Division Rules 1973, have conferred on the High Court Division appellate jurisdiction. ④

c. Revisionary Jurisdiction: (a) Section 115 of the Code of Civil Procedure, 1908, has conferred revisionary jurisdiction on the High Court Division. The High Court Division may examine the decisions of the courts subordinate to it. (b) Section

---

①   Annual Report 2014, the Supreme Court of Bangladesh, p. 66.

②   Ibid.

③   Ibid.

④   Ibid.

439 of the Code of Criminal Procedure 1898, has conferred on the High Court Division revisionary jurisdiction as to criminal matters of the courts subordinate to it. Furthermore, the High Court Division has inherent power under Section 561A of the Code of Criminal Procedure to make such orders as may be necessary to give effect to any order under this Code or to prevent abuse of the process of any court or otherwise to secure the ends of justice. [1]

d. *Review jurisdiction*: Section 114 of the Code of Civil Procedure 1908, has conferred review jurisdiction on the High Court Division. Part II, Chapter X of the High Court Division Rules 1973, and Order XLVII of the Code of Civil Procedure 1908, deal with the procedural matters relating to review. [2]

e. *Jurisdiction as to superintendence and control over courts subordinate to it*: Article 109 of the Constitution provides that the High Court Division shall have superintendence and control over all courts and tribunals subordinate to it. As part of its supervisory power over the subordinate judiciary, the Hon'ble Ex-Chief Justice Mr Md Muzammel Hossain visited several courts of subordinate judiciary in the year 2014. Twenty Judges, appointed by the Chief Justice inspected all the Courts and Tribunals of subordinate judiciary in 31 Districts in 2014. [3]

f. *Transfer of cases from subordinate courts to the High Court Division*: Under Article 110 of the Constitution if the High Court Division is satisfied that a case pending in a subordinate court involves a substantial question of law as to the interpretation of the Constitution or on a point of general public importance, the determination of which is necessary for the disposal of the case, it shall withdraw the case from that court and may: either (a) dispose of the case itself; or (b) determine the question of law and return the case to the court from which it has been so withdrawn (or transfer it to another subordinate court) together with a copy of the judgment of the Division on such questions, and the court to which the case is so returned or transferred shall, on receipt thereof, proceed to dispose of the case in conformity with such judgment. Apart from the above, Section 113 of the Code of Civil Procedure, 1908, grants jurisdiction to the High Court Division to give an opinion and order on a case referred to it by any subordinate Court by way of reference. Under Section 160

---

[1]   Annual Report 2014, the Supreme Court of Bangladesh, p. 66.
[2]   Annual Report 2014, the Supreme Court of Bangladesh, p. 67.
[3]   Ibid.

of the Income Tax Ordinance, 1984 the High Court Division is empowered to hear income tax references. Section 24 of the Code of Civil Procedure provides for transfer of cases of the civil Courts and Section 526 of the Code of Criminal Procedure provides for transfer of cases under criminal jurisdiction of the subordinate Courts. [1]

8. 1. 1. 3   A snapshot of the Bangladesh Supreme Court[2]

Established	16 December 1972 under Article 94 of the Constitution of the People's Republic of Bangladesh.
Authorised by	Part VI, Chapter I of the Constitution of Bangladesh.
Territorial Jurisdiction	Whole of Bangladesh.
Location	Dhaka, the capital of the Republic.
Area	55. 05 Acres of Land. Floor Area: (i) Main Building 1,65,026. 54 sqft. (ii) Annex Building 83,684. 00 sqft. (iii) Old Building 78,81. 83 sqft. (iv) New Annex Building(A,B and C)1,57,000. 00 sqft
Composition of Court	As per Article 94 (2) of the Constitution the Supreme Court, comprising the Appellate Division and the High Court Division, consists of the Chief Justice and such number of other Judges as the President may deem it necessary for each Division.
Appointment of Judges	(i) The Chief Justice and Judges of both the Divisions of the Supreme Court are appointed as per Article 95 of the Constitution; (ii) Additional Judges of the High Court Division and *ad hoc* Judges of the Appellate Division of the Supreme Court are appointed as per Article 98 of the Constitution.
Present Strength of Judges	(i) Appellate Division: 09 (Nine) Judges including the Chief Justice. (ii) High Court Division: 90(Ninety) Judges.
Tenure of Office of the Judges	Until he reaches the age of 67 years; unless (i) removed by the President of the Republic pursuant to a resolution of Parliament supported by a majority of not less than two-thirds of the total number of members of Parliament, on the ground of proved misbehaviour or incapacity; or (ii) resigns his office by writing under his hand addressed to the Hon'ble President of the Republic (Article 96 of the Constitution).

---

[1]   Annual Report 2014, the Supreme Court of Bangladesh, p. 67.

[2]   Annual Report 2014, the Supreme Court of Bangladesh, p. iv.

Jurisdiction	A) The Appellate Division shall have jurisdiction to hear and determine appeals from judgments, decrees, orders or sentences of the (ⅰ) High Court Division, (ⅱ) Administrative Appellate Tribunal and (ⅲ) International Crimes Tribunals. An appeal to the Appellate Division from a judgment, decree, order or sentence of the High Court Division shall lie: (a) as of right where the High Court Division—(ⅰ) certifies that the case involves a substantial question of law as to the interpretation of the Constitution or, (ⅱ) has sentenced a person to death or to imprisonment for life, or (ⅲ) has imposed punishment on a person for contempt of that Division; and in such other cases as may be provided for by Act of Parliament. [Article 103(1) and (2) of the Constitution]; and (b) by leave of the Appellate Division. B) The High Court Division shall have such original, appellate and other jurisdictions, powers and functions as are or may be conferred on it by the Constitution or any other law. (Article 101 of the Constitution)
Court Rooms	The Appellate Division: 03 (in the Main Building). The High Court Division: 21 (in the Main Building), 34 (in the Annex Building), 04 (in the Old Building) Total = 62
Contact	The Registrar Supreme Court of Bangladesh, Shahbagh, Dhaka-1000. Phone: (+ 88 02) 9562941-5, 9567307. Fax: (+ 88 02) 9565058. Website: www. supremecourt. gov. bd. Email: registrar@ supremecourt. gov. bd.

8. 1. 2   The lower courts of Bangladesh

The lower courts are divided into criminal and civil courts extending over 64 districts. The civil courts are classified as courts of Assistant Judge, Senior Assistant Judge, Joint District Judge, Additional District Judge and District Judge respectively. Criminal matters are heard by the courts of Sessions Judge, Additional Sessions Judge and Joint Sessions Judge. In metropolitan areas, sessions courts are termed as Metropolitan Court of Sessions. ① The criminal court is a two-tier system: Sessions Court is the apex one in case of criminal matters in district level. A Session Judge's Court and Additional Session Judge's Court have jurisdiction in respect of offences punishable with more than 10 years imprisonment. A Joint Session Judge can try offences punishable up to 10 years. While magistrates' courts have sentencing authority for up to seven years. ②

The judiciary also includes several Special Courts and Tribunals. For example:

---

① Judiciary, National Integrity System Assessment Bangladesh, Policy Brief 25, September 2014, p. 2.

② Bangladesh: Justice in Disarray, Country Reports on Judicial Corruption, Transparency International, 2005, p. 180.

Family Courts hear matrimonial matters; the Special Tribunal on Violence Against Women and Children deals with certain offences involving violence against women and children; the Acid Crimes Tribunal set up under the Acid Offences Prevention Act 2002 tries acid crimes; the Labour Court hears cases relating to labour and employment matters; the Anti-Corruption Tribunal tries corruption cases; and the Speedy Trial Tribunal deals with matters that demand immediate disposal and so on. [1]

8. 2   Arbitration mechanism

The impression among foreign investors is that the Bangladesh judiciary is not strong enough to enforce contracts and there are long delays of 10 years or more before a case is resolved. [2] It is also said that corruption is common in courts especially in the lower courts. [3] The failure of the government to comply with a Supreme Court decision in 1999, which in the absence of a constitutional protection of independence of the judiciary went on to set out 12 directives that it urged the government to implement, and the unabated executive interference with the judicial process came under criticism in 2005. [4] Nevertheless, the Supreme Court has robustly maintained its reputation for being fair and competent. This chapter demonstrates that dispute resolution mechanisms relating to trade and investment have improved tremendously in the last few years and the present legal system offers arbitration as a means of avoiding complicated court proceedings.

Arbitration is a non-judicial process for the settlement of disputes where an independent third party, an arbitrator, makes a decision that is binding. [5] It is an institution of international law, though it has a long pedigree that has been developed in the 19th century. [6] The growth of arbitration has become a reality around the world. It is now one of the most important and flexible means to resolve both private

---

[1]   Judiciary, National Integrity System Assessment Bangladesh, Policy Brief 25 September 2014, p. 2.

[2]   For details see, World Development Report (2005), pp. 86 – 90.

[3]   Ibid.

[4]   Ibid. In 2007 the interim caretaker government declared the separation of the judiciary and enacted four sets of rules to effect this separation. Through these directives the government separated the judiciary from the executive by making necessary rules and also set up Judicial Service Commission for appointment of judges of the subordinate courts.

[5]   Arbitration. http://www. ciarb. org/dispute-appointment-services/das-arbitration.

[6]   For details see J. H. Ralston, *International Arbitration from Athens to Locarno*, London, 1929.

and public disputes relating to international business, more particularly disputes between private investors from different states or between investors and the governments of countries in which they carry out their business. However, the government of the host state may work both in private or sovereign capacity. There is no such binding international law on arbitration; rather it is governed mostly by national laws or international set of laws chosen by respective parties. Besides, public disputes like investor-state arbitrations are governed by public international law that is largely practiced in the present globalised economy; hence arbitration has been proved as one of the most effective means to solve both public and private disputes. For the purpose of the present report public dispute implies investment arbitration between states or between investors and states, where private dispute denotes to commercial arbitration between investors or between investors and states while states work in private capacity.

It is crucial that Bangladesh promotes arbitration as arbitration is gaining popularity all over the world for the resolution of commercial disputes. Arbitration, as an alternative to judicial process, is an effective and efficient system of dispute resolution especially in the field of foreign investment. The arbitral award in *Saipem SpA v The People's Republic of Bangladesh* of 30 June 2009 is a good example of the role of commercial dispute arbitration in Bangladesh, where New York Convention and not the national law of Bangladesh is applicable. This chapter is an effort to articulate the national legal framework of Bangladesh to settle both commercial and investment disputes in line with international legal framework.

8. 2. 1   Investor-Investor/Commercial arbitration

International commercial arbitration is believed to contribute to market integration by safeguarding and improving the efficiency of international private transactions. [1] International commercial arbitration should be seen as a key instrument in the structuring of international markets. [2] Commercial arbitration has a long history[3] and offers an attractive and flexible method to resolve trade disputes among

---

① Alessandra Casella, " On Market Integration and the Development of Institutions: The Case of International Commercial Arbitration" (1996), *European Economic Review* 40, p. 155.

② Dezalay and Brayant G. Garth, *Dealing in Virtue: International Commercial Arbitration and the Construction of a Transnational Legal Order* (University of Chicago Press, Chicago and London, 1996), p. 7.

③ For details see R Bernstein and D Wood, *Handbook of Arbitration Practice* (3rd ed., London, 1998; E. E Bergsten, International Commercial Arbitration, New York, 1991).

parties which is cheap and swift. ①Many institutions across the world have drafted rules for the conduct for the conduct of arbitration in the hope of attracting lucrative arbitration business to their centres. ②To provide internationally uniform standard to settle dispute with foreign investors, Bangladesh follows UNCITRAL Model Law, ICSID Convention and New York Convention.

(A) International legal framework

The first significant international agreement regarding international commercial arbitration was the 1923 Geneva Protocol. ③ The Protocol was ratified by 30 states including the British Empire and the most important instrument in context of international commercial arbitration was the 1927 Geneva Convention on the Execution of Foreign Arbitral Awards. ④ After the Second World War, the 1953 proposal of ICC relating to the direct enforcement of arbitral award in national courts was rejected by world community and the result was the 1958 New York Convention on the Recognition and Enforcement of Foreign Arbitral awards. ⑤ This Convention provides a simplified procedure for recognition and enforcement of arbitral award and it has proved a great success as its list of states parties indicates, ⑥ and ratification becomes essential for countries whose traders are willing to participate in global trade. Bangladesh has ratified this Convention on 6 May 1992. ⑦

Development of arbitration laws follows multilevel efforts both from individuals and states. The International Chamber of Commerce (ICC) was founded in 1919 and thousands of arbitrations have been conducted under its rules. ⑧ UNCITRAL, the United Nations Commission on International Trade Law was established in 1966 to

---

① M Mustill, "Arbitration; history and background" (1989)6, *Journal of International Arbitration*, p. 43.

② John Collier and Vaughan Lowe, *The Settlement of Disputes in International Law: Institutions and Procedures* (Oxford; Oxford University Press, 2009), p. 46.

③ The Geneva Protocol 1923, 27 LNTS 157.

④ Geneva Convention on the Execution of Foreign Arbitral Awards 1927, 92 LNTS 301.

⑤ 1958 New York Convention on the Recognition and Enforcement of Foreign Arbitral Awards, 330 UNTs. For details see A J van den Berg, the New York Arbitration Convention of 1958: Towards a Judicial Interpretation (Daventer, 1981).

⑥ It has been ratified by 156 countries by the end of 2014.

⑦ Ratification status is available at http://www. newyorkconvention. org/countries.

⑧ ICC is the largest international business organisation in which arbitrations are supervised by the ICC International Court of Arbitration. The procedure of dispute settlement is being regulated through the Statute of International Court of Arbitration 1997, 36 ILM 1625 and Bangladesh is member of national committee of ICC. For details see http://www. iccwbo. org/worldwide-membership/national-committees/icc-bangladesh/.

harmonise and unify the laws on international trade and the UNCITRAL Arbitration Rules were adopted in 1976. [1]

UNCITRAL adopted a model law on international commercial arbitration in 1985 to harmonise the wide disparities in different national legislations of member states. [2] The Model Law seeks to strike a proper balance between the will of party autonomy and the right of state to regulate dispute settlement within its territory. [3] It requires that every national court should refuse to hear proceedings covered by a written arbitration agreement and should refer the parties to arbitration, unless it finds that the agreement is null and void, inoperative or incapable of being performed. [4]

Since Bangladesh follows dualist approach to international laws, the provisions of international laws relating to arbitration would not be directly applicable in Bangladesh unless expressly adopted by national legislation. To integrate arbitration into the regular state legal system it is necessary for there to be domestic legislation governing the relationship between arbitral tribunals and the courts.

(B) National laws of Bangladesh

In tune with the modernisation of international commercial arbitration, Bangladesh enacted the Arbitration Act 2001, which came into force on 10 April 2001[5] repealing the previous Act of 1940, [6] a common heritage of all the countries of Indian sub-continents. [7]Both Bangladesh and India developed their arbitration laws in line with UNCITRAL model law, and in certain aspects Bangladeshi law has drawn on the Indian Arbitration and Conciliation Act 1996.

The 2001 Act has been made in compliance with the Model Law to consolidate and codify national and international commercial arbitration law. In addition this Act

---

[1]   UNCITRAL Rules 1976, 15 ILM 701. UNCITRAL rule was considered as a neutral set of rules acceptable to all states and parties from all regions including those who suspected ICC rules prepared by western arbitration institutions and somehow coloured capitalist origins.

[2]   UNCITRAL Model Law 1985, UN Doc. A/40/17, annex 1, 1985, 24 ILM 1302. For details see CF. A. Broches, "1985 UNCITRAL Model Law on International Commercial Arbitration: An Exercise in International Legislation" 1987, 18 *Netherlands Year Book of International Law* 3.

[3]   UNCITRAL Model Law, Art. 5 as follows: "In matters governed by this law, no court shall intervene except where so provided in this law. "

[4]   Ibid, Arts. 7, 8.

[5]   Arbitration Act 2001.

[6]   Section 59 of 2001 Act.

[7]   A. F. M. Maniruzzaman, "The New law of International Commercial Arbitration in Bangladesh: A Comparative Perspective", *The American Review of International Arbitration*, 2003(14), p. 140.

has created a single and unified legal regime for arbitration in Bangladesh that reflects the latest trend elsewhere of the world to settle disputes with foreign entities. [1]

In comparison with UNCITRAL Model Law, Bangladeshi Act seems to allow more freedom to the parties, e. g. unlike UNCITRAL Model Law Article 17 of the Act provides a non-exhaustive list of questions that an arbitral tribunal may resolve, such as whether there was a valid arbitration tribunal or whether the arbitral tribunal is properly constituted. [2] Again in defining international commercial arbitration the Act has adopted verbatim the definition of the Indian Act 1996, [3] but has deviated from UNCITRAL Model. [4] This means that a commercial dispute between two Bangladeshi nationals having places of business even elsewhere cannot be considered the subject matter of international commercial arbitration under Bangladeshi Act, which would be otherwise possible under the Model Law.

In settling international commercial disputes, Bangladesh has also embraced some other methods in addition to arbitration. Manifesting a typical Asian approach to dispute resolution[5] the Act has encouraged other alternative dispute resolution mechanisms including mediation and reconciliation. Article 22 of Arbitration Act 2001 states as follows: "It shall not be incompatible with an arbitration agreement for an arbitral tribunal to encourage settlement of the dispute otherwise than by arbitration and with the agreement of all the parties. The arbitral tribunal may use mediation, conciliation or any other procedures at any time during the arbitral proceedings to encourage settlement"[6]. The Act also provides: "If during arbitral proceedings, the parties settle the dispute, the arbitral tribunal shall, if requested by the parties, record the settlement in the form of an arbitral award on agreed terms"[7]. So in Bangladesh there is no distinction between an award of agreed terms and any other award. [8]

---

[1]　I. e. the German Arbitration Act 1998 and the Indian Arbitration and Conciliation Act 1996.

[2]　Art. 17 of 2001 Act.

[3]　The Indian Arbitration Act 1996 Section 2(1)(f).

[4]　UNCITRAL Model Law, Art. 1(3).

[5]　A. F. M. Maniruzzaman, "International Commercial Arbitration in the Asia-Pacific: Asian Values, Culture and Context", (December 2002) 30 Int'l Business Lawyer, p. 508; see also A. F. M. Maniruzzaman, "The Problems and Challenges facing Settlement of International Energy Disputes by ADR Methods in Asia: The Way Forward", Int'l Energy Law and Taxation Review, 2003(6), p.193.

[6]　Arbitration Act 2001, Sec 22(1).

[7]　Arbitration Act 2001, Sec 22(2).

[8]　Arbitration Act 2001, Sec 22(4).

The Arbitration Act 2001 ensures freedom of choice of the parties allowing them to choose any law, not necessarily the law of the country as regards the substance of the dispute[1]. Professor Maniruzzaman observes that this choice is so expansive that the parties can choose the *lex mercatoria* or the rules of transnational commercial law, rules of specific trade or anything which is not characteristic of the legal system of a particular country. [2]Here the choice of seat law simply means the application of substantive law not the rules of conflict of law,[3] mainly to avoid the *renvoi* situation. [4] The Act allows the tribunal, in absence of the parties' choice, to apply the rules of law it considers to be appropriate given all the circumstances surrounding the dispute. [5]The arbitral proceedings shall be terminated by the final award or on order of the tribunal[6], and such award shall be final and binding on both the parties[7].

The Act of 2001 deals with recourse against an arbitral award in both a domestic arbitration and an international commercial arbitration held in Bangladesh. [8] An application to set aside a domestic arbitral award must be made to the court within the local limits of whose jurisdiction the arbitral award was made and signed,[9] and for awards made in international commercial arbitration to the High Court Division of the Bangladesh Supreme Court. [10] Section 43 of the Act contains an exclusive list of limited grounds on which an award may be set aside and no other ground should be

---

[1]   Arbitration Act 2001, Sec 36(1).

[2]   A. F. M. Maniruzzaman, "The Lex Mercatoria and International Contracts: A Challenge for International Commercial Arbitration?" (1999) 14(3), *AM. U. Int'l L. Rev.* 657.

[3]   Arbitration Act 2001, Sec 36(1).

[4]   A. F. M. Maniruzzaman, " The New Law of International Commercial Arbitration in Bangladesh: A Comparative Perspective", *op. cit.* , p. 162.

[5]   Arbitration Act 2001, Sec 36(2).

[6]   Arbitration Act 2001, Sec 41.

[7]   Arbitration Act 2001, Sec 39.

[8]   Arbitration Act 2001, Secs 42 – 43.

[9]   Arbitration Act 2001, Sec 42(1).

[10]   Arbitration Act 2001, Sec 42(2).

entertained for such purpose. ①

Domestic and foreign arbitral awards are directly enforceable under the law of Bangladesh. The Act provides that "the award shall be enforced under the Code of Civil Procedure, in the same manner as if it were a decree of the Court. "② Hence, domestic and foreign awards are given the status of a decree of the court. The court for the purpose of enforcing foreign arbitral awards under section 45 is the district court exercising the jurisdiction within the district of Dhaka. ③ For the purpose of setting aside an arbitral award made in an international commercial arbitration held in Bangladesh, recourse must be had to the High Court division. ④

Before the enactment of the present legislation on arbitration there existed no legal mechanism for enforcement of a foreign arbitral award in Bangladesh. Although Bangladesh acceded to the New York Convention on 6 July 1992, the country had not enacted any legislation to give effect to the convention. Consequently, the practice of Bangladeshi judiciary showed that judges were hesitant to deal with recognition and enforcement of foreign arbitral award. ⑤ However the 2001 Act incorporated the mechanism of New York Convention within *corpus juris* of Bangladeshi law and section 46 of the Act⑥ reproduces from New York Convention the grounds on which

---

①   Arbitration Act 2001, Sec 43 (1) states as follows: "Grounds for setting aside arbitral award. (1) An arbitral award may be set aside if—(a) the party making the application furnishes proof that-(i) a party to the arbitration agreement was under some incapacity; (ii) the arbitration agreement is not valid under the law to which the parties have subjected it; (iii) the party making the application was not given proper notice of the appointment of an arbitrator or of the arbitral proceedings or was otherwise unable due to some reasonable causes to present his case; (iv) the arbitral award deals with a dispute not contemplated by or not falling within the terms of the submission to arbitration or it contains decision on matters beyond the scope of the submission to arbitration. . . ".

②   Arbitration Act 2001, Secs 44 and 45(1)(b).

③   Arbitration Act 2001, Sec 45.

④   Arbitration Act 2001, Sec 42(2).

⑤   See *Haji Azam v Singleton Binda & Co.* , (1975) 27 DLR 583; *Bangladesh Air Service PVT v British Airways PLC* (1997) 49 DLR 187(AD).

⑥   Arbitration Act 2001, Sec 46 provides for grounds for refusing recognition or execution of foreign arbitral awards: " (1) Recognition or execution of foreign arbitral award may be refused only on the following grounds, namely(a) if the party against whom it is invoked furnishes proof to the Court that (i) a party to the arbitration agreement was under some incapacity; (ii) the arbitration agreement is not valid under the law to which the parties have subjected it; (iii) the party against whom the award is invoked was not given proper notice of the appointment of the arbitrator or of the arbitral proceedings or was otherwise unable due to some reasonable causes to present his case; or(iv) the concerned foreign arbitral award contains decisions on matters beyond the scope of the submission to arbitration. "

a court may refuse to recognise and enforce an arbitral award. ① Section 45 of the Act underlines the proceedings to execute a foreign arbitral award in Bangladesh. An application for the execution of a foreign arbitral award must be accompanied with: "(a)the original arbitral award or a copy thereof duly authenticated in the manner required by the law of the country in which it was made;(b)the original agreement for arbitration or a duly certified copy thereof and (c) such evidence as may be necessary to prove that the award is a foreign award."② The requirement under sub clause(c) is neither found in New York Convention nor in Model Law: it is an addition in Bangladeshi law.

The 2001 Act has incorporated fundamental principles of international commercial arbitration such as party autonomy, minimal judicial intervention in arbitration,independence of the tribunal and effective enforcement of arbitral awards. The Act has endorsed certain principles of natural justice which leads to the fair and impartial settlement of dispute. ③ The Act is unique because it has both retrospective and prospective effect. ④ Bangladesh has made a positive step towards attracting foreign investment through providing adequate access for foreign investors to settle commercial disputes in line with international standards.

Apart from the statutory protection the country also offers an institutional mechanism to solve commercial disputes in Bangladesh. The Bangladesh International Arbitration Centre(BIAC) was launched in 2011,the country's first arbitration centre for the settlement of commercial disputes. ⑤ BIAC is an initiative of the ICC in partnership with Dhaka Chamber of Commerce and the Metropolitan Chamber of Commerce and Industry. As a first organisation in Bangladesh, BIAC offers viable ADR means particularly arbitration and it has formulated Arbitration Rules and developed state-of-the-art facilities.

---

①   The New York Convention, Art V.

②   Arbitration Act 2001, Sec 45(2).

③   Arbitration Act 2001, Sec 23 states as follows: "(a)each party shall be given reasonable opportunity to present his case orally or in writing or both, and(b)each party shall be given reasonable opportunity to examine all the documents and other relevant materials filed by other party or any other person concerned before the tribunal".

④   Arbitration Act 2001, Sec 3(4)states as follows: "where any arbitration agreement is entered into before or after the enforcement of this Act, the provisions thereof shall apply to the arbitration proceedings in Bangladesh relating to the dispute arising out of that agreement."

⑤   *BIAC Quarterly Bulletin*, Volume 2, No. 2(Dhaka, April-June 2013).

8.2.2　Investor-State/Investment treaty arbitration

Unlike commercial arbitration as discussed above, Investment treaty arbitration①
is not a purely private dispute settlement mechanism that is entirely subject to party
autonomy and limited to its effects to the parties to the proceedings. Rather, it fulfils a
public function in influencing the behaviour of foreign investors, states and civil
society. Thus, it works and operates as part of public system of investment protection.
It is one of the most vibrant and fastest growing fields of international dispute
settlement, while the total number of known treaty-based cases reached 608.② It is the
result of both an unprecedented increase in foreign investment flows, in particular
since the end of the Cold War, and an expansion of substantive and procedural
protection for foreign investors under international law.③

The number of International Investment Agreements existing today is more than
3,000.④ International Investment Agreements (IIAs) are treaties between two states
thereby agreeing to protect the investments made by the investors of both states in
each other's territory, by undertaking certain obligations and restrictions in respect of
the treatment and regulation of the investments made by the investor of the other state
party.⑤ IIAs impose a number of obligations and restrictions on the host states in
order to protect the rights of a foreign investor. The obligations and the restrictions
placed on the host states by the IIAs include obligations: to create a favourable
environment for investments; to provide most-favoured nation treatment to investors
and investments of the other party; to provide fair and equitable treatment and full
protection and security to foreign investors and their investments; to refrain from
expropriating the investments of a foreign investor except for public purpose, without

---

①　Investment treaty arbitration is the arbitration between foreign investors and host states about rights and
obligations arising under international investment treaties.

②　UNCTAD, Latest Development in Investor-state Dispute Settlement, available at http://
investmentpolicyhub. unctad. org/Publications/Details/132.

③　Stephan W Schill, "Crafting the International Economic Order: The Public Function of Investment
Treaty Arbitration and Its Significance for the Role of the Arbitrator" (2010) 23: 2 *Leiden Journal of
International Law* at 401.

④　International Investment Navigator, http://investmentpolicyhub. unctad. org/IIA, accessed 23 November
2015.

⑤　For a general discussion on Bilateral Investment Treaties, see Rudolf Dolzer and Christoph Schreuer,
Principles of International Investment Law (2nd ed., Oxford University Press 2012); Jeswald W Salacuse, *The
Law of Investment Treaties* (Oxford University Press 2013); Andrew Newcombe and Lluis Paradell, *Law and
Practice of Investment Treaties: Standards of Treatment* (Wolters Kluwer 2009).

adequate compensation; to allow repatriation of the profits and returns on the investments; to refrain from discriminating the foreign investments against the investments made by the domestic investors; to allow the foreign investors access to justice through administrative or judicial tribunals; and most significantly, to allow individuals to bring cases against the host states for the breaches of the standards of treatment ensured by the IIAs (i. e. investor-state dispute settlement or investor-state arbitration). The basic rationale for the states accepting obligations and restrictions of the kind aforementioned lies in the assumption that the framework that is created by the IIAs leads to the increased flow of foreign investments. [1]

International investment law is designed to promote and protect activities of private foreign investors. [2] The perception for IIAs is that it boosts investor's confidence that results in greater inflows of FDI. [3] Developing countries enter into IIAs primarily to attract foreign investors and thereby to increase FDI inflow. [4] Like any other developing country Bangladesh is keen to attract foreign investors and it is quite evident from the number of IIAs more particularly BITs, the country entered into. In the beginning of 1980s there was only one BIT [5] and it has now reached 29. [6] In 1980, the Government enacted the Foreign Private Investment (Promotion and Protection) Act which contains provision relating to protection and equitable treatment, indemnification, expropriation and nationalisation and repatriation of investment, etc. [7] Further significant reforms were made after 1991, which included progress on tariff reforms, reformation of import clearance procedure and movement towards a uniform tariff structure. [8] Recognising the role of foreign investment in its comprehensive Industrial Policy of 1999, the Government of Bangladesh recognised

[1]   M Sornarajah, *The International Law on Foreign Investment*, 3rd ed. Cambridge University Press 2010, p. 187.

[2]   Rudolf Dolzer and Christoph Schreuer, *Principles of International Investment Law*, 2nd ed. , Oxford University Press 2012, p. 46.

[3]   Jennifer L. Tobin and Marc L. Busch, "A BIT is better than A Lot; Bilateral Investment treaties and Preferential Trade Agreements", *World Politics*, 2010(62), p. 1.

[4]   Eric Neumayer and Laura Epess, "Do Bilateral Investment Treaties Increase Foreign Direct Investment to Developing Countries?" *London; LSE Research* (online).

[5]   Bangladesh-German BIT.

[6]   IIA Database.

[7]   Foreign Investment in Bangladesh. http://www. sdnbd. org/sdi/statisticapocketbook/Chap01/0114. htm, accessed 25 November 2015.

[8]   Bandara and McGillivray (n 2) p. 886.

the importance of " promoting private sector to lead the growth of industrial production and investment" and "attracting foreign direct investment in both export and domestic market oriented industries to make up for the deficient domestic investment resources, and to acquire evolving technology and gain access to export markets". ①

The Prime Minister's message on the website of Board of Investment as follows: "We want to turn Bangladesh into a middle-income country by 2020 for which foreign investment is a significant component. "② which implies that the Government is trying to create a more open and completive climate for the foreign investment. ③

As of 2015 the total number of IIAs signed by Bangladesh is 30 whereof 24 are in force. Out of these 30 IIAs, by 1993 only 9 were signed, and the rest 21 were signed thereafter. The total GDP of Bangladesh in 2013 is USD 152. 8 billion④ and the total FDI inflow in 2013 is USD 1,599 million, thereby forming a meagre 1. 09 percent of the total GDP. However, despite FDI forming a small percentage of GDP, the inflow of FDI has substantially increased from USD 14 million in 1993 to USD 1, 599 million in 2013,⑤ thereby suggesting that foreign investment has increased substantially.

All the IIAs so far Bangladesh entered into have provisions on the settlement of investment disputes between investor and the host state or between contracting parties. In most of the agreements three options are left to the foreign investors to settle disputes with host state. First, an investor can submit the dispute in the competent national court; second, he can submit the dispute to ICSID tribunal⑥ subject to membership of investor's home state to the convention; third, he can

①　Foreign Investment in Bangladesh, http://www. sdnbd online website. org/sdi/statisticapocketbook/Chap01/0114. htm, accessed 16 November 2015.

②　PM's Message(Statement at Bangladesh Investment Summit, New York, USA, September 2009, Board of Investment, Bangladesh) online.

③　Foreign investment in Bangladesh.

④　Country-wise Nominal and Real GDP, total and per capita, annual, 1970 – 2013, UCNTAD stat 〈unctadstat. unctad. org/wds/TableViewer/tableView. aspx〉accessed 25 November 2015.

⑤　Ibid.

⑥　International Centre for the Settlement of Investment Dispute (ICSID) Convention 1965 which is also known as Washington Convention provides mechanism for conciliation and arbitration of investment disputes. ICSID as an institution facilitates dispute settlement in accordance with the convention which is distinct from inter-state and international commercial arbitration, while sharing features of both. For details see Salacuse, pp. 369 –390; John Coller, pp. 59 – 76.

submit the dispute to an ad hoc arbitration tribunal established under the Arbitration Rules of Procedure of the United Nations Commission for International Trade Law. It is hereby important to note that the choice of one of these proceedings is final. Bangladesh has become member state of ICSID on 26 April 1980.

All IIAs signed by Bangladesh including that of China① mandate that awards shall be final and binding for all parties in dispute, and the country has committed itself to execute the award according to its national law. To illustrate it further, the India-Bangladesh investment provisions underlines as follows: " the arbitral award shall be made in accordance with the provisions of this Agreement and shall be binding for the parties in dispute. "②

However, as a result of the obligations undertaken under the IIAs, Bangladesh has been involved in two investor-state dispute in the case of *Saipem SpA v People's Republic of Bangladesh*③ and *Niko Resource(Bangladesh) LTD v People' s Republic of Bangladesh.*

Lastly, the present paradigm seems to create Bangladesh as an attractive place for dispute resolution in the field of international trade, commerce and investment. The new legislative step was urgent in the face of increasing foreign investment in Bangladesh in various sectors, especially in natural gas and power, and its ever-growing export trade with the rest of the world. Since the new Act embodies the modern practices of arbitration, it is considered to help build confidence in prospective foreign investors in Bangladesh. ④ The Arbitration Act was a much desired step from the perspective of foreign investors for the legal security of their investments by way of international settlement of commercial disputes.

---

① Agreement between the Government of the People' s Republic of China and the Government of the People's Republic of Bangladesh for the Promotion and Protection of Investments, 25 March 1997.

② Agreement between the Government of the Republic of India and the Government of the people's Republic of Bangladesh for the Promotion and Protection of Investments, 7 July 2011, Art 5(3c).

③ ICSID Case No ARB/05/7, Decided in favour of the Investor(Home Country-Italy) : The dispute arose because of the refusal of the domestic courts of Bangladesh to recognize and enforce and ICC arbitral award in favour of Saipem, the investor, against Petrobangla. The ICSID arbitral tribunal decided in favour of the investor, holding that Bangladesh had violated the obligations under Italy-Bangladesh IIA.

④ A. F. M Moniruzzaman "Modernisation of International Arbitration Law in the Age of Globalisation: A Bangladesh Perspective" OPINION: [2004] I. C. C. L. R. 133.

Conclusions

It is clear that over the past decades Bangladesh has shown a serious commitment to ensuring non-discriminatory treatment to foreign investors on both pre and post-establishment basis. The existing legal and institutional frameworks of the country guarantee fair and equitable treatment for foreign investment. Trade has become an integral part of the total developmental effort and national growth of all economies including Bangladesh. Trade plays a central role in the development plan of Bangladesh where a major hurdle is foreign exchange scarcity. Export trade can largely meet foreign exchange gap, and export growth would increase the import capacity of the country that in turn would increase industrialization as well as overall economic activities. Despite structural limitations in the Bangladesh economy, the export sector performed well throughout the 1990s, more interestingly, during the last few years the export growth rate of Bangladesh was higher than that of the World and SAARC countries.

This report is a unique effort to examine the legal and institutional framework of Bangladesh and to check whether the country is willing to open up its market to foreign investment. The report made it clear that Bangladesh launched in earnest a wide-ranging trade reform strategy in the early 1990s. This included substantial reduction and rationalization of tariffs, removal of quantitative restrictions, movement from multiple to a unified exchange rate system, convertible current account and an overall outward orientation of trade policy regime. The role of private sector driven export growth and diversification has been emphasised in Bangladesh's PRSP, making export-led growth a key thrust of its poverty reduction and growth strategies. Bangladesh has proved itself as an active advocate of free trade at the global level and currently the country is heading LDCs in WTO forum, as an LDC, Bangladesh first challenged the anti-dumping measure imposed by India before the Dispute Settlement Body of WTO.

So far as customs laws are concerned, Bangladesh has already taken steps to reform the existing customs laws of the country to comply with WTO standards under

TFA 2013. The draft of the new Customs Act 2014 has been approved by the Cabinet and will soon be placed in the National Parliament for approval. Bangladesh will soon ratify the Trade Facilitation Agreement (TFA) of the World Trade Organisation as more than 50 nations have already approved the deal to simplify their trade rules. Bangladesh has been actively advocating to simplify the customs procedure in international trade. Since the beginning of the 1990s Bangladesh emphasised the simplified customs procedure in both export and import. The current Export Import Policy Order 2015 – 2018 endeavours to remove all possible barriers to international trade. The country has made significant improvement in making customs system up to the mark in recent times. The consistent inclination of the country to sign and ratify numerous bilateral and multilateral investment treaties also hint that she is open for foreign entities and committed to provide protection to foreign investment in accordance with international standards.

The Government of Bangladesh actively seeks foreign investment, particularly in energy, power and infrastructure projects. Bangladesh offers generous opportunities for investment under its relaxed industrial policy and export-oriented, private sector-led growth strategy. More interestingly foreign investors are allowed to own up to 100 percent of the equity in Bangladeshi companies except for certain regulated entities and there are also no restrictions on ownership of land by 100 percent foreign owned companies. The country has signed more than 30 bilateral treaties and some other international investment treaties to facilitate foreign direct investment. Bangladesh is keen to attract foreign investors and thereby the country has been gradually developing local laws to provide satisfactory safeguards to foreign investment.

A continuous six percent growth of economy during the last 12 or so years shows that Bangladesh has the proper mechanism to manoeuvre its economic system. The central bank with the help of a number of laws monitors foreign exchange, banking, non-bank financial institution and money flowing sectors. The laws relating to the monetary and banking system create a favourable environment for investment, banking and money flow. On the other hand these laws have set out a stringent penal system to deal with violations of investor's rights.

To illustrate Bangladesh as a paradise for investment, the Government of Bangladesh is working closely with the private authorities. The Government promotes public private partnership methods under the Office of the Prime Minister. The Office of the Prime Minister considers foreign investment in the public sector giving it highest priority. The new Public Private Partnership Act provides the best possible facilities to investors and protects their investment. Currently there are several enormous public infrastructure projects under different public private partnership model. It can surely be said that Bangladesh welcomes foreign investors and provides opportunities for investment in the public infrastructure sector and the Government is ready to share profits according to international norms.

As a signatory to several international instruments, Bangladesh is determined to provide a good working environment for workers who may enjoy labour rights. The Labour Act 2006, is designed to protect and promote the interests of both workers and employers. The investment pattern and rapid growth of garments sector is an indicator of labour and investor friendly environment in Bangladesh. Moreover, the country is committed to protecting its environment from the impact of unplanned industrialisation. The Government has devised several laws relating to the environment. Proper application of these laws can ensure protection of its environment from hazardous pollution.

Lastly the report shed brief light on the dispute settlement mechanism relating to foreign investors in Bangladesh and it is now auspicious that the country is committed to provide safeguards to foreign investors in line with international standards. The Arbitration Act 2001 was framed to comply with 1958 New York Convention on the Recognition and Enforcement of Foreign Arbitral Swards, UNCITRAL Arbitration Rules 1976, UNCITRAL Model Law 1985 and some other international laws relating to commercial and investment arbitration. The country now has been turned into an attractive destination for the foreign investors.

Pakistan

Mr Mohammad Saqib Jillani

About the Author

Saqib Jillani is an advocate and managing partner of Jillani & Co (Advocates & Legal Consultants). The firm is based in Pakistan and advises companies on a variety of corporate and commercial matters. His practice covers major sectors such as industries (textiles, chemicals, beverages and others), power generation, cement, oil & gas, information technology, intellectual property, competition law, property and areas of civil and commercial disputes.

Introduction

The Islamic Republic of Pakistan was founded in 1956. It has a long border with India on the east. On the west, it is bordered by Iran and Afghanistan and on the north by China. To the south of Pakistan is over, 1000 kilometres of coastline. Pakistan, which has a landmass of over 800,000 square kilometres, enjoys a hot and dry climate in the south and a cold and temperate climate in the north. It has a population of 191. 71 million[①] out of which 75. 19 million live in urban areas. Pakistan has a diverse ethnic mix consisting of Punjabis, Sindhis, Pakhtoons or Pathans, Baluchis, and immigrants from India who dominate in Urban Sindh. It has four provinces, i. e. Punjab, which is the most populous, Sindh, Khyber Pakhtunkhwa and Baluchistan. Baluchistan has the largest land mass and is rich in minerals and petroleum resources. Urdu is the national language of the country but English is widely spoken in most government ministries. Pakistan's population is predominantly Muslim (97 percent), with Christians and Hindus constituting small but vibrant minorities. Pakistan's GDP is around USD 270 billion and the real GDP growth rate is projected to be in excess of four percent annually. Its major exports include textile products such as cotton cloth, knitwear and cotton yarn. It is also a major exporter of rice products. Major imports include petroleum products, palm oil and telecommunication equipment.

Political System

Pakistan is a democratic federal republic, with a parliamentary system of government. The Constitution of Pakistan provides for a bicameral legislature, consisting of a National Assembly (lower house) and a Senate (upper house). The executive is headed by the Prime Minister who is also the head of the government. The President of Pakistan is a nominal head of state and acts on the advice of the

---

① Pakistan Economic Survey, 2014 – 15 by Ministry of Finance, Government of Pakistan p. 199.

Prime Minister. All government contracts are executed in the name of the President of Pakistan. The Prime Minister acts in consultation with the Cabinet which consists of ministers and advisors appointed by the President on the advice of Prime Minister. Each of the four provinces of Pakistan has its own provincial government, a cabinet of provincial ministers and a provincial legislature. Following the constitutional amendments in 2010, a number of powers and areas which were previously vested in the Federal Government have been devolved to the provincial legislatures. There is a comprehensive federal list[1] which delineates the competence of the federal legislature, i. e. the subjects/areas on which the federal legislature has the power to legislate. All other subjects/areas are within the competence of the provincial legislatures.

---

[1]   4th Schedule of the Constitution(Article 70(4)).

Chapter 1   Customs Laws in Pakistan

1. 1   Introduction

Customs is a general term used to define imposts, levies and duties imposed on the import and export of goods to and from a country and the term is used in contradistinction to internal taxes, such as excise duties and sales taxes. [1] The administration of customs duties in Pakistan falls within the ambit of a customs department which is a wing under the domain of the Federal Board of Revenue (FBR)[2]. The powers, duties and the extent of the authority of the customs department are laid down in the Customs Act 1969, which consolidated the then existing three customs laws dealing separately with sea[3], land[4] and air[5] customs.

The customs department provides an important source of revenue to the Government of Pakistan in the form of taxes levied on the goods traded across its borders. The stated government policy which is implemented through the customs department is to protect the domestic industry and discourage consumption of imported luxury goods by imposing higher customs duties. The Customs Act is a major law that regulates all customs related processes and procedures. It lays down extent of jurisdiction and power of customs authorities and describes the dispute resolution mechanisms pertaining to customs disputes. The customs authorities enjoy wide range of powers under the Customs Act, such as power to search, screen, arrest, stop convoys, break locks, summon persons to give evidence, seize and confiscate goods and impose penalties. It also provides for import checking and clearance procedures as well as the import and export documentation requirements.

---

[1] See *The Customs Act, 1969 with Commentary by Najib A. Chaudhry* (Lahore: Tariq Najib Corp, 1983).

[2] FBR is an attached department of the Ministry of Finance and Revenue and operates under the Revenue Division.

[3] Sea Customs Act, 1878.

[4] Land Customs Act, 1924.

[5] Air Ships Act, 1911.

1. 2   Customs authorities in Pakistan

The FBR has the power to appoint customs officers for any specified area in Pakistan. According to Section 3 of the Customs Act, the FBR may appoint a Chief Collector of Customs, a Collector of Customs, a Collector of Customs(Appeals), an Additional Collector of Customs, a Deputy Collector of Customs, an Assistant Collector of Customs and an Officer of Customs with any other designation.

1. 2. 1   Officers of Customs

Chief Collector of Customs

The principal officers of the customs department are the Chief Collector of Customs for north and south regions. ① The areas falling within the ambit of Chief Collector of Customs North include Model Customs Collectorate, Peshawar, Rawalpindi, Lahore, Multan, Sambrial and Faisalabad. The areas falling within the ambit of Chief Collector of Customs South include Model Customs Collectorate of PACCS (Pakistan Automated Customs Computerised System), Custom House Karachi, Model Customs Collectorate of Appraisement, Custom House Karachi, Model Customs Collectorate of Exports, Custom House, Karachi, Model Customs Collectorate of Port Muhammad Bin Qasim, Karachi, Model Customs Collectorate of Preventive, Custom House, Karachi, Model Customs Collectorate of Post Clearance Audit, Custom House, Karachi, Model Customs Collectorate, Hyderabad, Model Customs Collectorate, Quetta, Model Customs Collectorate, Gwadar. The Chief Collector of Customs is the focal person for implementation of all reform initiatives and programs under Tax Administration Reform Program(TARP). They may exercise all powers of officers of customs subordinate to them in their respective jurisdiction. They are responsible for supervision and monitoring of collectorates under their jurisdiction.

Collector of Customs

He is the head of the customs department at Sea Ports and Collectorates and is the Chief Executive Officer for the purposes of the Customs Act. He is responsible to the FBR for the efficient administration, and has quasi-judicial authority in

---

① See SRO No. 967(I)/2007, 20 September 2007.

adjudication and appeal matters.

Collector of Customs(Appeals):He hears the customs-related appeals.

Additional Collector of Customs:He is subordinate to the Collector of Customs. His statutory powers are both executive and quasi-judicial.

Deputy Collector of Customs:He is also subordinate to the Collector of Customs and his statutory powers are both executive and quasi-judicial.

Assistant Collector of Customs: He is also subordinate to the Collector of Customs and is responsible to the Collector of Customs for the efficient administration of the circles or divisions under his charge. He also enjoys executive and quasi-judicial powers.

Officer of Customs with any other designation. [1]

Clause(g) of Section 3 of Customs Act provides that the FBR may appoint any officer of customs with any other designation in relation to a certain area.

Collector of Customs, Collector of Customs (Appeals), Deputy Collector of Customs, Assistant Collector of Customsare assisted by Superintendents, Deputy Superintendents, Preventing Officers and Inspectors, etc. in running of the administration.

1.2.2   Directorates under Customs Act

Directorate General of Intelligence and Investigation,FBR

The Directorate General of Intelligence and Investigation consists of a Director General and as many Directors, Additional Directors, Deputy Directors, Assistant Directors and such other officers as the FBR may, by notification in the official Gazette, appoint. [2] These officers have the power to detain, seize and confiscate goods imported in violation of any prohibition or restriction under the Customs Act. [3]

Directorate General of Transit Trade

The Directorate General of Transit Trade consists of a Director General and as many Directors, Additional Directors, Deputy Directors, Assistant Directors and such

---

[1]   Section 3 of the Customs Act 1969.

[2]   Section 3A of Customs Act.

[3]   See SRO No. 486 (I)/2007,9 June 2007, for powers, functions and jurisdiction of the officers of the Directorate Genera, Intelligence and Investigation.

other officers as the Board may, by notification in the official Gazette, appoint. ① This Directorate is responsible for the enforcement of all transit trade agreements, law and procedures. ②

Directorate General of Internal Audit

The Directorate General of Internal Audit consists of a Director General and as many Directors, Additional Directors, Deputy Directors, Assistant Directors and such other officers as the Board may, by notification in the official Gazette, appoint. ③ This directorate is responsible for internal inspection and audit functions. ④

Directorate General of Reform and Automation

The Directorate General of Reform and Automation consists of a Director General and as many Directors, Additional Directors, Deputy Directors, Assistant Directors and such officers as the Board may, by notification in the official Gazette, appoint. ⑤ The Directorate General of Reform and Automation is responsible for automation within the customs department. ⑥

Directorate General of Risk Management

The Directorate General of Risk Management consists of a Director General and as many Directors, Additional Directors, Deputy Directors, Assistant Directors and such other officers as the Board may, by notification in the official Gazette, appoint. ⑦ This Directorate is responsible for assessment of risk and its management. ⑧

Directorate General of Training and Research

The Directorate General of Training and Research consists of a Director General and as many Directors, Additional Directors, Deputy Directors and Assistant Directors and such other officers as the Board may, by notification in the official Gazette,

---

①   Section 3AA of Customs Act.
②   See SRO No. 932(I)/2012,1 August 2012.
③   Section 3B of the Customs Act.
④   See SRO No. 75(I)/2006,26 January 2006.
⑤   Section 3BB of the Customs Act.
⑥   See SRO No. 767(I)/2014,12 August 2014, amended by Notification No. 859(I)/2014,30 September 2014.
⑦   Section 3BBB of the Customs Act.
⑧   See SRO No. 769(I)/2014,12 August 2014.

appoint. ① The Directorate General of Training and Research is responsible for effective training of personnel in the customs department.

Directorate General of Intellectual Property Rights Enforcement

The Directorate General of Intellectual Property Rights Enforcement consists of a Director General and as many Directors, Additional Directors, Deputy Directors, Assistant Directors and such other officers as the Board may, by notification in the official Gazette, appoint. ② The Directorate General of Intellectual Property Rights Enforcement is responsible for the intellectual property rights related issues. ③

Directorate General of Valuation

The Directorate General of Valuation consists of a Director General and as many Directors, Additional Directors, Deputy Directors, Assistant Directors and such other officers as the Board may, by notification in the official Gazette, appoint. ④ The functions of the Directorate General of Valuation is to ensure uniformity and neutrality of valuation practices across the country. ⑤

Directorate General of Post Clearance Audit(PCA)

The Directorate General of Post Clearance Audit(PCA) consists of a Directors-General and as many Directors, Additional Directors, Deputy Directors, Assistant Directors and such other officers as the Board may, by notification in the official Gazette, appoint. ⑥ The Directorate General of Post Clearance Audit is responsible for post clearance audit, to develop a comprehensive monitoring mechanism to verify the correctness of trade related declarations and to detect and investigate commercial and trade related frauds and propose measures to prevent their occurrence. ⑦

Directorate General of Input Output Co-efficient Organisation(IOCO)

The Directorate General of Input Output Co-efficient Organisation consists of a Director General and as many Directors, Additional Directors, Deputy Directors,

---

① Section 3C of the Customs Act.
② Section 3CC of the Customs Act.
③ See SRO No. 768(I)2014,12 August 2014.
④ Section 3D of the Customs Act.
⑤ See SRO No. 494(I)2007,9 June 2007.
⑥ Section 3DD of the Customs Act.
⑦ See SRO No. 496(I)/2009,13 June 2009, SRO No. 500(I)/2009,13 June 2009 and Customs General Order No. 13/2008,18 October 2008.

Assistant Directors and such other officers as the Board may, by notification in the official Gazette, appoint. ① The Directorate General of Input Output Co-efficient Organisation is primarily related to IOCO industrial unit or registered persons under the Sales Tax Act,1990. ②

1.3   Duties and powers of Customs authorities

1.3.1   General duties of Customs officers③

To ensure that every amount of customs duty is correctly levied, realised, collected and duly accounted for;

To prevent smuggling and ensure that everything that enters into or goes out of the country is brought or sent strictly in accordance with the provisions of the law for the time being in force;

To supervise the movement of goods from one foreign country to another in transit through Pakistan and thereby eliminate chances of such goods entering into Pakistan illegally for home consumption;

To seize anything liable to confiscation under the Act in any place either upon land or water and thereafter adjudicate such cases; and

To see that the parties concerned in the importation and exportation of goods, conform to the obligations imposed on them by the Act and further that offences against the Act are prevented and, if committed, are suitably dealt with.

1.3.2   General powers of Customs officers

The officers of Customs are armed with legal powers under the Customs Act so as to enable them to enforce the requirements of the Act which they are expected to administer. Some of the legal powers of Customs officers under the Customs Act are as follows:

Power of search and arrest

Customs officers have the power to search and arrest any person with or without warrant. ④ They may do so only if they have reason to believe that a person is

---

① Section 3DDD of the Customs Act.
② See SRO No. 811(I)/2013,20 September 2013.
③ See *The Customs Act,1969 with Commentary by Najib A. Chaudhry* (Lahore: Tariq Najib Corp,1983).
④ Sections 158,161,162,163 and 167 of the Customs Act.

carrying illegal goods (which are liable to be confiscated) or documents relating to them. Such a search or arrest can only be made if such person has landed from or is on board or is about to board a vessel within the Pakistan customs-waters, or if he has alighted from, or is about to get into or is in any other conveyance arriving in or proceeding from Pakistan, or if he is entering or about to leave Pakistan, or if he is within the limit of any customs-area. [1]

Whenever any officer of Customs not below the rank of an Assistant Collector of Customs or any other officer of like rank duly employed for the prevention of smuggling has reasonable grounds for believing that any goods liable to confiscation or any documents or things which in his opinion will be useful for or relevant to any proceeding under the Customs Act are concealed or kept in any place and that there is a danger that they may be removed before a search can be effected under Section 162, he may, after preparing a statement in writing of the grounds of his belief and of the goods, documents or things for which search is to be made, search or cause search to be made for such goods, documents or things in that place. [2]

The appropriate Customs officer is also empowered to search a person, if he has reason to believe that such person is carrying smuggled Platinum, any radioactive mineral, gold, silver or precious stones, manufactures of Platinum, any radioactive mineral, gold, silver or precious stones, or currency, or any other goods or class of goods notified by the Federal Government in the official Gazette, or any documents relating to any one or more of the aforementioned goods. [3] Any authorised officer of customs, who has reason to believe that any person has committed an offence under the Customs Act or an offence of smuggling, may arrest such person. [4] The Customs officers may arrest a person afterwards, if that person is not arrested at the time of committing the offence. [5]

Power to screen and X-Ray bodies of suspected persons

Where the appropriate Customs officer has reason to believe that any person has any goods liable to confiscation secreted inside his body, he may detain such person

---

[1]   Section 158(1).

[2]   Section 163(1) of Customs Act.

[3]   Section 158(2) of Customs Act.

[4]   Section 161(1) & (2) of Customs Act.

[5]   Section 167 of Customs Act.

and produce him without unnecessary delay before an officer of Customs not below the rank of an Assistant Collector of Customs. The suspected person may then be held to be screened or X-Rayed. [1]

Where on the basis of a report from a radiologist, the Customs officer is satisfied that the suspected person has any goods liable to confiscation secreted inside his body, he may direct suitable action for bringing such goods out of his body to be taken on the advice and under the supervision of a registered medical practitioner and such suspected person is bound to comply with such a direction.

Power to stop and search conveyances, compel aircrafts to land and to break locks

Where an appropriate Customs officer has reason to believe that within the territories of Pakistan (including territorial waters) any conveyance has been, is being or is about to be, used in the smuggling of any goods or in the carriage of any smuggled goods, he has the power to stop any such conveyance or, in the case of an aircraft, compel it to land, and

(a) rummage and search any part of the conveyance;

(b) examine and search any goods thereon; and

(c) break open the lock of any door, fixture or package for making a search.

If it becomes necessary to stop any conveyance other than a vessel or aircraft, the appropriate Customs officer has the power to use or cause to be used all lawful means for stopping it or preventing its escape including, if all other means fail, firing upon it. [2]

Power to summon persons to give evidence

During the course of an inquiry in connection with the smuggling of any goods, an appropriate Customs officer may require any person to produce or deliver any document or thing to such officer and examine any person acquainted with the facts and circumstances of the case. In this context, any gazetted officer of Customs has power to summon any person whose attendance he considers necessary either to give evidence or to produce documents or any other thing in any inquiry which such officer is making. [3]

---

[1]   Section 160 of Customs Act.

[2]   Section 164 of Customs Act.

[3]   Section 165 of Customs Act.

Power to seize or detain things liable to confiscation

An appropriate customs officer has the power to seize any goods liable to confiscation under the Customs Act and where it is not practicable to seize any such goods, he may serve on the owner of the goods or any person holding them in his possession or charge an order that he must not remove, part with, or otherwise deal with the goods except with the previous permission of such officer. The officer may seize any documents or things which in his opinion will be useful as evidence in any proceeding under the Customs Act. Any authorised Customs officer may also detain any package, brought whether by land, air or sea into Pakistan which is suspected to contain any newspaper or book, any documents containing any treasonable or seditious matter. [1]

Power to impose penalties and to confiscate goods

Customs officers are empowered to confiscate goods, adjudicate upon them, and award punishments under Sections 179, 156 and 157 of the Customs Act.

In cases involving confiscation of goods or recovery of duty and other taxes not levied, short levied or erroneously refunded, imposition of penalty or any other contravention under the Customs Act or the rules made thereunder, the jurisdiction and powers of the officers of Customs in terms of amount of duties and other taxes involved, excluding the conveyance, are as follows: [2]

- Collector — no limit
- Additional Collector — not exceeding three million rupees
- Deputy Collector — not exceeding one million rupees
- Assistant Collector — not exceeding five hundred thousand rupees
- Superintendent — not exceeding fifty thousand rupees.
- Principal Appraiser — not exceeding fifty thousand rupees.

Powers of Customs officers under other Acts

Customs officers are also empowered perform duties imposed by other relevant legislation. Some of such functions performed by the officers of Customs are as follows:

Recovery of sales tax on goods imported into or exported from the country,

---

[1] Sections 168 and 172 of Customs Act.

[2] Section 179 of Customs Act.

which may be levied under the Sales Tax Act,1990;

Recovery of the cotton/tea cesses(cess is a tax) and various other cesses on agricultural produce exported out of the country, on behalf of the Cess Committees concerned;

Recovery of lighthouse dues, on behalf of the Ministry of Commerce;

To arrest without warrant any citizen of Pakistan who has contravened or attempted to contravene or against whom a reasonable suspicion exists that he has contravened the provision of any order made under Sub-Rule(1) of Rule 31 of the Defence of Pakistan Rules,1971;

To arrest without warrant any person who has contravened or against whom a reasonable suspicion exists that he has contravened the provisions of the Passport Act,1974 and of the Pakistan(Control of Entry) Act,1952;

To report offences of unauthorsied import of arms and ammunition within the meaning of the Arms Act;

To enforce certain allied Acts,Ordinances and Regulations, etc. ;

To assist other revenue collecting agencies such as Income Tax,Central Excise and Sales Tax.

Under Chapter 3 of the Customs Act, the FBR has a number of powers in relation to declaration of ports,airports and land customs stations. It may:

- declare any place that alone can be the customs port or customs airports or land customs stations for clearance of goods or any class of goods to be imported or exported;[1]
- declare routes by which alone goods or any class of goods specified may pass by land or inland water ways into or out of Pakistan;[2]
- specify the limits of any customs station and approve proper places in any customs station for the loading and unloading of goods or any class of goods;[3]
- declare places to be warehousing stations at which alone public warehouses may be appointed and private warehouses may be licensed;[4]

The Collector of Customs has the power to appoint or license public or private

[1]   Section 9 of Customs Act.
[2]   Section 9 of Customs Act.
[3]   Section 10 of Customs Act.
[4]   Section 11 of Customs Act.

warehouses wherein dutiable goods may be deposited without payment of customs duty. ①

1.4   Prohibitions, valuation for the purposes of Customs Act and dispute resolution

According to Section 15 of the Customs Act, there is a general prohibition on the following goods which cannot be brought into or taken out from Pakistan:

- counterfeit coins;
- forged or counterfeit currency notes or any other counterfeit products;
- any obscene book, paper, drawing, painting, representation, figure, photograph, film or article, video or audiorecording or any other material;
- any goods having applied thereto a counterfeit trademark within the meaning of Pakistan Penal Code or False Trade Description, Layout Designs of Integrated Circuits Ordinance, the Patent Ordinance, 2000 and the Trademark Ordinance, 2001;
- goods made or produced outside Pakistan and having applied thereto any name or trademark being or purporting to be name or trademark of any manufacturer or dealer or trader in Pakistan;
- goods involving infringement of copyrights, layout designs of integrated circuits, industrial designs, patents within the meaning of Copyright Ordinance, Registered Designs Ordinance and Patent Ordinance respectively.

The Federal Government has the power to prohibit or restrict the bringing into or taken out of Pakistan any goods of any specified description by air, sea or land. ②

According to Section 18, customs duties may be levied at such rate as specified in First Schedule or under any other law for the time being enforced on:

- goods imported into Pakistan;
- goods brought from any foreign country to any customs station and without payment of duty there transshipped or transported for, or thence carried to, and imported at any other customs station;
- goods brought in bond from one customs station to another.

Section 18 of the Customs Act provides that the Federal Government may

---

① Sections 12 and 13 of Customs Act.

② Section 16 of Customs Act.

subject to conditions, limitations or restrictions, levy a regulatory duty on all or any of the goods imported or exported as specified in the First Schedule at a rate not exceeding 100 percent of the value of such goods as determined under Section 25 or 25(A) of the Customs Act. Cumulative incidents of customs duties which may be levied under Section 18 must not exceed the rate agreed to by the Government of Pakistan under trade agreements. The Federal Government has the power by notification in the *Official Gazette* to exempt any good imported into or exported out of Pakistan or into or from any specified port or station from customs duty. It may exercise such power following an approval of the Economic Coordination Committee of the Cabinet and only in situations of national security, national disasters, national food security in emergency situations, protection of national economic interest in situations arising out of abnormal fluctuation in international commodity prices, removal of anomalies in duties, development of backward areas, and implementation of bilateral and multilateral agreements, subject to such other conditions and limitations or restrictions as it may deem fit to impose. [1]

Value of Imported and Exported Goods for the purposes of Customs Duty[2]

Transaction value: The customs value of imported goods is the transaction value, that is, the price actually paid or payable for the goods when sold for export to Pakistan. In determining the customs value, the following are added to the price actually paid or payable:

- ghe cost of transport to the port, airport or place of importation;
- loading, unloading and handling charges;
- cost of insurance;
- commissions including indenting commission and brokerage, except buying commissions;
- cost of containers;
- cost of packing whether for labour or material.

Added to the price is also the value of following goods and services where supplied directly or indirectly by the importer or his related person free of charge or at reduce cost for use in connection with the production and sale for export of the

---

① See Section 19 of the Customs Act.
② See Section 25 of the Customs Act.

imported goods:

- materials, components, parts and similar items incorporated in the imported goods;
- tools, dies, moulds and similar items used in the production of the imported goods;
- material consumed in the production of imported goods; and
- engineering, development, art-work, design work, and plans and sketches undertaken elsewhere than in Pakistan and necessary for the production of the imported goods.

The following will also be added to such price: royalties and license fees related to the goods being valued to the extent such royalties and fees are not included in the price actually paid or payable; and the value of any part of the proceeds of any subsequent resale, disposal or use of the imported goods that accrues directly or indirectly to the seller.

If sufficient information is not available with respect to any adjustment as referred to above, the transaction value of the imported goods must be treated as one that cannot be determined. If the customs value of the imported goods cannot be determined, then the customs value is the transaction value of identical goods sold for export to Pakistan and exported at or about the same time as the goods being valued.

If the customs value of the imported goods cannot be determined as above, the customs value of the imported goods must be based on the unit price at which the imported goods or identical or similar imported goods are sold in the greatest aggregate quantity at or about the time of importation of goods being valued to person who is not related to the person from whom they buy such goods.

If the customs value of the imported goods cannot be determined as above, it must be based on computed value consisting the sum of:

- costs of value of materials and fabrication or other processing employed in producing the imported goods;
- an amount of profit and general expenses equal to that usually reflected in the sale of goods on the same class or kinds as the goods being valued which are made by producers in the country of exportation;
- cost of value of all other expenses including transport, loading, unloading and cost of insurance.

Where any customs valuation has been determined by the Collector of Customs or Director of Valuation, then a revision petition may be filed before the Director General of Valuation within 30 days from the determination of customs value. [1]

Duty Drawback

Customs Act allows duty drawback on goods on which duties were paid at the time of import into Pakistan and they are within the period of two years bound out of Pakistan for export. [2]

Offences

Chapter XXII provides for the offences and penalties under the Customs Act.

Dispute resolution

The Customs Act provides for an appeal to Collectors (Appeal) by any person who is aggrieved by a decision made or order passed in relation to a refund of customs duty, an assessment under Section 79 of the Customs Act, a decision under Section 80 of the Customs Act relating to a goods declaration by an importer and an adjudication under Section 179 of the Customs Act by an officer of Customs. Under Section 194, the Federal Government has constituted an appellate tribunal to be called Customs Appellate Tribunal to hear appeals against decisions made or orders passed by Collector (Appeals) or Additional Collector or FBR or a Collector of Customs under Section 195.

1.5   Clearing procedures

1.5.1   Declaration and assessment

The owner of any imported goods is required to make entry of such goods for home consumption or warehousing or transshipment or for any other approved purposes, within 15 days of the arrival of the goods, by:

(a) filing a true declaration of goods, giving complete and correct particulars of such goods, duly supported by commercial invoice, bill of lading or airway bill, packing list or any other document required for clearance of such goods in such form and manner as the FBR may prescribe; and

(b) assessing and paying his liability of duty, taxes and other charges, in case of

---

[1]   Section 25D of Customs Act.

[2]   Section 35 of Customs Act.

a registered user of the Customs Computerised System.

A declaration of goods may not be made prior to 10 days of the expected time of arrival of the vessel. An officer of Customs, not below the rank of Assistant Collector of Customs, may in case of goods requiring immediate release allow their release thereof prior to presentation of a goods declaration, subject to such conditions and restrictions as may be prescribed by the FBR. ①

1.5.2   Checking of goods declaration by the Customs

On the receipt of goods declaration, an officer of Customs must satisfy himself regarding the correctness of the particulars of imports, including declaration, assessment, and, in case of the Customs Computerised System, payment of duty, taxes and other charges. An officer of Customs may examine any goods that he may deem necessary at any time after the import of the goods into the country and may requisition relevant documents, as and when and in the manner deemed appropriate, during or after the release of the goods by Customs. If during the checking of goods declaration, it is found that any statement in such declaration or document or any information so furnished is not correct in respect of any matter relating to the assessment, the goods are then to be reassessed to duty taxes and other charges levied. ②

1.5.3   Discharge of goods by conveyances other than vessels

When, on arrival of a conveyance other than a vessel at a land customs-station or customs-airport, the person-in-charge of such conveyance has delivered the import manifest and the documents required, such person must forthwith take the conveyance to the examination station at the land customs-station or customs-airport and remove all goods carried in such conveyance to the custom-house in the presence of the appropriate officer or some person duly authorised by him in that behalf. ③ No imported goods required to be shown in the import manifest may, except with the permission of the appropriate officer, be unloaded from any conveyance at any customs-station unless they are specified in the import manifest or amended or

---

①   Section 79 of the Customs Act.
②   Section 80 of the Customs Act.
③   Section 74 of the Customs Act.

supplementary import manifest for being unloaded at that customs-station.① This rule, however, does not apply to the unloading of mail bags, or baggage accompanying a passenger or a member of the crew.

1. 5. 4   Responsibilities of a person in charge of a conveyance

The person in charge of the conveyance, master, agent for conveyance and owner of the conveyance are jointly and individually responsible to submit the following information to the Collector of Customs, namely:

(a) loading or unloading of any container of package, etc. , which is believed to contain any other goods or has different weight or quantity or freight than declared in the bill of lading or any other document in the knowledge of such person;

(b) the name and full address with telephone number of the person who stuffed the goods in the container if he is other than the actual owner of the goods;

(c) the name and full address with telephone number of the person who issued a consignment note or the house bill of lading in case of a person other than licensed by the Customs as Customs agent; and

(d) full details and photocopies of a corrigendum or instructions issued by the owner of the goods or by the other persons for change in the name of the consignee or consignor or destination or regarding weight, value, description and quantity of the goods loaded on the conveyance arriving or leaving Pakistan. ②

1. 5. 5   Declaration by passenger or crew of baggage

The owner of any baggage whether a passenger or a member of the crew is required to make a verbal or written declaration of the contents of the baggage to the appropriate officer and is further required to answer such questions as the said officer may put to him with respect to his baggage and any article contained therein or carried with him and shall produce such baggage and any such articles for examination. ③

The import checking and clearing procedures have been simplified by a new Web-Based One Customs (WEBOC) system which allows for all of the above referred to steps through an online system. An importer may file online a bill of

---

① Section 75 of the Customs Act (Imported goods not to be unloaded unless entered in the import manifest).

② Section 72A of the Customs Act.

③ Section 139 of the Customs Act.

lading or airway bill, certificate of origin, commercial invoice, packing list and insurance certificate in relation to processing and release of imported goods. An importer must have a national tax number and sale tax registration number.

1.6   Export checking and clearance procedure

1.6.1   Permission before loading

No goods other than passengers' baggage or mail bags or ballast urgently required for a vessel's safety are to be loaded or water-borne on a conveyance at a place in a customs-station until an order in respect of the conveyance has been given or permission in this behalf in writing has been granted by the appropriate officer. ①

1.6.2   Clearance requirements for export

Section 31 provides that no goods can be loaded for exportation until their owner has made a declaration by filing a goods declaration to Customs containing correct and complete particulars of his goods, and assessed and paid his liability of duty, taxes and other charges. Any claim of duty drawback, if any, has to be calculated and reflected in the declaration filed for export through Customs Computerised System. For this purpose, the officials of Customs must satisfy themselves regarding the correctness of the particulars of export, including declaration, assessment, and payment of duty, taxes and other charges and also verify the admissibility of the duty drawback claimed.

The WEBOC system is also applicable to export and an exporter can complete all the filing and declarations online.

---

①   Section 130 of the Customs Act.

Chapter 2   Foreign Trade
System and Laws in Pakistan

2. 1   Introduction

Foreign trade is the exchange of capital, goods and services across international borders. Trade has been the bedrock of global economic system since General Agreement on Tanffs and Tariffs (GATT) 1947 and nations across the world have made attempts to make their trade laws conform to the principles enunciated in GATT. Being a founding member of GATT in 1947 and the WTO in 1995, Pakistan has supported an open, transparent and rule-based multilateral trading system. Pakistan extends "most favoured nation" (MFN) treatment to all WTO members except India and Israel. Since 2013, any product may be imported from India unless it is listed in the "negative list" of about 1,200 that Pakistan has compiled, whereas previously only those 2,000 or so products listed in the "positive list" could be imported. [1] As a result of this change, bilateral trade between the two countries has increased exponentially. Pakistan has a transparent legislative regime on anti-dumping measures, countervailing duties and safeguards related measures which are fully compliant with the relevant WTO agreements. It also has a sanitary and phytosanitary measures law which is also broadly compliant with Agreement on Application of Sanitary and Phytosanitary Measures.

2. 2   Trade law—No license system

Pakistan operates a liberal trade regime, and importers and exporters are not required to obtain a license to engage in their trade. Any legal person registered under the laws of Pakistan may import and export goods. The FBR has recently introduced the Web-Based One Customs system (WEBOC) [2] which is a paperless system and

[1]   See Appendix-G of the Import Policy Order, 2013.
[2]   www. weboc. gov. pk.

allows online manifest filing and goods declaration. An importer can file online the bill of lading or airway bill, certificate of origin (in case of concessionary import under a FTA/PTA), commercial invoice, packing list and insurance certificate in relation to the processing and release of imported goods. An importer or an exporter must have a national tax number and a sales tax registration number. Manual interference for customs examination and clearance times have been substantially reduced.

The import of goods into Pakistan is governed by the Import Policy Order of 2013, which provides that imports can be made against all modes of payments subject to procedures prescribed by the State Bank of Pakistan. For imports under loans or credits or bilateral assistance requiring contracts to be approved by Economic Affairs Division or some other agencies, letters of credit must be opened within 60 days of registration of a contract with the bank designated by the State Bank of Pakistan. As a general rule, imports of all goods are allowed from worldwide sources unless otherwise banned, prohibited or restricted by the Import Policy Order.

The export of goods from Pakistan is governed by the Export Policy Order of 2013. It provides that the export from Pakistan shall be made under the foreign exchange rules, regulations and procedures notified by the State Bank of Pakistan from time to time upon submission of documents as may be prescribed. As a general rule, export of all goods is allowed except those specified in Schedule-I. Exports of goods which are specified in Schedule-II, are subject to conditions therein. ①

2.3　Rules on origin of goods

Rules of origin are those laws, regulations and administrative determinations of general application which a country uses to determine the country of origin of goods. Rules of origin add to the complexity of the trade regimes and are generally not viewed favourably. Pakistan does not have any rules of origin requirements for MFN treatment. ② However, rules of origin exist in respect of a number of bilateral and plurilateral trade agreements. These agreements include: the South Asian Free Trade Area (SAFTA), Pakistan-Sri Lanka FTA, Pakistan-China FTA, Pakistan-Malaysia FTA, Pakistan-Iran Preferentiad Trade Agreement (PTA), Pakistan-Mauritius PTA,

---

① See Export Policy Order, 2013.

② As per its notification to the WTO. See WTO document G/RO/N/16.

Global System of Trade Preferences and Pakistan-Indonesia PTA. Almost all of these agreements require the products to be wholly produced or obtained in the country of origin. The minimum value addition requirements in respect of goods range from 35 percent to 50 percent of free on board(FOB).

2.4   Sanitary and phytosanitary measures

The Agreement on the Application of sanitary and phytosanitary measures allows a WTO member to apply Sanitary or Phytosanitary(SPS) measures to protect animal or plant life from risks arising from the entry of pests, diseases and disease carrying organisms. Similarly, SPS measures are allowed to protect human or animal life from risks arising out of additives, contaminants, toxins or disease-carrying organisms in food, beverages or feedstuffs. Pakistan does not have unified legislation dealing with the SPS measures; a number of statutes empower Pakistan to impose SPS measures should the need arise. Some of the statutes covering the SPS measures are as follows;

Agricultural Products(Grading and Marking) Act,1937;

Agricultural Pesticides Ordinance,1971;

Plant Quarantine Act,1976;

Pakistan Animal Quarantine Ordinance,1979;

Pakistan Fish Inspection and Quality Control Act,1997;

Pakistan Animal Quarantine(Import and Export of Animal Products) Act,1970 and Rules made under it.

It must be noted that work is under way on a National Sanitary and Phytosanitary Authority Act as the primary law dealing with all permissible SPS measures under the WTO law. We understand from the relevant authorities that this draft bill will be placed before the National Parliament in due course. Currently, there is a National Animal and Plant Health Inspection Services(NAPHIS) notified under the Ministry of National Food Security and Research of Pakistan, which is functioning as an inquiry point under the SPS Agreement. [1]

The SPS Agreement in Annex A provides certain recommendations regarding the international standards and guidelines which WTO member may follow. In respect of food safety it recommends the standards, guidelines and recommendations established by Codex Alimentarius Commission relating to food additives, veterinary drug and

[1]   WTO Trade Policy Review of Pakistan(Report by the Secretariat),17 February 2015.

pesticide residues, contaminants, methods of analysis and sampling, and codes and guidelines of hygienic practice. For animal health and zoonoses, it recommends the standards, guidelines and recommendations developed under the auspices of International Office of Epizootics(World Organisation for Animal Health). In respect of plant health, it recommends the international standards, guidelines and recommendations developed under the auspices of the Secretariat of International Plant Protection Convention (IPPC). Pakistan is a member of all of the above organisations and follows their recommended standards and guidelines.

Pakistan has signed and ratified the Cartagena Protocol on Biosafety to the Convention on Biological Diversity, which is an international agreement which aims to ensure the safe handling, transport and use of living modified organisms(LMOs) resulting from modern biotechnology that may have adverse effects on biological diversity, taking also into account risks to human health.

The Department of Customs and the Department of Plant Protection are responsible for regulating food imports. The Department of Plant Protection, the competent authority for plant health, is the designated national plant protection organisation. It regulates the country's international trade in agro-commodities through plant quarantine outposts in all seaports, international air terminals, and international borders. Physical inspection is mandatory for imported and exported goods. Laboratory testing is risk- based and may be performed either at the border or inland. Bilateral agreements and protocols regarding specific commodities have been concluded with many countries.

Plant quarantine work is done by Plant Quarantine Division in the Department of Plant Protection, which has legal authority and management responsibility. The organisational arrangements are as per Article IV of the International Plant Protection Convention,1997. The objective of the Plant Quarantine Division is to protect crop and forest wealth through legislative means and to facilitate the trade of plants and plant products. It is not used as a barrier to trade. The main principles governing the procedures are as follows:

- import from a country where the pests, which are to be guarded against, are either absent or under official control;
- import from a country with an efficient quarantine service;
- obtain a phytosanitary certificate according to Guidelines for phytosanitary certificate(ISPM Publication No.7,FAO,Rome);

- inspect material on arrival and treat as required;
- inspect material prior to exportation and treat where necessary;
- assessment of compliance by the exporters as to pest freedom, treatment, packing and packaging;
- issue a phytosanitary certificate and provide information to the importing country;
- maintain transparency and fair play;
- share information and experience.

Papers such as import permits, certificates of origin, phytosanitary certificates, treatment certificates, bills of lading, invoice, letters of credit, anchorage permits, in respect of the consignment are checked for genuineness and proper entry. Violations and infringements are adequately dealt with.

The Animal Quarantine Department[1] is responsible for regulating imports and exports of animals. It performs the following key functions: regulating the import, export and quarantine of animals and animal products, in order to prevent the introduction or spread of exotic diseases; maintaining quarantine services of high standards, to protect the livestock industry of Pakistan and other countries; providing certifications services to the exporters and importers.

There is a National Veterinary Laboratory which performs the following functions:

- serve as National Reference Laboratory, especially for the Transboundary Animal Diseases(TADs) having economic and trade significance;
- test residues of livestock and livestock products to meet EU and WTO sanitary and phytosanitary conditionalities;
- provide vaccine quality control and analysis;
- develop active disease surveillance and virus typing;
- offer training and refreshers in lead laboratory technology and disseminate;
- coordinate, investigate and help contain the highly pathogenic emerging diseases(HPED) as they arise;
- evaluate veterinary drugs for quality, safety, potency and efficacy.

Pakistan's only notification under the SPS Agreement was in 2000 when it

---

[1]   Department under the Ministry of National Food Security & Research of Pakistan(see www. mnfsr. gov. pk).

required dioxin-free certificates in respect of livestock and livestock products imported from Belgium, to ensure that livestock products imported from Belgium are dioxin free.

Acting under the Import Policy Order of 2013, Pakistan has banned the import of live animals particularly from countries infected with bovine spongiform encephalopathy (BSE, or cow disease as commonly known) as well as poultry products originating from certain countries as an SPS measure. According to the WTO Trade Policy Review, no specific trade concerns have been raised with respect to Pakistan's SPS measures.

2. 5   Anti-dumping laws

Article VI of the GATT 1994 condemns the practice of dumping whereby products of one country are introduced into the commerce of another country at less than the normal value of the products and when such introduction causes or threatens material injury to an established industry in the territory of a contracting party or materially retards the establishment of a domestic industry. Pakistan has recently promulgated a new Anti-Dumping Duties Act 2015 (Anti-Dumping Act). This law reforms and consolidates the earlier law on the subject which was promulgated in 2000. [1]

Section 3 of the Anti-Dumping Act authorsies the National Tariff Commission (NTC) [2] to impose anti-dumping measures on products imported to Pakistan when it determines, pursuant to an investigation initiated and conducted in accordance with the provisions of the Anti-Dumping Act that an investigated product is being dumped in Pakistan and that injury is being caused to the domestic industry. A product may be considered to be dumped if it is introduced into the commerce of Pakistan at a price which is less than its normal value. [3] The NTC must determine the normal value of an investigated product on the basis of the comparable price paid or payable, in the ordinary course of trade, for sales of a like product when destined for consumption in

---

①   Anti-Dumping Ordinance 2000.

②   NTC has been established pursuant to the National Tariff Commission Act 2015. NTC was originally established under the National Tariff Commission Act 1990. Section 3 of the National Tariff Commission Act 2015 provides that the earlier NTC established under the 1990 shall be deemed to have been established under the new Act and notwithstanding the repeal of the 1990, it shall be deemed to have been validly constituted.

③   Section 4 of the Anti-Dumping Act.

an exporting country. The NTC may also establish normal value of an investigated product on the basis of comparable price paid or payable in the ordinary course of trade for sales of like product when destined for consumption in the country of origin of the investigated product if such products are not produced in an exporting country or there is no comparable price for them in the exporting country. [1]

Where there is no sale of a like product in the ordinary course of trade in the domestic market of an exporting country, or where such sales do not permit a proper comparison because of any particular market situation, then the NTC must establish normal value of the investigated product on the basis of either a comparable price of the like product when exported to an appropriate third country provided that this price is representative or the cost of production in the exporting country plus a reasonable amount for administrative, selling and general costs and for profits. [2]

For determining the injury, the NTC must make an objective examination of all the relevant factors including: (i) the volume of the dumped imports; (ii) the effect of dumped imports on prices in the domestic market for like products; and (iii) any consequent impact of dumped imports on domestic producers of such products. [3]

An application on behalf of the domestic industry can be initiated by means of a written application to the NTC. The application must include evidence of dumping and injury and the causal link between the dumped imports and the injury, including any other relevant information on which the domestic industry would be relying. [4] After receiving an application, the NTC is bound to give a notice to the government of each exporting country of the receipt of the application. If satisfied that sufficient evidence is not available to indicate dumping or an injury to justify initiation of an investigation, the NTC will reject the application. It must be noted that NTC may initiate an investigation, of its own motion, without having received a written application by or on behalf of the domestic industry if it has sufficient evidence of dumping and injury.

According to Section 24(2) of the Anti-Dumping Act, no investigation may be initiated when domestic producers expressly supporting an application account for less than 25 percent of the total production of a domestic product produced by domestic

[1] Section 5 of the Anti-Dumping Act.
[2] Section 6 of the Anti-Dumping Act.
[3] Section 15 of the Anti-Dumping Act.
[4] Section 20 of the Anti-Dumping Act.

industry.

The NTC may terminate an investigation at any time if it is satisfied that there is not sufficient evidence of either dumping or injury to justify proceeding with an investigation. It may also terminate an investigation if it determines that dumping margin is negligible or that volume of dumped imports, actual or potential, or injury is negligible. The dumping margin shall be considered to be negligible if it is less than two percent of the export price. Volume of dumped imports shall be regarded as negligible if the volume of dumped imports of an investigated product is found to account for less than three percent of the total imports of a like product unless imports of the investigated product from all countries under investigation which individually account for less than three percent of the total imports of a like product collectively account for more than seven percent of imports of a like product. ①

The NTC has the power to impose provisional measures if it makes an affirmative preliminary determination of dumping and injury, and determines that provisional measures are necessary to prevent injury from being caused during the course of investigation. When the NTC has established the existence of dumping and injury in accordance with the provisions of the Act, it must impose anti-dumping duties. Anti-dumping duties imposed under the Anti-dumping Act take the form of *ad valorem* or specific duties, and may be imposed in addition to other import duties levied on an investigated product; be, collected in the same manner as customs duties under the Customs Act, and levied and collected on a non-discriminatory basis on imports of such product from all sources found to be dumped and causing injury.

Any interested party may prefer an appeal to an Appellate Tribunal constituted under the Anti-Dumping Act against the initiation of an investigation or a preliminary determination where the same have not been done in accordance with the law. An appeal also lies against an affirmative or negative final determination of the NTC. An appeal against the decision of the Appellate Tribunal may be made to the High Court.

2.6   Countervailing duties law

The Agreement on Subsidies and Countervailing Measures (Agreement on

---

① Section 41 of the Anti-Dumping Act.

Subsidies) prohibits (subject to exceptions provided in the Agreement on Agriculture) subsidies that require recipients to meet export targets or use domestic goods instead of imported goods, as they distort international trade. Where the WTO settlement procedure confirms that the subsidy is a prohibited subsidy, it must be withdrawn. If it is not withdrawn, the affected WTO member may take countervailing measures. It may impose countervailing measures on the import of such subsidised goods which hurts its domestic industry.

Pakistan has recently promulgated the Countervailing Duties Act 2015 which gives effect to the Agreement on Subsidies. According to Section 3 of the Countervailing Duties Act, the NTC has the power to impose a countervailing duty on any imported goods which has been improperly subsidised by the exporting country directly or indirectly in its manufacture or production or exportation (including transportation to Pakistan).

According to Section 4 of the Countervailing Duties Act, a subsidy shall be deemed to exist if

(A) There is a financial contribution by a government, where

(i) the government practice involves direct transfer of funds including grants, loans and equity infusion, or potential direct transfer of funds or liabilities, or both;

(ii) government revenue that is otherwise due is forgone or not collected including fiscal incentives such as tax credits, provided that exemption of an exported product from duties or taxes borne by a like product when destined for domestic consumption, or remission of such duties or taxes in amounts not in excess of those which have accrued, are not deemed to be a subsidy provided that such exemption is granted in accordance with the provisions of the First, Second and Third Schedules;

(iii) the government provides goods or services other than general infrastructure or purchases goods; or

(iv) the government makes payments to a funding mechanism, or entrusts or directs a private body to carry out one or more of the type of functions specified in sub-clauses (i), (ii) and (iii) which would normally be vested in the government and the practice in, no real sense, differs from practices normally followed by governments;

(B) There is any form of income or price support within the meaning of Article XVI of the General Agreement on Tariffs and Trade, 1994; and

(C) A benefit is thereby conferred.

Subsidy is subject to countervailing measures under the countervailing duties and only if the NTC determines that such subsidy is specific towards a certain enterprise, industry or group of enterprises. It must be noted that the setting or changing of generally applicable tax rates by all levels of the government entitled to do so is not deemed to be a specific subsidy. A determination of injury by NTC must be based on positive evidence and involve an objective examination of the volume of any subsidised imports and their effects on prices in the domestic market for like products and the consequent impact of subsidised imports on the domestic industry. [1]

The NTC must initiate an investigation to determine the existence, degree and effect of any alleged subsidy upon their receipt of a written application by or on behalf of the domestic industry. The application must include sufficient evidence of the existence of a subsidy and if possible its amount, injury within the meaning of the Act, and a causal link between the subsidised imports and the alleged injury.

The NTC has the power to impose provisional countervailing duties provided a public notice of initiation of investigation has been given, interested parties have been given adequate opportunity to submit information, and a provisional affirmative determination has been made by the NTC that a subsidy exists and that there is a consequent injury to domestic industry.

If during an investigation the NTC determines that the prohibited subsidy, or the volume of subsidised imports or the injury is negligible, it must immediately terminate the investigation. Where NTC has established the existence of prohibited subsidies and consequent injury, it may impose a definitive countervailing duty. A definitive countervailing is an amount equal to or less than the amount of prohibited subsidies from which any exporters have been found to have benefited, as established by the NTC in accordance with the provisions of this Act. There is provision for an appeal before the Appellate Tribunal against the initiation of an investigation or a preliminary determination where it does not satisfy the requirements of Section 11 and Section 13 of the Countervailing Duties Act, against an affirmative or negative final determination by the NTC and against an order of termination of investigation by the

---

[1] Section 9 of the Countervailing Duties Act.

NTC. The decision of the Appellate Tribunal is appealable in the High Court.

2.7   Safeguard measures law

The Agreement on Safeguards enables a WTO member to apply safeguard measures to a product if such product is being imported into its territory in such increased quantities, absolute or relative to domestic production, and under such conditions as to cause or threaten to cause serious injury to the domestic industry that produces like or directly competitive products. A WTO member may only apply a safeguard measure following a proper investigation by the competent authorities of that member.

Pakistan's law implementing the agreement on safeguards is contained in the Safeguard Measures Ordinance of 2002.

Section 3 of the Safeguard Measures Ordinance provides that the Federal Government may apply a safeguard measure on an investigated product imported into Pakistan if it has been determined by the NTC pursuant to an investigation conducted by it that as a result of unforeseen developments and the effect of WTO obligations assumed by Pakistan, the investigated product is being imported in such increased quantities absolute or relative to domestic production and under such conditions as to cause serious injury or threat of serious injury to domestic industry producing like or directly competitive products. In determining whether the importation has caused serious injury or threat of serious injury, the NTC must evaluate all relevant factors of an objective and quantifiable nature having a bearing on the situation of the domestic industry.

2.8   Technical barriers to trade[①]

The Technical Barriers to Trade Agreement of the WTO aims to ensure that technical regulations, standards and conformity assessment procedures are non-discriminatory and do not create unnecessary obstacles to trade. It provides that technical regulations must not be more trade-restrictive than necessary to fulfil a legitimate objective, taking account of the risks non-fulfilment would create. Such legitimate objectives are, *inter alia*, national security requirements, plant life or

---

① See Trade Policy Review of WTO, 17 February 2015.

health, or the environment. Considerations relevant to an assessment of such risks include vailable scientific and technical information, related processing technology and intended end-uses of products.

The Pakistan Standards and Quality Control Authority(PSQCA) was established pursuant to an Act of Parliament in 1996. It is the national standard-setting body responsible for the formulation and enforcement of Pakistan's Standards regarding many essential sectors such as agriculture and food, chemicals, electronics, mechanical, automobile and textile sectors, the PSQCA develops and adopts standards and provides conformity/testing assessments. It also advises the government on standardisation policies, programmes and activities, and, endeavours to promote industrial efficiency and development as well as consumer protection. PSQCA is a member of the International Organisation for Standardisation(ISO), the International Electro-technical Commission (IEC) and the International Organisation of Legal Metrology(OIML). It is the focal point for National Enquiry Point(NEP) for the WTO Agreement on Technical Barriers to Trade(TBT). [1]

As a member of ISO, IEC, and OIML, Pakistan strives to make its national standards conform to international requirements. It has some 30,927 standard specifications covering mainly agriculture, foodstuffs, chemicals, civil and mechanical engineering and textiles. These are generally harmonised with international/regional standards. Of these, 15,700 are ISO standards, 6,370 are IEC/OIML standards and 8,857 are national standards which, according to the authorities, are often based on regional or UK standards. [2]

Imports are subject to the same quality standards or regulations which are applicable to similar goods produced in Pakistan. Appendix N of the 2013 Import Policy Order contains a list of products under the Compulsory Certification Mark License Scheme which must meet at the import stage Pakistan standards on human safety and public health. These goods must have a Certification Mark issued by the PSQCA to be made, stocked or sold domestically. All domestic manufacturers and exporters from Pakistan must be registered with the PSQCA to ensure compliance. Imports and domestic goods undergo the same conformity testing procedures. PSQCA also sets mandatory standards, generally in line with international requirements(e. g.

---

[1]   Trade Policy Review of WTO, 17 February 2015, p. 43.

[2]   Ibid.

WHO and CAC) for public health and safety (mainly on food and exports). The PSQCA has some 52 registered inspection agencies and a total of 22 laboratories undertaking quality control services. ①

The Pakistan National Accreditation Council (PNAC) is the national accreditation body for testing laboratories and other conformity assessment facilities and operates under the administrative control of the Ministry of Science and Technology. The standards are elaborated by one of the PSQCA's 11 national entities and their technical committees. Draft standards are circulated among stakeholders for comments. PNAC has Mutual Recognition Arrangements with the International Laboratory Accreditation Cooperation (ILAC) and the Asia Pacific Laboratory Accreditation Cooperation (APLAC). Pakistan has concluded 11 mutual recognition agreements with other countries and is included in the list of countries having equivalent status for accreditation of testing and calibration laboratories and certification bodies for Quality Management Systems (QMS), i. e. ISO9000, and Environmental Management Systems (EMS), i. e. ISO14000. PNAC applies international standards and has accredited 59 testing and calibration laboratories, including in pharmaceuticals, textiles, chemicals, engineering and food. Another agency, the Pakistan Council of Scientific and Industrial Research (PCSIR) also provides testing facilities (mainly to exporters). ②

Pakistan has submitted 59 notifications to the WTO under the TBT Agreement covering health and safety standards adopted, covering mainly sampling and testing procedures as well as labelling, packaging, storage and transport of a number of food and other products. The authorities indicate that additional notifications are under preparation. No specific trade concerns have been raised with respect to Pakistan's TBT measures. ③

---

① Trade Policy Review of WTO, 17 February 2015, pp. 43 – 44.
② Ibid.
③ Ibid.

Chapter 3　Foreign Direct Investment Related Laws

3.1　Introduction

Foreign direct investment(FDI) refers to long-term investment by an investor of one country in another country. It may be in the shape of management, joint ventures, transfer of technology, licenses and expertise. FDI is a measure of foreign ownership of assets, such as industries and land, etc., in a host country. Today FDI is considered to be an important means of achieving economic integration among countries.

Pakistan has had a liberal investment regime since 1997 when the first investment policy was laid out by the Board of Investment(BOI) of Pakistan. This policy opened services, social infrastructure and agricultural sectors to foreign investors which were previously restricted to manufacturing sector only. [1] The latest investment policy issued by the Federal Government of Pakistan is the Investment Policy 2013. This policy not only reinforces the liberal regime set up in 1997 but further liberalises the investment climate of the country by further incentivising both foreign and domestic investors making investments in Pakistan.

The Investment Policy 2013, Foreign Private Investment (Promotion & Protection) Act 1976 and the Protection of Economic Reforms Act 1992 set out the broad principles relating to FDI, the sectors in which foreign investments may be made, and how foreign investors are treated as compared with local investors. The Foreign Private Investment(Promotion & Protection) Act 1976 and the Protection of Economic Reforms Act 1992 also provide protection by facilitating easy repatriation of foreign exchange from Pakistan.

The recent introduction of the Special Economic Zones Act 2012 (SEZ ACT 2012) offers huge incentives to foreign and domestic investors who set up industries

---

[1]　See generally Investment Policy 2013.

in Special Economic Zones. These incentives include duty free import of capital goods for establishment of zones and projects therein and exemption from income tax for a period of 10 years for zone developers and zone enterprises

Pakistan firmly believes in bilateral, regional and multilateral trade regimes and has implemented national legislation to ensure legal protection of incentives offered to trade regimes in Pakistan.

All investments in Pakistan must be channelled through corporate entities, mostly companies established under the Companies Ordinance 1984. The Securities and Exchange Commission of Pakistan(SECP) is the apex regulator of corporate bodies including private, public and public non-listed companies. It is the sole body responsible for incorporation, monitoring and regulation of all types of companies incorporated in Pakistan under the Companies Ordinance 1984.

The regulatory authorities in Pakistan operate on the principle of non-discrimination to ensure that foreign and domestic investors are treated in a like manner. There are no onerous financial or other obligations which are imposed on foreign investors as opposed to domestic investors, except some security related measures which may be imposed on foreign nationals.

3. 2   Salient features of Pakistan's investment regime[1]

3. 2. 1   Free entry of foreign investors

All sectors and activities are open to foreign investment unless specifically prohibited for reasons of national security and public safety. The specified restricted industries include arms and ammunitions; high explosives, radioactive substances; securities, currency, and mint; and consumable alcohol. There is no minimum equity requirement for foreign investment in any sector. There is no upper limit on the share of foreign equity allowed, except in specific sectors including airline, banking, agriculture and media.

3. 2. 2   National treatment principle[2]

As a member of the WTO, Pakistan adheres to the national treatment principle on internal taxation and regulation. Foreign investors are not subject to internal taxes

---

① See Investment Policy 2013.
② See Article 3 of the General Agreement on Tariffs and Trade(GATT 1947).

or internal charges more burdensome than those applicable to investments made in similar circumstances by citizens of Pakistan and are accorded equal treatment in respect of their investments in Pakistan. ① Similarly, any industrial undertaking having foreign private investment must be accorded the same treatment as accorded to similar industrial undertakings having no such investment, in the application of laws, rules and regulations relating to importation and exportation of goods.

3.2.3　Ease of registration and entry

Pakistan has an open-admission system that does not require pre-screening and approval for entrants. Foreign companies which comply with the Companies Ordinance 1984 and other laws of Pakistan do not require any separate approval for their investments. Merger with or acquisition of a company operating within Pakistan requires a pre-merger or pre-acquisition approval from the Competition Commission and certain procedures under the Companies Ordinance 1984, have to be followed. Additionally, certain sector-specific regulatory approvals are required for any business undertaking in a specific sector. These approvals are required as a matter of Pakistani law and are applicable equally to both foreign and domestic investors in a non-discriminatory manner. ②

The BOI has instituted an online registration procedure for foreign companies entering and operating in Pakistan. Registration serves as a notification to the Government of Pakistan of the presence of the investor and guarantees to the investor the entitlements specified in the Investment Policy. This is not an approval mechanism. For rendering efficient services, BOI charges a nominal fee.

The typical way of setting up or undertaking a business in Pakistan is by means of setting up, or acquiring shareholding in, a private limited company or public limited company by following the applicable registration procedures provided in the Companies Ordinance 1984. A foreign investor can also acquire shares in public companies listed on the Pakistan Stock Exchange(PSX) in accordance the applicable rules and regulations provided by the SECP and the Stock Exchange. Similarly, a foreign entity can set up a branch or a representative or liaison office in accordance with the applicable procedures specified by the BOI. The BOI charges a fee for these services. Foreign investors may freely sell shares, transfer ownership, and wind up

---

① See Section 8 of the Foreign Private Investment(Promotion & Protection) Act 1976.

② See below Section 7 Regulators of Pakistan.

under Companies Ordinance 1984.

Foreign Investors are free to obtain foreign currency loans from banks/financial institutions abroad, parent companies of the foreign investors and as supplier credit including credits for projects covered by the Government Investment Policy. Private entities may negotiate foreign currency loans to import plant and equipment for export-oriented industries either for the establishment of new industrial units or for balancing, modernising, replacement and expansion of existing export oriented units. In addition to the above, foreign currency loans may also be obtained to finance exports or to provide working capital, subject to certain conditions. All foreign currency private loan agreements and supplier credit agreements are required to be submitted to the State Bank of Pakistan (SBP) for registration.

Foreign investors are now entitled to hold land for development purposes subject to applicable federal or provincial regulations. A foreign investor is allowed to hold 60 percent of a stake in agricultural projects. For corporate agricultural farming 100 percent ownership is permissible.

3.3   Establishment of Special Economic Zones

The Special Economic Zones Act 2012 provides for the creation, development and efficient operation of Special Economic Zones to encourage and promote domestic and foreign investors, and for the establishment of industrial infrastructure in Pakistan.

The salient features and incentives under the SEZ Act are as follows:

It allows a minimum of 50 acres of land in any province of Pakistan to be qualified as a Special Economic Zone(SEZ).

It extends to the whole of Pakistan and overrides any other law.

The government must establish SEZs by itself, or in collaboration with private parties under various modes of collaboration including public-private partnership, or accord recognition to the privately established economic activity zones as SEZ to be governed under this Act.

Board of Approvals under the SEZs Act is headed by the Prime Minister of Pakistan with the Minister for Finance as the Vice Chairman and includes the Chief Minister of each province, heads of economic ministries, executive heads of the Provincial Investment Boards and representatives of private sector.

Board of Approvals may grant additional benefits to a particular category of

SEZ, zone enterprise, regions or certain sector if justified on the basis of an economic impact assessment.

Approvals Committee set up by the SEZ Act is chaired by the chairman of the BOI and comprises the representatives of the federal/provincial economic ministries and private sector representatives.

Every province must have its own SEZ authority which is a legal entity headed by Chief Minister of the province or a person nominated by the Chief Minister.

Any existing zone may apply to the SEZ authority in which they are located to become eligible for SEZ but can benefit from only one set of incentives.

Incentive/exemptions once granted to SEZ clusters, SEZ developers and zone enterprises cannot be withdrawn.

Zone developers and zone enterprises import duty-free capital goods for the establishment, maintenance of zones and projects therein.

Zone developers and zone enterprises enjoy tax exemption for a period of 10 years.

All utilities and infrastructure shall be given by the government till zero point of the zone.

Zone developers may be permitted to undertake captive power generation and sell any excess.

There shall be a One-Window-Facility operated by the BOI. The government shall provide dry ports facilities. The security arrangements shall be provided by the provincial government.

3.4   Visa facilitation

Pakistani missions abroad are authorised to grant multiple entry business visas valid for five years within 24 hours to the businessmen of 69 countries of Business Visa List (BVL), provided that necessary documents such as an invitation from a Pakistani company, the BOI, or a Provincial Investment Promotion Agency are presented. The visa holder may stay in Pakistan for a maximum of three months during each visit.

Visa-on-Arrival for 30 days validity and stay will be given to the businessman of 69 countries of BVL mentioned above on production of documents for business visa.

Pakistan missions abroad are also authorised to grant work visas to foreign technical and managerial personnel as defined by BOI for the purpose of imparting technical know-how and skills to the local population. The duration of a work visa is one year and may be renewed annually. A visa extension application will be processed by BOI in four weeks.

A foreigner who has been issued a work visa is exempt from registration with the police, except nationals of countries on the negative list.

3.5   Protection of foreign investment

The Government of Pakistan offers full protection to investments made by a foreign investor. The Foreign Private Investment(Promotion & Protection) Act 1976 and the Protection of Economic Reforms Act 1992 are the key statutes which guarantee protection to foreign investors. Some of the key protections are stated below.

3.5.1 Protection against expropriation

If the Federal Government takes over the management of an industrial undertaking having foreign private investment or acquires the ownership of shares of a Pakistani citizen in such industrial undertaking, any agreement approved by the Federal Government relating to such undertaking between a foreign investor or creditor and any person in Pakistan is not affected by such takeover or acquisition. [1]

Similarly, any foreign capital or foreign private investment in any industrial undertaking is not acquired except under the due process of law which provides for adequate compensation in the currency of the country of origin of the capital or investment and specifies the principles on and the manner in which compensation is to be determined. [2] According to Section 7 of the Protection of Economic Reforms Act 1992, the ownership, management and control of any banking, commercial, manufacturing or other company, establishment or enterprise transferred by the government to any person under any law may not again be compulsorily acquired or taken over by the government for any reason whatsoever.

Similarly, according to Section 8 of the Protection of Economic Reforms Act 1992, "No foreign, industrial or commercial enterprise established or owned in any

---

[1]   Section 5 of the Foreign Private Investment(Promotion & Protection) Act 1976.

[2]   Ibid.

form by a foreign or Pakistani investor for private gain in accordance with law, and no investment in share or equity of any company, firm, or enterprise, and no commercial bank of financial institution established, owned or acquired by any foreign or Pakistani investor, may be compulsorily acquired or taken over by the Government. "

3.5.2 Repatriation of profits[1]

Foreign investors in any sector must at any time repatriate profits, dividends or any other funds(including loans and interest charges) in the currency of the country from which the investment originated, subject to procedural requirements set under the Foreign Exchange Manual 2002 of the SBP. Similarly, foreign employees/foreign nationals employed in any industrial undertaking having foreign private investment may make remittances for the maintenance of their dependents in accordance with the rules and regulations of the SBP.

Any foreign investor who holds a foreign currency account enjoys immunity against any enquiry from the income tax department or any other taxation authority as to the source of financing of the foreign currency accounts. The balances in the foreign currency accounts and income therefrom continue to remain exempt from wealth tax and income tax and compulsory deduction of Zakat (Zakat is a tax applicable only to Muslims) at source. There are no restrictions on deposits in and withdrawals from the foreign currency accounts. The banks are under obligation to maintain complete secrecy in respect of transactions in foreign currency accounts. [2]

3.5.3 Protection of financial obligations

According to Section 10 of the Protection of Economic Reforms Act 1992, all financial obligations incurred, including those under any instrument, or any financial and contractual commitment made by or on behalf of the government, continue to remain in force and may not be altered to the disadvantage of the beneficiaries.

3.5.4 Protection of fiscal incentives for setting up of industries

Section 6 of the Protection of Economic Reforms Act 1992 provides that fiscal incentives for investment provided by the government through statutory orders listed in Schedule or otherwise notified continue in force for the term specified therein and

---

[1] See Section 6 and 7 of the Foreign Private Investment(Promotion & Protection) Act 1976.

[2] Section 5 of the Protection of Economic Reforms Act 1992.

may not be altered to the disadvantage of the investors.

It must be noted that the Protection Economic Reform Act 1992, has an overriding effect as far as other laws are concerned and has effect notwithstanding anything to the contrary contained in other law.

3.6   Bilateral investment treaties (BITs) between Pakistan and other countries

Pakistan has signed double taxation and investment treaties with a number of countries (see Table 1). These treaties were signed and ratified by the executive branch of the government and finally were made part of the Pakistani law by means of a Statutory Revisionary Order (SRO). An SRO is a subordinate legislation and carries the full force of law. The features of these BITs include:

- encouragement of investments between the contracting parties;
- non-discrimination between local investors and foreign investors and fair and equitable treatment of foreign investors;
- easy repatriation of profits, dividends, royalties and technical fees and interest;
- settlement of disputes under the International Convention for Settlement of Investment Disputes (ICSID);
- equal/non-discriminatory treatment in case of compensation for losses owing to war, other armed conflicts or a state of national emergency.

The BITs between Pakistan and other contracting countries have been signed over a period of last 50 years, and not all BITs are uniform in their content. The BOI is working on a model document which will ensure the protection of investment from the contracting country on the basis of reciprocity. The aim is to make existing BITs conform to the model document to the extent possible and for new BITs to adhere to the new model document.

It must be noted that Pakistan applies the same non-discriminatory and equality principles with respect to other non-contracting countries provided those countries treat investment from Pakistan in a similar fashion.

Table 1. List of Countries/Union with BITs with Pakistan

S. No.	Name of Country	Signing Date	S. No.	Name of Country	Signing Date
1	Australia	07. 02. 1998	25	Malaysia	07. 07. 1995
2	Azerbaijan	09. 10. 1995	26	Mauritius	03. 04. 1997
3	Bahrain	18. 03. 2014	27	Morocco	16. 04. 2001
4	Bangladesh	24. 04. 1995	28	Netherlands	04. 10. 1988
5	Belarus	22. 01. 1997	29	Oman	09. 11. 1997
6	Belgo-Luxemburg Economic Union	23. 04. 1998	30	Philippines	23. 04. 1999
			31	Portugal	17. 04. 1995
7	Bosnia	04. 09. 2001	32	Qatar	06. 04. 1999
8	Bulgaria	12. 02. 2002	33	Romania	10. 07. 1995
9	Cambodia	27. 04. 2004	34	Singapore	08. 03. 1995
10	China	12. 02. 1989	35	Republic of Korea	25. 05. 1988
11	Czech Republic	07. 05. 1999	36	Spain	26. 04. 1994
12	Denmark	18. 07. 1996	37	Sri Lanka	20. 12. 1997
13	Egypt	16. 04. 2000	38	Sweden	12. 03. 1981
14	France	01. 06. 1983	39	Switzerland	11. 07. 1995
15	Germany	01. 12. 2009	40	Syria	25. 04. 1995
16	Indonesia	08. 03. 1996	41	Tajikistan	13. 05. 2004
17	Iran	08. 11. 1995	42	Tunisia	18. 04. 1996
18	Italy	19. 07. 1997	43	Turkey	22. 05. 2012
19	Japan	10. 03. 1998	44	Turkmenistan	26. 10. 1994
20	Kazakhstan	08. 12. 2003	45	U. A. E.	05. 11. 1995
21	Kuwait	14. 02. 2011	46	United Kingdom	30. 11. 1994
22	Kyrgyz Republic	23. 08. 1995	47	Uzbekistan	13. 08. 1992
23	Lebanon	09. 01. 2001	48	Yemen	11. 05. 1999
24	Laos	23. 04. 2004		—	—

3. 7   Regulators of Pakistan and foreign investors

3. 7. 1   State Bank of Pakistan (SBP)

The central bank of Pakistan is the State Bank of Pakistan. The State Bank of Pakistan Act 1956 provides that SBP was established "to regulate the monetary and credit system of Pakistan and to foster its growth in the best national interest with a view to securing monetary stability and fuller utilisation of the country's productive resources". SBP has the exclusive authority to regulate the banking sector, to conduct an independent monetary policy and to set limits on government borrowing. Most importantly, the SBP has the primary regulatory role in supervising banking companies in Pakistan. Any new foreign bank intending to set up operations in Pakistan whether as a Branch office or by incorporating as an independent company has to obtain a license from the SBP. [1] At present, a foreign banking company is allowed a maximum 49 percent ownership in a banking company in Pakistan.

3. 7. 2   Pakistan Telecommunication Authority(PTA)

PTA is the sole regulatory authority of telecommunications companies in Pakistan. It was set up in 1996 pursuant to the Pakistan Telecommunications (Re-organiastion) Act 1996. Its core function is to regulate the establishment, operation and maintenance of telecommunication systems and the provision of telecommunication services in Pakistan. The PTA has the power to grant and renew license of any telecommunication system on payment of such fees and charges as it may specify from time to time. It has the power to monitor, supervise and enforce the terms and conditions of the licenses of telecommunications companies. The new Telecommunications Policy 2015 was issued by the Government of Pakistan with an aim to transform Pakistan into an information society and knowledge-based economy. The policy visions are: " Universally available, affordable and quality telecommunications services provided through open, competitive, and well managed markets and ubiquitously adopted to the benefit of the economy and society". The Telecommunications Policy provides for a level playing field for foreign and domestic players in the field of telecommunications and does not provide for any obligations and commitments to foreign investors which are more onerous as compared to the

---

[1]   See Section 27 of the Banking Companies Ordinance 1962.

domestic investors.

3.7.3 Oil and Gas Regulatory Authority(OGRA)

Oil and Gas Regulatory Authority(OGRA) has been set up under the Oil and Gas Regulatory Authority Ordinance 2002 to foster competition, increase private investment and ownership in the midstream and downstream petroleum industry, protect the public interest while respecting individual rights and provide effective and efficient regulations. As laid down in the Ordinance, the Authority comprises one Chairman and three members. The Government of Pakistan has promulgated the Petroleum Policy of 2012 and offered huge pricing incentives for both domestic and international exploration companies for any hydrocarbons found in Pakistan. The government allows 100 percent foreign ownership of exploratory blocks in the country. The government is particularly keen to attract foreign investment in this sector in order to increase the production of oil and gas, as foreign oil imports into Pakistan constitute a huge strain on the foreign exchange reserves of the country.

3.7.4 Pakistan Electronic Media Regulatory Authority(PEMRA)

PEMRA has been established pursuant to the Pakistan Electronic Media Regulatory Authority Ordinance 2002 and entrusted with the responsibility for "regulating the establishment and operation of all broadcast media and distribution services in Pakistan established for the purpose of international, national, provincial, district, local or special audiences".

3.7.5 National Electric Power Regulatory Authority(NEPRA)

NEPRA was established pursuant to the Regulation of Generation, Transmission and Distribution of Electric Power Act 1997. Its main responsibilities are to:
- issue licenses for generation, transmission and distribution of electric power;
- establish and enforce standards to ensure quality and safety of operation and supply of electric power to consumers;
- approve investment and power acquisition programs of utility companies; and
- determine tariffs for generation, transmission and distribution of electric power.

NEPRA is responsible for the regulation of the electric power sector to promote a competitive structure for the industry and to ensure a coordinated, reliable and adequate supply of electric power. NEPRA is mandated by law to ensure that the interests of the investor and the customer are protected through judicious decisions based on transparent commercial principles and that the sector moves towards a competitive environment.

3.7.6   Civil Aviation Authority(CAA)

CAA is a regulatory authority to provide for the promotion and regulation of civil aviation activities and to develop an infrastructure for a safe , efficient , adequate , economical and properly coordinated civil air transport service in Pakistan. The Government of Pakistan recently issued the National Aviation Policy 2015 , pursuant to which it has encouraged foreign investment in a number of aviation related activities in respect of maintenance , repair and overhaul services. 100 percent ownership is permissible. However , a foreign airline may own up to 49 percent of stake in a domestic airline company.

3.8   Business structures for foreign investors

3.8.1   Foreign company liaison office

A foreign company , desiring to establish its office in Pakistan , may choose to open a Liaison or Branch office as its extension in Pakistan. A foreign company may open liaison/representative offices in Pakistan which may be used for the promotion of products , provision of technical advice and assistance , exploring the possibility of joint collaboration and export promotion. A liaison office is not allowed to undertake any commercial or trading activities in Pakistan and expenses have to be met through remittances received from its head office.

3.8.2   Branch office

A foreign company having a valid contract with a public or private sector entity in Pakistan is allowed to set up a branch office in Pakistan to fulfil its contractual obligations. The activities of the branch are confined to those which are stated in such contract. It cannot engage in any commercial or trading activities. It has to meet all its expenses out of contractual receipts and remittances from head office. A non-resident company while establishing its branch office in Pakistan retains its constitutional framework under which it is incorporated. The process involves two stages , permission from BOI and registration with SECP. Appointment of a principal officer and resident officer is a mandatory requirement. The maintenance of local registered address is also required.

Permission has to be obtained from the BOI for establishing a branch. The application to the BOI must be submitted along with copies of the contract awarded to the foreign company in Pakistan. The BOI grants permission to the foreign company for establishing a branch, after obtaining clearance from various agencies of Ministry of Interior (MOI). The process normally takes seven to eight weeks, after submission of the application to the BOI. Initial permission to operate a Branch office is issued for one year, subsequent renewals to continue are allowed for a period of three to five years. To register a branch of the foreign company in Pakistan, specified information in the prescribed form together with the relevant documents must be filed with the SECP, within 30 days of BOI permission.

3.8.3　Private limited company

A foreign investor may establish a 100 percent owned subsidiary in Pakistan in the shape of a private limited company. Under the Company Law the private limited company must have a minimum of two members and a minimum two directors. Subject to any sector specific regulatory approval, it may commence its business immediately after incorporation. A private limited company, through its Articles of Association (AoA) restricts the right to transfer its shares, limits the number of its members to 50 and prohibits any invitation to the public to subscribe for its shares. The process of incorporation of a private limited company involves preparation of Memorandum and Articles of Association and identity documents of the investing company and directors of the proposed company, and their submission to the SECP. The process of incorporation starts from reservation of company's name and ends with the issuance of a Certificate of Incorporation. The SECP usually does not require more than one week for incorporation, from the filing of the required documents and payment of the prescribed fee. It must be noted, however, that there is a security clearance step (in case of a foreign national as director or shareholder of the company) undertaken by the relevant agencies which may require sometime. Previously, the incorporation of companies with foreign directors or shareholders use to take seven to eight weeks because of security clearance issues. However, SECP is now mandated to issue a certificate of incorporation, before formal security clearance, provided the foreign national gives an undertaking that in case its security clearance is not approved, he must offer a suitable replacement for director/shareholder in the company.

3.8.4　Single member company

Single member company as is evident from the name is a type of company with only one member who is the sole director of the company as well. All the shares are vested in the single member; however, it is mandatory for the single member to nominate an individual as nominee director to act as director in case of his death, and an alternative nominee director who will act as nominee director in case of non-availability of the nominee director. A corporate entity cannot become its member or director.

3.8.5   Public Limited Company

A public unlisted company must have at least three members and three directors. It is not entitled to commence business unless it obtains a "Certificate of Commencement of Business" from the Registrar of Companies, SECP. There is no restriction on the maximum number of members and transfer of shares.

A public company has the option to list its securities/shares at any stock exchange in Pakistan. It must then have at least seven members and seven directors. Its minimum paid-up capital should be Rs. 200 million and it is also required to make a public offer/issue of its shares, which must be subscribed by at least 500 applicants. The post issue paid up capital is required to be at minimum Rs. 500 million.

Chapter 4   Monetary and Banking System and Law in Pakistan

4.1   Introduction

Pakistan has a robust banking and monetary system. The banking sector of Pakistan has remained healthy with steady earnings and a strong capital position. Its profits after tax surged by 52 percent year on year on the back of both interest and non-interest income, while capital adequacy ratio remained strong at 17.2 percent well above the local requirement of 10 percent and the international benchmark of 8 percent. A decent increase in the asset base came from an increase in investment in government securities, seasonal public sector commodity financing and some growth in private sector lending. Non-remunerative current deposits formed a major source of funding while financial borrowings decreased as a result of improved liquidity position. [1]

4.2   Foreign exchange system and rules on movement of funds

Foreign exchange policy in Pakistanis is formulated and regulated in accordance with the provisions of the Foreign Exchange Regulation Act 1947(FERA 1947). The object of this Act is to regulate, in the economic and financial interest of Pakistan, certain payments, dealings in foreign exchange, securities, import/export of currency and bullion. Under the Act, the basic regulations are issued by the Government of Pakistan and the State Bank of Pakistan(SBP) in the form of notifications which are published in the *Official Gazette*.

Sections 3,4 and 5 of the FERA 1947 make it clear that dealings involving foreign exchange may not be undertaken unless duly authorised. Section 3 provides that the SBP may, on an application made to it, authorise any person to deal in all or some foreign currencies and transaction of all or some transactions in foreign

---

[1]   Quarterly Performance Review of the Banking Sector(April-June 2015) by State Bank of Pakistan.

currency. The SBP may also specify the period for which the authorisation is valid. An authorised dealer must comply with all general or special directions issued by the SBP from time to time. There is a general prohibition on foreign exchange dealings by any person in Pakistan to buy or borrow or sell or lend any foreign exchange in Pakistan or outside without general or special permission granted by the SBP. No person resident in Pakistan is permitted to(a) make any payment to or for the credit of any person resident outside Pakistan; (b) draw, issue or negotiate any bill of exchange or promissory note or acknowledge any debt, so that an actual or contingent right to receive a payment is created or transferred in favour of any person resident outside Pakistan. However, this rule is not applicable to situations where specific exemptions or authorisations have been granted under the FERA. Similarly, this rule would also not contravene the concessions given to foreign investors who seek to repatriate foreign currency out of Pakistan through a person (such as a bank) authorised to deal in foreign exchange. ①

Authorisation to deal in all foreign currencies and in approved transactions of every description has been given to scheduled banks which conduct all types of banking transactions. ② An application for grant of a licence must be made by the head office of a bank or the principal office in Pakistan of a foreign bank, to the director of exchange policy department SBP stating the nature of transactions that it desires to deal with. The application should confirm that trained staff and the required systems and equipment to handle foreign currency transactions are available. Once the head office/principal office of a bank has obtained authorisation to deal in foreign exchange, it would be free to decide which of its branches would conduct foreign exchange business. Every branch of a bank authorised to deal in foreign exchange is authorised to purchase foreign currency notes, coins, travellers' cheque and demand drafts. Such transactions must be reported to a branch designated by its head office for consolidation and reporting to SBP. ③

An authorised bank may open foreign currency accounts of any person resident in and outside Pakistan as well as of foreign nationals whether residing abroad or in Pakistan.

---

① Sections 4 and 5 of FERA Act 1947.
② Foreign Exchange Manual of SBP, para. 1 of Chapter 2.
③ Foreign Exchange Manual of SBP, para. 2 of Chapter 2.

4.3   Banking system and essential rules on banking operations

4.3.1   SBP—The Central Bank

State Bank of Pakistan is the central bank of the country. While it was founded by the State Bank of Pakistan Order 1948, its formal role as the central bank of the country was established by the State Bank of Pakistan Act 1956 (SBP Act 1956). This Act forms the basis of its operations today. The main object of the SBP is "to regulate the monetary and credit system of Pakistan and to foster its growth in the best national interest with a view to securing monetary stability and fuller utilisation of the country's productive resources". SBP has full and exclusive authority to regulate the banking sector, to conduct an independent monetary policy and to set limits on government borrowings from the State Bank of Pakistan. According to Section 27 of the Banking Companies Ordinance, no banking company can operate in Pakistan unless it has obtained a license from the SBP.

The Governor of SBP is its chief executive and, on behalf of the Board of Directors directs and controls all affairs of the Bank. [1] The general superintendence and direction of the affairs and business of the Bank is entrusted to its Board of Directors consisting of the Governor, Secretary of the Finance Division of the Government of Pakistan and eight directors including at least one from each province, who must be eminent professionals from the fields of economics, finance, banking and accountancy, appointed by the Federal Government. Those appointed to the Board must have no conflict of interest with the business of the Bank. [2] There is a Monetary and Fiscal Policies Coordination Board responsible for the monetary and exchange rate policies, consisting of Federal Minister for Finance, Federal Minister for Commerce or Secretary, Minister of Commerce, Deputy Chairman of the Planning Commission, the Governor, Secretary of the Finance Division of the Government of Pakistan and two eminent macro or monetary economists with proven record of research and teaching, appointed by the Federal Government. The Coordination Board is also responsible for ensuring consistency among macro-economic targets of growth, inflation and fiscal, monetary and external accounts. In addition, the

---

[1]   Section 10 of SBP Act 1956. The Governor of SBP shall be fully independent, i. e. he shall not be member of any legislature in Pakistan or currently in service of any federal or provincial government or any other bank.

[2]   See Section 9 of SBP Act 1956.

Coordination Board is to consider limits on the government borrowing as revised from time to time. The Coordination Board is prohibited from taking any measure that would adversely affect the autonomy of the SBP.

Section 9C of the SBP Act places a limit on borrowing by the Federal Government and provides that its borrowing must be brought to zero at the end of each quarter. This requirement does not apply to the ways and means limit that is determined by the Board of Directors of SBP from time to time. It also places an obligation on the Federal Government to settle its debts as of 30 April 2011 not later than 12 years from that date. If Federal Government fails to comply with any of these two requirements, it must make a statement in Parliament giving detailed justifications for such failure.

There is a Monetary Policy Committee of the SBP consisting of the Governor of SBP, three senior executives of the SBP, three members of the Board, three external members who shall be economists appointed by the Federal Government. The Monetary Policy Committee supports the general economic policies of the Federal Government and is required to (i) formulate, support and recommend the monetary policy, including, appropriate, decisions relating to intermediate monetary objectives, key interest rates and supply of reserves in Pakistan and may make regulations for their implementation; (ii) approve and issue the monetary policy statement and other monetary policy measures; (iii) perform any other functions conferred on it by law; and (iv) carry out any ancillary activities incidental to the exercise of its functions.

The SBP performs a number of functions on behalf of the Federal Government. It purchases or holds the shares and debentures of any banking company on the direction of the Federal Government. It acts as an agent of the Federal Government in the purchase and sale of gold or silver or approved foreign exchange, in the purchase, sale, transfer and custody of bills of exchange, securities or shares in any company and in the management of public debt and transaction of special drawing rights with the IMF. Its functions include the issue of notes, regulation and supervision of the financial system, acting as the bankers' bank and the lender of the last resort. It is the banker to the government and formulates monetary policy. It also advises the government on policy matters and maintains close relationships with international financial institutions.

One of the fundamental responsibilities of the SBP is regulation and supervision of banks and the financial system to ensure their soundness and stability as well as to protect the interests of depositors. Banking activities are now monitored through a system of "off-site" surveillance and "on-site" inspection and supervision. Off-site surveillance is conducted by the State Bank through regular checking of various returns regularly received from banks. On-site inspection is undertaken by the State Bank in the premises of the concerned banks, as and when required.

Aside from prescribing credit and risk exposure limits, "prudential regulations" for banks also prescribe guide lines relating to classification of short-term and long-term loan facilities, set criteria for management, prohibit criminal use of banking channels for the purpose of money laundering and other unlawful activities, lay down rules for the payment of dividends, direct banks to refrain from window dressing, and prohibit them from extending fresh loans to defaulters of old loans. The existing format of balance sheet and profit-and-loss account was changed to conform to international standards, ensuring adequate transparency of operations. Section 25 of the Banking Companies Ordinance authorises the SBP to determine the policy to be followed by the banking companies in granting advances. This policy may include the credit ceilings to be maintained by a banking company, sectors and regions to which advance may or may not be made, the margins to be maintained in respect of advances, rates of interest, prohibition of giving of loans, advances and credit to any borrower or a group of borrowers, etc.

The SBP has the power to collect credit information from a bank in relation to the amounts and the nature of its loans or advances or other credit facilities, including bills purchased or discounted, letters of credits and guarantees, etc. , extended to any borrower or class of borrowers. ①

4. 3. 2   Laws governing banking companies

Banking Companies Ordinance 1962 is the key legislation in relation to banking operations in Pakistan. Banking has been defined in the Ordinance as "the accepting, for the purpose of lending or investment, of deposits of money from the public, repayable on demand or otherwise, and withdrawable by cheque, draft, order or otherwise". Section 7 of the Ordinance provides an exhaustive list of activities that a

---

① Section 25 A of the Banking Companies Ordinance.

banking company may engage in, in addition to its banking business. The list includes:①

- the borrowing, raising, or taking up of money; the lending or advancing of money either upon or without security; the drawing, making, accepting, discounting, buying, selling, collecting and dealing in bills of exchange, *hundi* (an informal remittance instrument), promissory notes, coupons, drafts, bills of lading, railway receipts, warrants, debentures, certificates, scrips (participation term certificates, term finance certificates, musharika certificates, (Islamic finance instrument) modaraba certificates (Islamic finance instrument) and such other instruments as may be approved by the State Bank) and other instruments, and securities whether transferable or negotiable or not; the granting and issuing of letters of credit, traveller's cheques and circular notes; the buying, selling and dealing in bullion species; the buying and selling of foreign exchange including foreign bank notes; the acquiring, holding, issuing on commission, underwriting and dealing in stock, funds, shares, debentures, debenture stock, bonds, obligations, securities (participation term certificates, term finance certificates, musharika certificates, modaraba certificates and such other instruments as may be approved by the State Bank) and investment of all kinds; the purchasing and selling of bonds, scrips or other forms of securities (participation terms certificates, term finance certificates, musharika certificates, modaraba certificates and such other instruments as may be approved by the State Banks) on behalf of constituents or others, the negotiating of loans and advances; the receiving of all kinds of bonds, scrips of valuables on deposit or for safe custody or otherwise; the providing of safe deposit vaults, the collecting and transmitting of money and securities;
- carrying on and transacting every kind of guarantee and indemnity business;
- purchase or acquisition in the normal course of its banking business any property, including commodities, patents, deigns, trademarks and copyrights, with or without buy-back arrangements by the sellers or for sale in the form

---

① See Section 7(1) of the Banking Companies Ordinance for the exhaustive list of banking activities which may be performed by the Banks. Banks may not perform any other activity which is not specified in Section 7 (1).

of hire-purchase or on deferred payment basis with markup or for leasing or licensing or for rent-sharing or for any other mode of financing;

- managing, selling and realising any property which may come into the possession of the company in satisfaction or part satisfaction of any of its claims;
- acquiring and holding and generally dealing with any property or any right, title or interest in any such property which may form the security or part of the security for any loans or advances or which may be connected with any such security;
- undertaking and executing trusts;
- establishing associations, trusts, funds for employees and ex-employees doing all such other things as are incidental or conducive to the promotion or advancement of the business of the company;
- any other form of business which the SBP may by circular specify.

A banking company is prohibited from employing a person who has been declared insolvent, or has suspended payment or has compounded with creditors, or who is or has been convicted by a criminal court of an offence involving moral turpitude. [1]

No banking company shall remove from Pakistan any record relating to the bank or any of its branches without the permission of the SBP. [2]

According to Section 13, a banking company can only commence business in Pakistan if it has a minimum paid-up capital as determined by the SBP, the latest capital requirement being Rs. 23 billion. A foreign banking company is required to maintain the minimum required paid-up capital with the SBP in an interest-free deposit in cash in Pakistani Rupees or an interest free deposit in a freely convertible approved foreign exchange as specified by SBP or a deposit of unencumbered approved securities. Where a foreign banking company ceases to exist for any reason, the deposit with the SBP shall be regarded as an asset of the foreign banking company on which claims of all the creditors of such banking company in Pakistan shall be the first charge.

According to Section 14, a banking company incorporated in Pakistan must

---

[1]   Section 11 of Banking Companies Ordinance.
[2]   Section 12 of Banking Companies Ordinance.

satisfy the following requirements:

- subscribed capital of the company is not less than one-half of the authorised capital and the paid up capital is not less than one-half of the subscribed capital;
- the capital of the company consists of ordinary shares and perpetual non-cumulative preference shares;
- that the voting rights of any one shareholder are strictly proportionate to the contribution made by him to the paid-up capital of the company;
- voting rights of any particular shareholder, except those of Federal Government, do not exceed five percent of the total voting rights of all the share-holders. It must be noted that the later provisions in the same Section 14 imply that a person can hold more than five percent of the shareholding of a banking company subject to approval from the SBP.

The SBP has the power to direct a banking company to call a general meeting of shareholders and to elect new directors of the banking company. A director of a banking company shall not hold office for more than six consecutive terms. [1] There is a prohibition on appointment as director a person who is a director in another banking company. [2]

A banking company is not permitted to create a floating charge on the undertaking or any property of the company unless approval has been obtained from the SBP. [3] Similarly, a banking company is not permitted to make any loan or advance against the security of its own shares; or grant an unsecured loan or advances to its directors or any family members of the directors or make loans and advances on the guarantee of, its directors or any family members of the directors. [4]

Banking companies are obliged to create a reserve fund. If the amount in such fund together with the amount in the share premium account is less than the paid-up capital of the banking company, it is required to maintain in the fund a sum equivalent to not less than 20 percent of the balance of profit of each year as disclosed in the profit and loss account and before any dividend is declared; and if the amount in such fund together with the amount in the share premium account is equal

---

[1]   Section 15 of Banking Companies Ordinance.
[2]   Section 20 of Banking Companies Ordinance.
[3]   Section 18 of Banking Companies Ordinance.
[4]   Section 24 of Banking Companies Ordinance.

to or exceeds the paid-up capital of the banking company, it must maintain in the fund a sum equivalent to not less than 10 percent of the balance of profit and before any dividend is declared. ①

Every banking company in Pakistan is required to maintain in Pakistan in cash, gold or unencumbered approved securities valued at a price not less than 20 percent of the total of its time and demand liabilities in Pakistan. ② Every banking company is also required to furnish to SBP a monthly return in the prescribed form and manner showing particulars of its assets maintained in accordance with Section 29 and its time and demand liabilities in Pakistan during the month. It must be noted that the value of the assets of the banking company must not be less than 85 percent of the time and demand liabilities in Pakistan. ③

Every banking company is required to file with the SBP a half-yearly return in the prescribed form and manner showing its assets and liabilities in Pakistan for the half-yearly period. ④ In addition, every banking company is also required to file an annual balance sheet and profit and loss account for the year. This obligation is also applicable to foreign banking companies operating in Pakistan through branches. The annual accounts must be audited by any of the panel of auditors approved by the SBP. ⑤ Every banking company including a foreign banking company is required to display a copy of its audited balance sheet and profit and loss account at a conspicuous place in its principal office and in every branch office in Pakistan. ⑥ The SBP has a right to inspect the books of accounts of any banking company in Pakistan. It is the statutory responsibility of SBP to systematically monitor the performance of every banking company to ensure that it is complies with the applicable statutory criteria and banking rules and regulations. ⑦

The SBP is empowered to give directions to banking companies generally or to any banking company in particular if it considers that it is necessary to so (a) in the

---

①   Section 22 of Banking Companies Ordinance.
②   Section 29 of Banking Companies Ordinance.
③   Section 30 of Banking Companies Ordinance. Time demand liability is liability to pay at a specific time, such as in the case of a fixed term deposit account. Demand liability is to pay on demand as in the case of a current account.
④   Section 32 of Banking Companies Ordinance.
⑤   Sections 34 and 35 of Banking Companies Ordinance.
⑥   Section 38 of Banking Companies Ordinance.
⑦   Section 40A of Banking Companies Ordinance.

public interest or (b) to prevent the affairs of the banking company from being conducted in a manner detrimental to the interests of depositors or (c) to secure the proper management of the banking company generally. ① The SBP has the power to remove from a banking company a director, chief executive or a person in a managerial position if it considers that it is necessary to so(a) in the public interest or(b) to prevent the affairs of the banking company from being conducted in a manner detrimental to the interests of depositors or (c) to secure the proper management of the banking company generally. ②It also has the power to supersede (suspend) the board of directors of a banking company if for reasons to be recorded it considers it necessary to do so. All powers and duties of the board of directors shall during the period of such supersession be exercised and performed by such person as the SBP may from time to time appoint for this purpose. ③ SBP has the power to direct prosecution of a director or chief executive or another officer who in its opinion has knowingly acted in a manner causing loss of depositors' money or the income of the banking company. ④ Under Section 42 of the Banking Companies Ordinance, SBP has extensive powers in relation to all affairs relating to any banking matter.

The Banking Companies Ordinance also provides for the procedure regarding restructuring, amalgamation and merger of banking companies. ⑤ A provincial High Court is empowered to wind up a banking company if it is unable to meet its debts or if an application for its winding up has been made by the SBP.

There is a Banking Mohtasib (a banking Ombudsman) appointed under the Banking Companies Ordinance. It has the power to enquire into (i) complaints of banking malpractices; (ii) perverse, arbitrary or discriminatory actions; (iii) violations of banking laws, rules, regulations or guidelines; (iv) inordinate delays or inefficiency; and (v) corruption, nepotism and other forms of maladministration.

4.3.3   Financial Institutions(Recovery of Finances) Ordinance

This ordinance provides for the establishment of Banking Courts in Pakistan to

---

① Section 41 of Banking Companies Ordinance.
② Section 41 A of Banking Companies Ordinance.
③ Section 41 B of Banking Companies Ordinance.
④ Section 41 D of Banking Companies Ordinance.
⑤ Sections 47 and 48 of Banking Companies Ordinance.

provide for the speedy disposal of banking suits brought by banks or customers in relation to the default in any obligations with regard to any finance facility. It provides for the procedure of filing of suits by the plaintiffs and replies by the respondents. The procedure is mostly summary in nature, except when substantial questions of law or fact have been raised in respect of which evidence needs to be recorded.

4.3.4 Anti-Money Laundering Act 2010

The Anti-Money Laundering Act was promulgated for the prevention of money laundering, combatting the financing of terrorism, and forfeiture of property derived from or involved in money laundering or financing of terrorism. This law has established a Financial Monitoring Unit (FMU) within the SBP which has independent decision-making power. Every bank in Pakistan is required to file with the FMU a "suspicious transactions report" when it knows, suspects or has reason to suspect that a particular transaction involves funds derived from illegal activities or is intended or conducted in order to hide or disguise proceeds of crimes or involves financing of terrorism. Whoever wilfully fails to comply with the suspicious transaction reporting requirement or gives false information is liable for imprisonment or fine or both. Where a reporting entity is convicted of such an offence, it may have its license or registration revoked.

4.3.5 Payment Systems and Electronic Fund Transfers Act 2007

The Act provides for the regulation of payment systems and electronic funds transfer in Pakistan and for the protection of consumers and determination of rights and liabilities of financial institutions and other service providers, their customers and participants; and the designation of a Payment System as a Designated Payment System. It provides for the establishment and operation of one or more Real Time Gross Settlement Systems and empowers the SBP to nominate one or more Clearing Houses to provide clearing or settlement services for a Payment System. The Act also has provisions dealing with documentation of transfers and error notification and correction.

It must be noted that there is an Electronic Transaction Ordinance 2002, which provides for the legal recognition and facilitation of documents, records, information, communications and transactions in electronic form. According to Section 3 of this Ordinance, "no document, record, information, communication or transaction shall be denied legal recognition, admissibility, effect, validity, proof or enforceability on the ground that it is in electronic form and has not been attested by any witness".

4.4　Restrictions on foreign banks and financial institutions

Foreign branches and wholly foreign-owned locally incorporated subsidiaries are permitted, provided that the foreign bank's home country belongs to a regional grouping in which Pakistan is a member or it has global tier 1 minimum paid-up capital of USD 5 billion. Otherwise, foreign banks may operate only as a locally incorporated subsidiary, with foreign equity capped at 49 percent. Existing foreign banks, as well as those formed under the above criteria, are allowed to open up to 100 branches as per Branch Expansion Plans submitted and approved by the SBP. Commercial banks with over 100 branches must open 20 percent of their branches in regional centres where no bank branch exists. ①

---

① Trade Policy Review of WTO, 17 February 2015, para. 4. p. 99.

Chapter 5   Laws Relating to
Construction of Infrastructure

5. 1   Introduction

A major indicator of a country's development is the quality of its infrastructure. A good infrastructure has a direct impact on the social and economic well-being of the people. It reduces the cost of doing business for enterprises by bringing efficiency and certainty into their operations. A population which has access to quality and affordable health, education and basic utility services such as water and sanitation, energy and road network, is always a content society. With a population close to 200 million, Pakistan has an enormous demand for infrastructural developments. And this calls for significant monitory and human resources, which are scarce. For this reason, Pakistan has embraced the public private partnership (PPP) model of infrastructure development at a fierce pace. The Federal Government has put in place the Pakistan Policy on Public Private Partnerships 2010 (Pak-PPP) which delineates in detail the conceptual framework of PPP model for infrastructure development and the institutional support which the Federal Government will provide to the private sector in the implementation of these projects. Similarly, the provincial governments have promulgated PPP laws to institutionalise the PPP model and provide legal cover to concession agreements between the government and the private sector. The PPP laws and policies in Pakistan adopt a market-oriented approach and has in place incentives to attract the private sector to participate in infrastructure development projects.

There is no restriction on foreign participation in infrastructure development projects and Pakistan treats domestic and international investors equally without discrimination.

Pakistan and China signed an agreement on 20 April 2015 to commence work on the China-Pakistan Economic Corridor (CPEC) development projects worth over USD 46 billion, which amount to roughly 20 percent of Pakistan's annual GDP. The corridor aims to connect Gwadar port in Balochistan to China's Xinjiang region via a network of highways, railways and pipelines spread over 3,000 km. The first phase of the CPEC comprising energy projects is estimated to be completed by December 2017. Chinese companies involved in the project are working tirelessly to complete energy projects in time, aimed at generating about 10,000MW of electricity. ①

5.2   Pakistan Policy on Public Private Partnerships(Pak-PPP)

The Economic Coordination Committee (ECC) of the Cabinet② approved the Pak-PPP on 26 January 2010. The key objectives of the Policy are: (a) promotion of inclusive social and economic development through the provision of infrastructure; (b) leveraging of public funds with private financing from local and international markets; (c) encouragement and facilitation of investment by the private sector by creating an enabling environment in PPP in infrastructure; (d) protection of the interests of all stakeholders including end users, affected people, government and the private sector; (e) setting up of efficient and transparent institutional arrangements for identification, structuring and competitive tendering of projects; (f) development of efficient risk sharing mechanisms such that the party best equipped bears the appropriate level of risk; and (g) providing a viability gap funding where the projects' viability is insufficient to attract private sector funding.

The Pak-PPP covers a wide spectrum of areas which include:

Transport and Logistics including federal, provincial and municipal roads, rail, seaports, airports, fishing harbours as well as warehousing, wholesale markets, slaughter houses and cold storage;

Mass Urban Public Transport including integrated bus systems as well as intra- and inter-city rail systems;

Local Government Services including water supply and sanitation, solid waste management, low-cost housing, and healthcare/education and skills development facilities;

Energy Projects including hydroelectric and captive power generation projects;

Tourism Projects including cultural centres, entertainment and recreational facilities and other tourism related infrastructure;

Industrial Projects including industrial parks, special economic zones and related projects;

---

① http://www.boi.gov.pk/ViewNews.aspx? NID = 972.
② Cabinet consists of federal ministers from all government ministries.

Irrigation Projects some of which are combined with power generation;

Social Infrastructure which includes education, culture and health infrastructure.

Regardless of the sector or level of government, PPPs under the Pak-PPP will be pursued where they represent priority projects or are affordable to the government and consumers and represent value for money, i. e. provide a better approach than public procurement.

The eligibility criteria and investment incentives for PPP are listed and made available to all PPP participants.

The following institutions play key roles in these arrangements:

The Ministry of Finance including various departments and bodies under Ministry of Finance, specifically

- The inter-ministerial PPP Taskforce(TF) with working groups;
- The Infrastructure Project Development Facility(IPDF);
- The Debt Policy Coordination Office(DPCO);
- Project Development Fund (PDF), the Viability Gap Fund (VGF) and Infrastructure Project Financing Facility(IPFF);
- The Planning Commission and its Central Development Working Party;
- Line Ministries and relevant departments at federal, provincial and local levels as Contracting Authorities.

The Infrastructure Project Development Facility (IPDF) and the Infrastructure Project Finance Facility (IPFF) are two major institutions established by the Government of Pakistan under the Ministry of Finance which are responsible for the promotion, development, regulation and financing of infrastructure projects.

The IPDF's mandate is to: (i) facilitate the preparation and improvement of PPP proposals submitted by public implementing agencies to ensure that the projects are viable; (ii) ensure that only superior proposals with value for money will be supported; (iii) oversee the preparation and implementation of PPP projects consistent with prudent financial, environmental and social safeguards; (iv) build on the job experience of implementing agencies and private partners; and (v) act as the secretariat to the PPP Task Force, and coordinate with other agencies and public and private stakeholders.

IPFF is an organisation which complements the IPDF to assist in the financial aspects of PPP development. It is a non-banking finance company established under Companies Ordinance and is responsible for providing long-term financing for the

PPP project.

Although the PPP policy was formally established in 2010, in practice the federal and the provincial governments have been using the PPP model much earlier in two key infrastructure sectors which are road and transportation and power generation. In Sections 5. 4 and 5. 5 of this sub chapter on the laws of construction of infrastructure, these two sectors have been discussed in greater detail so as to shed light on the PPP model in practice in Pakistan.

5. 3   PPP Infrastructure Development Laws in provinces of Pakistan

Most provinces of Pakistan have in place PPP Infrastructure Development Laws. They are the Sindh Public Private Partnership Act 2010 (SPPP Act), the Punjab Public Private Partnership Act 2014(PPPP Act) and the Khyber Pakhtunkhwa Public Private Partnership Act 2014(KPPPP Act). All these laws have the same predominant objective of expanding the provision of infrastructure services and improving their reliability and quality to achieve the social and economic objectives of the government and to mobilise private sector resources for financing, construction, maintenance and operation of infrastructure projects. We will take the PPPP Act to illustrate how provincial infrastructural developments are handled.

5. 3. 1   The Punjab Public Private Partnership Act 2014(The PPPP Act)

Under the PPPP Act a Government Agency①may enter into a PPP agreement with a private party for the performance of functions relating to the design and construction of a project, services relating to it, and provision of finance for design, construction, operation or others. Schedule I of the PPPP Act enumerates the infrastructure sectors where PPP approach may be adopted. The sectors include canals or dams, education facilities, health facilities, housing, industrial estates, information technology, land reclamation, mining, power generation facilities, roads (provincial highways, district roads, bridges or bypasses), sewerage or drainage, solid waste management, sports or recreational infrastructure, public gardens or parks, trade fairs, conventions, exhibitions or cultural centres, urban transport including mass transit or

---

① Government Agency means a department, attached department, body corporate, autonomous body of the Federal Government, local government or any organisation or corporation owned or controlled by the Federal Government.

bus terminals, water supply or sanitation, treatment or distribution, wholesale markets, warehouses, slaughter houses or cold storages, grain silos and street lights. Schedule II of the PPPP Act enumerates the types of PPP agreements which can be used for the purposes of the PPPP Act. They are:

- *Build and Transfer (BT)*: A contractual arrangement whereby the private party undertakes the financing and construction of an infrastructure project and after its completion hands it over to the Government Agency. The Government Agency will reimburse the total project investment, on the basis of an agreed schedule. This arrangement may be employed in the construction of any infrastructure project, including critical facilities, which for security or strategic reasons must be operated directly by the Government Agency.

- *Build Lease and Transfer (BLT)*: A contractual arrangement whereby the private party undertakes the financing and construction of an infrastructure project and upon its completion hands it over to the Government Agency on a lease arrangement for a fixed period, after the expiry of which ownership of the project is automatically transferred to the Government Agency.

- *Build Operate and Transfer (BOT)*: A contractual arrangement whereby the private party undertakes the financing and construction of an infrastructure project and the operation and maintenance thereof. The private party operates the facility for a fixed term during which it is allowed to collect from project users' appropriate tariffs, tolls, fees, rentals, or charges not exceeding those proposed in the bid or negotiated and incorporated in the PPP agreement, to enable the private party to recover its investment and operating and maintenance expenses for the project. The private party transfers the facility to the Government Agency at the end of the fixed term that shall be specified in the PPP agreement. This BOT model shall include a supply and operate situation, which is a contractual arrangement whereby the supplier of equipment and machinery for an infrastructure project operates it, providing in the process technology transfer and training of the nominated individuals of the Government Agency.

- *Build Own and Operate (BOO)*: A contractual arrangement whereby the private party is authorised to finance, construct, own, operate and maintain an infrastructure project, from which the private party is allowed to recover its investment and operating and maintenance expenses by collecting user levies from project users. The private party owns the project and may choose to assign its operation and maintenance to a project operator. The transfer of the project to the Government Agency is not envisaged in this arrangement. However, the Government Agency may terminate its obligations after the specified time period.

- *Build Own Operate Transfer (BOOT)*: A contractual arrangement similar to the BOT agreement, except that the private party owns the infrastructure project during the fixed term before its transfer to the Government Agency.
- *Build Transfer and Operate (BTO)*: A contractual arrangement whereby the Government Agency contracts out an infrastructure project to the private party to construct on a turn-key basis, assuming cost overruns, delays and specified performance risks. Once the project is commissioned, the private party is given the right to operate the facility and collect user levies under the PPP agreement. The title of the project always vests in the Government Agency in this arrangement.
- *Contract Add and Operate (CAO)*: A contractual arrangement whereby the private party expands an existing infrastructure facility, which it leases from the Government Agency. The private party operates the expanded project and collects user levies to recover the investment over an agreed period. There may or may not be a transfer arrangement with regard to the added facility provided by the private party.
- *Develop Operate and Transfer (DOT)*: A contractual arrangement whereby favourable conditions external to an infrastructure project, which is to be built by the private party, are integrated into the PPP agreement by giving it the right to develop adjoining property and thus enjoy some of the benefits the investment creates such as higher property or rental values.
- *Joint Venture (JV)*: Joint venture is a form of public private partnership in which both the Government Agency and the private party make equity contributions and pool their resources towards the project development and implement the project by forming a new company (joint venture company) or by assuming joint ownership of an existing company through the purchase of shares. When established, a joint venture company will have a separate legal identity and it is through this company that the common enterprise of the public and private partners will be carried out. The government agency and

the private party will own the shares of the joint venture company, and there will be a board of directors, usually made up of shareholder representatives.

- *Management Contract (MC)*: A contractual arrangement whereby the Government Agency entrusts the operation and management of an infrastructure project to the private party for an agreed period on payment of specified consideration. The Government Agency will directly, or through an agent, charge and collect user levies.

- *Rehabilitate Operate and Transfer (ROT)*: A contractual arrangement whereby an existing infrastructure facility is handed over to the private party to refurbish, operate and maintain it for a specified period, during which the private party collects user levies to recover its investment and operation and maintenance expense. At the expiry of this period, the facility is returned to the Government Agency. The term is also used to describe the purchase of an existing facility from abroad, importing, refurbishing, erecting and operating it.

- *Rehabilitate Own and Operate (ROO)*: A contractual arrangement whereby an existing infrastructure facility is handed over to the private party to refurbish, operate and maintain with no time limitation imposed on ownership. The private party is allowed in perpetuity to collect user levies to recover its investment and operation and maintenance expenses.

- *Service Contract (SC)*: A contractual arrangement whereby the private party undertakes to provide services to the Government Agency for a specified period with respect to an infrastructure facility. The Government Agency will pay the private party an amount according to an agreed schedule.

5.3.2 Institutional arrangements and project delivery process under PPPP Act

The PPPP Act provides for institutional arrangements through which all PPP projects must pass. There is a PPP Steering Committee which is empowered to approve, reject, or send for reconsideration the PPP project proposal submitted by a Government Agency. It is also empowered to approve/reject or send back for reconsideration the recommendations submitted by a Government Agency for the contract award to a private party. It is the final deciding Authority for all projects. Similarly, a PPP Cell has been established under Planning and Development Department to promote and facilitate PPP development in the province, and to assist a

Government Agency in preparing and executing high-quality projects.

The PPPP Act provides for the establishment of a Risk Management Unit in the Finance Department to act as a fiscal guardian for the projects using the PPP approach.

The PPPP Act provides that a Government Agency shall manage a PPP project throughout its life cycle consisting of identification, preparation, tendering, implementation and operation. It is required to:

- identify suitable projects and prioritise them within its sector or geographical area of responsibility;

- recruit transaction advisors for project preparation and tendering;

- supervise the preparation of a feasibility study and if its outcome is positive, submit the project proposal through the PPP Cell to the PPP Steering Committee;

- conduct a competitive tendering process consisting of pre-qualification and bidding to select the private party;

- carry out bid evaluation and submit its recommendation on contract award to the PPP Steering Committee;

- negotiate and sign the PPP agreement; and

- monitor and evaluate implementation and operation of the project.

The Government Agency may seek support and advice of the PPP Cell for the performance of any of the functions set out above.

Under the PPP arrangement, Government Agency may enter into a PPP agreement with a private party for the performance of functions in relation to the design and construction of a project, services relating to it or the provision of finance for the design, construction and operation. It may also arrange or provide for payment to the private party in accordance with the terms and conditions of the PPP agreement. It must be noted that the PPPP Act empowers the Government Agency to enter into an arrangement with any other Government Agency, the Federal Government, or a body, authority or entity owned or controlled by the Federal Government for a project.

The PPPP Act requires the Government Agency to identify and prepare a project proposal, obtain approval of the PPP Steering Committee for it and complete this phase before tendering. It must identify and conceptualise potential projects from its master plans and other planning documents, prioritising the projects within its sector or geographical area, using criteria such as supply and demand gaps, social and economic benefits, financial attractiveness, risks and uncertainties involved, and readiness for implementation. The Government Agency has to ensure that preparation of a project proposal consists of a feasibility study, initial environmental examination or environmental impact assessment, risk analysis and an analysis of the need for government support.

Once the project has been approved by the PPP Steering Committee, the Government Agency must select a private party for the project through competitive public tendering using the two stage process of pre-qualification and bidding. The PPPP Act provides in detail the process to be followed for the pre-qualification of a private party for a project.

5.3.3   Public private partnership acts in other provinces

It must be noted that the public private partnership laws of other provinces to have a comprehensive institutional framework to promote and implement the PPP projects. While there are differences in the terminology of the institutional framework in the SPPP Act, KPPPP Act and the PPPP Act, the underlying intention is same, i. e. to invite private sector in the development of public infrastructure services in an open, transparent and competitive manner.

5.4   Road and transport

National Highway Authority(NHA) is the national authority responsible for the construction and development of national highways and strategic roads in Pakistan. It was established pursuant to the National Highway Authority Act 1991 (NHA Act 1991) and its statutory purpose and function is "to plan, promote, organise and implement programs for construction, development operation, repairs and maintenance of National Highways and Strategic Roads specially entrusted to it by the Federal Government, or by a Provincial Government or other authority concerned"[1]. National Highways have been defined as those roads which are listed in Part I of the Schedule to the NHA Act and those which have been notified by the Federal Government as National Highways. Strategic Roads have been defined as those roads which are listed in Part II of the Schedule and those which the Federal Government has notified as Strategic Roads. The NHA is the main Federal body responsible for all

---

[1]   See Section 4 of the NHA Act 1991.

national highways, motorways and strategic roads. NHA has about 12,000 km of road network under its jurisdiction, which is only about 4.6 percent of the total road network but carries about 80 percent of the country's traffic. ①

There is a National High Council with the Minister of Communication of Government of Pakistan as its chairman, which is responsible for approving plans regarding the construction, development, repair and maintenance of national highways and strategic roads specially entrusted to the NHA by the Federal or Provincial Government. The general direction and administration of the NHA is vested in the Executive Board of the NHA. It has the power to consider and approve proposals and schemes not exceeding in value Rs. 100 million and it may recommend any project more expensive than that to the Central Development Working Party (CDWP) or Executive Committee of National Economic Council (ECNEC).

NHA has extensive powers to carry out the purposes of the NHA Act. It is responsible for advising the Federal Government on matters relating to National Highways and Strategic Roads. It is empowered to acquire land for the purposes of the NHA Act: such an acquisition is deemed to be an acquisition for a public purpose. It can levy, collect or cause to be collected tolls on national highways and strategic roads and other roads as may be entrusted to it. It may also, from time to time, raise funds through borrowings, floating of bonds, sharing or leasing of assets or any other means. ②

Under the NHA Act there is a National High Authority Fund (NHA Fund) to which must be credited all funds received by NHA including loans and grants from the Federal Government, income from tolls, foreign aid, grants and loans negotiated by the NHA and funds from floating bonds, shares or through any other means.

Under the Public Private Partnership Policy and Regulatory Framework 2009 (PPP Regulatory Framework 2009) issued by NHA and Ministry of Communications, the private sector is encouraged to participate in the development and construction of national highways and strategic roads on a public private partnership model. The scheme envisaged in PPP Regulatory Framework 2009 is that the investment of private capital to design, finance, construct, operate, and maintain a project for public use for a specific term during which a private investment consortium is able to collect

---

① The Pakistan infrastructure report by State Bank of Pakistan Infrastructure Taskforce.
② Section 10 of the NHA Act 1991.

revenue from the users of the facility. At the expiration of the period of time so specified title to the project reverts to the NHA at a nominal consideration of one Pakistani Rupee, or, the NHA may decide to extend the concession or retender as provided in the tender documents. By then, the consortium should have collected enough revenue to recover its investment and earn a profit, i. e. made a reasonable return on the investment. Projects under these models must be transparently tendered to invite competition; however, a different model may apply where a multilateral agency or government is involved which requires a different process. ①

The first step in any PPP project is procuring a pre-feasibility study through which NHA may satisfy itself that the project is technically, environmentally, economically and financially viable and in conformity with the principles of the PPP Regulatory Framework 2009. The pre-feasibility study has the following features:

A. a defined rationale, scope and description of the PPP project;

B. preliminary project cost estimates based on preliminary engineering designs;

C. robust traffic forecasts and revenue analysis from traffic and other sources;

D. an economic cost-benefit analysis;

E. a comprehensive social and environmental analysis including mitigation costs;

F. a financial and sensitivity analysis.

A private sector entity may submit an unsolicited project for PPP model. However, such projects will not be supported by the NHA, unless there are clear and overriding advantages such as a new technology, opening up of disadvantaged areas or other very strong reasons.

In a PPP project, a private sector participant is allowed to charge tolls (including any escalation) in accordance with an agreed formula under the concession agreement. When a PPP project is not financially viable, the government may provide a subsidy or support, in order to attract the private sector, either through the Ministry of Finance Viability Gap Fund or the PSDP. The government does not collect any local taxes within the Concession Area.

In any PPP project, pre-financial close costs are non-recoverable, and the concessionaire bears all costs associated with: (i) studies carried out by them to establish the financial and environmental viability of the project; (ii) legal and other expenses incurred by them in preparing concession agreements and arranging finance;

---

① PPP Regulatory Framework 2009.

(iii) construction and maintenance costs of the project (preferably including costs associated with relocation of utilities and construction supervision, where appropriate) ; (iv) and toll collection and operating costs (including the cost of providing breakdown services, and routine maintenance costs). Concession period shall be generally for a period of 25 years. If there is any public sector grant or other support, such as traffic guarantee or revenue guarantee, it shall be specified in the bidding documents.

To facilitate the tendering process, model concession agreements have been prepared as a basis for privately financed and operated highway, tunnel and bridge projects. The model agreements specifically cover the extension situations and force majeure risks and procedures for dealing with changes in costs and losses caused by changes in law which are not reflected in the general consumer price index. Such changes will be adjusted through suitable adjustments in the concession period. NHA will undertake to: (a) give appropriate assistance to the concessionaire in obtaining the necessary government approvals for a project; (b) make available land for projects free of cost and free of encumbrances; (c) obtain from utility companies agreement regarding the methods, costs and time-scales associated with any necessary removal or relocation of public utilities; (d) take appropriate steps to prevent encroachments onto the right of way, to control roadside facilities and advertising material, and to limit access to expressways and motorways to specific entry and exit points.

All PPP projects are tendered and pre-qualified bidders invited to submit bids in accordance with the bidding documents. The bids will be ranked in accordance with the pre-determined criteria including the extent to which the Outline Design has been met, the proposed level of equity and the proposed toll rates. The first ranked bidder will be given 60 days to negotiate an acceptable concession agreement.

A PPP Cell under the NHA is responsible for the promotion, facilitation and monitoring of the PPP projects.

5.5   Power sector

Power is another infrastructure sector in which the Government of Pakistan has provided huge financial incentives to both domestic and international investors since 1994. The latest Power General Policy of 2015 builds on the earlier power policies and offers attractive returns for power generation projects. It covers both hydropower and thermal power projects with priority given to hydropower projects as they are indigenous, cheap and clean. International competitive bidding is envisaged for these projects.

5.5.1   Hydropower projects

A hydropower project is awarded on the basis of lowest evaluated levelised tariff along with any other parameters specified in the RFP of the Project. Proposals will be sought where a feasibility study is available but a detailed engineering design has not been carried out. The project will be awarded to the highest ranked applicant. For raw-site projects, proposals will be solicited and the projects will be awarded to the highest ranked applicant. A letter of intent (LOI) will be issued for carrying out the feasibility study. Small hydropower projects may be processed under the upfront tariff regime where such tariff is announced by NEPRA. The hydropower projects are implemented on BOOT basis or any other mode and the term of concession period for the private sector is 30 years after which the project will be transferred to the Provincial Government for a nominal consideration of one Pakistani Rupee.

A Water Use Charge (WUC) at Rs. 0.425/kWh is payable by the private sector hydropower project to the province where the project is located. This rate will be reviewed every five years. The power purchaser (government) will bear the risk of availability of water for hydropower projects, by making payment of a fixed monthly Capacity Purchase Price (CPP) component of the tariff to the project company in accordance with the monthly average hydrology.

5.5.2   Thermal power projects

Thermal power projects are awarded through ICB based on lowest evaluated levelised tariff or solicitation of discount on the upfront or benchmark tariff determined by NEPRA.

5.5.3   Tariff structure and incentives

The tariff will be offered in two parts: (i) Energy Purchase Price (EPP) and (ii) Capacity Purchase Price (CPP). The EPP will comprise fuel cost/water use charge, variable O&M and any variable component determined by NEPRA. The EPP will be paid based on the amount of kWh (Rs/kWh) delivered at the point of delivery. The CPP will comprise Fixed O&M, Return on Equity, Debt Servicing, Insurance, Cost of Working Capital, and any fixed component determined by NEPRA.

In order to mitigate the exchange rate variation risk, specified adjustments are allowed for exchange rate variations of US Dollar, Pound Sterling, Euro and Japanese Yen. An adjustment related to debt servicing is allowed for such currencies. Adjustment is also permissible for local inflation, foreign inflation and interest rate variations.

Financing of the projects will be in the form of equity and debt, to be arranged by the sponsors. The minimum equity is 20 percent and the maximum is 30 percent. However, if the equity is more than 30 percent of the capital cost, equity in excess of 30 percent is treated as a debt.

To eliminate protracted negotiation, a standardised Implementation Agreement (IA) and a Power Purchase Agreement (PPA) must be prepared for private/public partnership power projects.

The Government will guarantee the payment obligations of the power purchaser if it is a federal entity and will also guarantee the payment obligations of provincial governments under the IA. Protection is given against specified force majeure events as contained in the standard IA as well against changes in the tax and duties regime.

The project company is entitled to delayed payment interest at the rate of three-month KIBOR plus 200 basis points to be specified in the PPA.

An attractive rate of return on equity/IRR is allowed in the tariff by NEPRA. Repatriation of equity along with dividends will be freely allowed.

Exemption from income tax is available to new IPPs and PPP projects and for any expansion of projects by IPPs already in operation. Sponsors of the power project will be allowed to import plant and equipment not manufactured locally at a concessionary rate of five percent customs duty. No turnover tax or withholding tax on imports will be charged.

100 percent foreign ownership of companies is permitted.

Chapter 6   Labour Laws in Pakistan

6.1   Introduction

Pakistan has a comprehensive Labour Code comprising a number of statutes at federal and provincial levels. The Constitution of the Islamic Republic of Pakistan 1973 which enshrines a bill of rights laying down a range of provisions with regards to labour rights. Article 11 of the Constitution prohibits all forms of slavery and forced labour and prohibits any child below the age of 14 from being engaged in any factory or mine or any other hazardous employment. Article 17 enshrines freedom of association and unions. Article 25 of the Constitution lays down the right to equality before the law and prohibits discrimination on the basis of sex. The 18th Constitutional Amendment of 2010 devolved legislative competence in the subject of labour to the four provinces. The four provincial legislatures have all enacted legislation dealing with labour: the Punjab Industrial Relations Act 2010, the Sindh Industrial Relations Act 2013, the Khyber Pakhtunkhwa Industrial Relations Act 2010, and the Baluchistan Industrial Relations Act 2012.

It must be noted that the Industrial Relations Act 2012 still exists at the federal level, which is applicable to Islamabad Capital Territory and trans-provincial establishments and industry. Pakistan's labour law effectively guards against unjust exploitation of labour and promotes fair labour practices in industrial and commercial establishments.

6.2   Labour laws in Pakistan

6.2.1   Industrial Relations Act 2012(IRA 2012)

This law provides for the law relating to the formation of trade unions and the improvement of relations between employers and workmen in Islamabad Capital Territory and trans-provincial establishments(establishments having branches in more than one province). It is applicable to workmen who are defined as persons engaged in manual or clerical or unskilled, semi-skilled or skilled work of a repetitive nature. It excludes employees working in managerial, executive or administrative capacities. The IRA 2012 allows workers to establish and join associations. It prescribes the requirements and minimum conditions for a trade union to be registered.

The law provides for a collective bargaining agent if there are more than one trade union in an establishment. The collective bargaining agent in relation to an establishment is entitled to bargain with the employer on matters connected with the employment of a workman. It represents all or any of the workmen in any matter or judicial proceedings under the act. It has the right to give notice of and declare a strike in accordance with the provisions of the IRA 2012. The IRA 2012 provides for the establishment of a National Industrial Relations Commission (NIRC) which consists of 10 full-time members including its chairman. The NIRC may adjudicate and determine an industrial dispute in the Islamabad Capital Territory to which a trade union or a federation of such trade unions is a party and which is not confined to matters of purely local nature and any other industrial dispute which is in the opinion of the government of national importance and is referred to it by that government. It also has been assigned the function of registering trade unions and industry-wide trade unions of an establishment or a group of establishments.

6.2.2   Provincial industrial relations laws

As discussed above, the four provinces have passed their own industrial relations act. The Punjab Industrial Relations Act 2010 provides for the right of workers to establish trade unions and provides that workers of an establishment employing not less than 50 may establish and subject to the rules of organisation, join an association of their own choice without previous authorisation. It sets out the requirements for the registration of a trade union in the province. It provides for the appointment of the collective bargaining agents and their rights and duties. It also provides for the establishment of labour courts for the adjudication of industrial disputes. The Khyber Pakhtunkhwa Industrial Relations Act 2010 follows a similar pattern to the Punjab Industrial Relations Act 2010. The Industrial Relations Acts of Baluchistan and Sindh, but not of Punjab and Khyber Pakhtunkhwa, provide for the creation of a State Industrial Relations Commission. Since all these statutes were passed soon after the 2010 Constitutional Amendment, there are many omissions, ambiguities and overlappings in relation to the scope of these provincial laws.

6. 2. 3　Workmen's Compensation Act 1923

The law provides for payment of compensation for injury or death arising out of accident in the course of employment. Schedule II contains a list of persons who are including in the definition of workmen. The law is applicable to all types of establishments(industrial or commercial), railways, mines and many others like road transport services. An employer is liable to pay compensation for personal injury to workmen caused by an accident arising out of and in the course of employment, except where the worker was drunk at the time the personal injury was caused, or, if the worker wilfully disobeyed the orders or safety rules and wilfully removed or disregarded the safety guard or other device provided for safety of workers. If death or permanent and total disablement of a worker results from the injury, the employer has to pay the dependents of that employee a sum of Rs. 200,000.

Schedule III of this law contains a list of occupational diseases against which compensation is payable by the employer if the workmen contract the same during the course of employment.

Compensation under this law will not be available if an injured workman has instituted a civil suit for damages. Similarly, no suit for damages is available if an injured workman has instituted a claim for compensation under this law or if there is an agreement between workman and his employer providing for the payment of compensation in respect of the injury.

6. 2. 4　W. P Industrial and Commercial Employment(Standing Order) Ordinance 1968(Standing Orders Ordinance)

The Standing Orders Ordinance is a law aimed at providing the basic minimum terms and conditions of employment in relation to workmen both in commercial and industrial establishments in Pakistan. It applies to all industrial and commercial establishments where 20 or more workmen are employed or were so employed during the preceding 12 months. The Standing Orders Ordinance does not apply to any industrial or commercial establishment carried on by or under authority of the Federal Government or a provincial government, where there are specific statutory rules of service, conduct and discipline.

Standing Order 2-A of the Standing Orders Ordinance requires that every workman, at the time of his appointment, transfer or promotion should be provided with an order in writing, showing the terms and conditions of his service. Similarly, the periods and hours of work of all classes of workmen shall be exhibited in Urdu in the principal language of workmen, employed in the industrial or commercial establishment on notice boards maintained at the main entrance of the establishment. There is also a requirement of prominently displaying on notice boards holidays and pay days. The establishments are also required to so display the rate of wages payable to all classes of workmen and for all classes of work.

Every industrial establishment, which is a factory and in which 50 or more workmen are employed, must introduce a group incentive scheme to provide incentive for greater production to groups of workmen employed in the factory. The scheme must provide the manner in which the performance of different groups of workmen shall be evaluated. The incentives take the form of additional wages or additional leave with wages or in both such forms. [1]

The Standing Orders Ordinance provides for payment of gratuity. Gratuity is a lump-sum amount of money payable to a worker on leaving service (through resignation, retirement, death or termination of service) based on salary (highest or the final salary) and period of service. Gratuity is a benefit for services rendered in the past. It is a reward for good, efficient and faithful service over a substantial period of time. According to 12 (6) of Standing Orders Ordinance, gratuity is paid for "every completed year of service or any part thereof in excess of six months". If a worker has worked for less than six months in a given year, he is not entitled to gratuity in that year. The six-month rule is also applicable to the first year of service. For example, if a worker resigns or is terminated after only seven months of service, he is eligible for gratuity of one year. No gratuity is payable if the termination from employment is on account of misconduct. The rate of gratuity is "thirty (30) days wages for every completed year of service or any period in excess of six months".

The employer is required to insure permanent workmen employed by him against natural death and disability and death and injury arising out of contingencies not covered by the Workmen's Compensation Act. The employer must in all cases be responsible for the payment of the amount of premium and all administrative arrangements regarding the insurance. The amount of insurance must not be less than the amount of compensation specified in Schedule-IV of the Workmen's Compensation Act 1924.

---

[1] Standing Order 10-A of Standing Orders Ordinance.

If the employer intends to terminate the contract of employment for any reason other than misconduct, he must give a one-month notice of termination. A contract may be terminated only by an order in writing stating the reasons for termination. A workman may be dismissed from service without payment of any compensation, for instance, if he is guilty of misconduct. Instances of misconduct include wilful insubordination or disobedience, theft, fraud or dishonesty, wilful damage to or loss of employer's goods or property, taking or giving bribes or illegal gratifications, habitual breach of any law applicable to the establishment, absence without permission, participation in an illegal strike, go-slow, etc. Every employee must be given an opportunity of being heard.

6. 2. 5   The Provincial Employees' Social Security Ordinance 1965

This ordinance lays down a Scheme of Social Security to provide benefits to certain employees or their dependents in the event of sickness, maternity, injury or death. The Ordinance establishes an Employees' Social Security Institution in each province of Pakistan. An employer must make a contribution on behalf of the employee, usually six percent of the monthly wage of the employee every month. These contributions must be paid into a fund maintained by the institution, and these funds are disbursed or utilised as sickness benefits, maternity benefit, death grant, injury benefit disablement gratuity, survivor pension, etc. There is an appeal procedure whereby an employer or an employee may prefer an appeal to a social security court against the decision of the Institution. An appeal from any order or decision of the Social Court lies in the High Court.

6. 2. 6   Factories Act 1934

This Act concerns the labour work force in a factory. It has detailed provisions regarding the health, safety and welfare of workmen. Some of the health and safety related provisions include cleanliness, disposal of wastes and effluents, ventilation and temperature, dust and fumes, overcrowding, lightening, drinking water, and lavatories. The Factories Act has detailed provisions which cater for prevention and precautions against contagious and infectious diseases, compulsory vaccination and inoculation, precautions in case of fire, fencing of machinery, work on or near machinery in motion, striking gear and devices for cutting power, self-acting machines and casing of new machinery, etc. The Act is the most essential regulatory framework for industries which employ workmen and is in most cases strictly enforced. For the enforcement of the provisions of this Act, the government has appointed inspectors who may visit a factory and inspect any premises including any plant or machinery.

Under this law, no adult employee can be required or permitted to work in any establishment in excess of 56 hours a week. Provision of a weekly holiday is a requirement. No worker may be required to work in a factory for more than nine hours in a day, provided that a male adult worker in a seasonal factory may work 10 hours in any day.

Every worker who has completed a period of 12 months of continuous service in a factory is allowed during the subsequent period of 12 months a holiday period of 14 consecutive days.

6.2.7   Payment of Wages Act 1936

This Act regulates the mechanism for payment of wages to certain employees of an establishment. It requires that the wages of a worker must be paid in a certain period of time not exceeding one month. The Act prohibits deductions from an employee's pay other than deductions which may be allowed under the Act, for instance, deductions made as fines, deductions for the absence of duty, deductions for damages to or loss of goods expressly entrusted to the employed person for custody, or for loss of money, etc. The enforcement under this Act may be carried out by an inspector appointed under Section 10 of the Factories Act 1934.

6.2.8   Minimum Wages Ordinance 1961

This Ordinance provides for the regulation of minimum wages for workers employed in certain industrial undertakings. The Ordinance provides for the establishment of a Minimum Wages Board for the province. The function of the board is to recommend to the government the minimum wages for adult unskilled workers and juvenile workers employed in industrial undertakings. The Board may also recommend different wages for different industries depending on the nature of the work and other relevant circumstances. The power to declare the minimum wages for a particular industry vests with the provincial government. The minimum wage for unskilled workers in Punjab, Baluchistan and Sindh is Rs. 13,000 while in Khyber Pakhtunkhwa it is Rs. 12,000.

6.2.9   Employees' Cost of Living(Relief)Act 1973

This law has been promulgated with a view to paying a cost of living allowance to employees in order to provide them with a cushion against inflation and/or rise in the cost of living. Since the promulgation of this Ordinance in August 1973, the government has, at various intervals, keeping in view inflation and rise in the cost of living, authorised a cost of living allowance benefit, which the employers are required to pay.

6.2.10   Companies Profits(Workers' Participation) Act 1968

The purpose of this Act is to facilitate participation of workers in profits of Companies. It has established a Workers' Participation Fund into which every company to which this Act applies, will pay 5 percent of its profits during the year. The fund is managed by a board of trustees consisting of representatives of both workers and the management of the company. The Act applies to a company which has 50 or more workers, the paid-up capital of which as on the last day of its accounting year is Rs. 2 million[1] or more and the value of the fixed assets of the company as on the last day of the accounting year is Rs. 4 million[2] or more. The fund maintained under this Act is used for the benefit of workers and the disbursement from the fund to the workers must be made in accordance with the procedures set out in the Schedule-I of the Act.

6.2.11   Employee's Old Age Benefits Act 1976

This Act deals with old age benefits for persons employed in industrial, commercial and other organisations. The Act establishes an Employees' Old Age Benefits Institution managed by a board of trustees. An employer must make a contribution to the Institution in respect of every person who is in his insurable employment, at a rate of six percent of his wages. No contribution is payable in respect of an insured person who is in receipt of old age pension or has reached the age of 60. The Act also provides for a discretionary contribution to be made by the Federal Government. The benefits under the Act to the insured person include old age pension benefit, old age grant (where an employee is not qualified to receive a pension), invalidity pension and, in case of the death of the insured person, a survivor pension.

6.2.12   Workers' Welfare Fund Ordinance 1971

This Ordinance provides for the establishment of a Workers' Welfare Fund. The

---

[1]   Rs. 5 million for companies established after July 2006.

[2]   Rs. 20 million for companies established after July 2006.

Ordinance calls for a contribution to be made to the fund equal to two percent of the total income of an industrial establishment whose total income is not the less than Rs. 500,000. There is a governing body of the Fund which is responsible for the allocation of funds collected under this Ordinance. It may sanction expenditure in respect of administration and management of the fund and invest the fund money in securities approved by the Federal Government. The money in the fund must be applied to the financing of projects connected with the establishment of housing estates for workers, financing of other welfare measures including educational training, reskilling, investment in government guarantees and non-government securities, etc.

6.2.13   The West Pakistan Factories Canteen Rules 1959

The provisions of this law apply to every factory where more than 250 workers are employed. The employers are required, by law, to provide in or near the factory a canteen, which is operated on a non-profit basis. The law provides that the canteen should have various facilities and equipment. The prices to be charged must be approved by a Canteen Managing Committee comprising representatives of collective bargaining agent and the employer and if the committee fails to agree on food prices, approval of the Chief Inspector of Factories must be obtained. The Managing Committee is required to ensure the quality and quantity of food to be served in the canteen and management of the menu.

6.2.14   The Disabled Persons(Employment and Rehabilitation)Ordinance 1981

This Ordinance provides for the employment rehabilitation and welfare of disabled persons. It is separately provided for in law that not less than one percent of the total number of persons employed by an establishment, at any time, must be disabled persons. If for any reason an establishment does not employ a disabled person satisfying the requirement of the one percent quota it must pay to a fund created by the Federal Government, each month, the same sum of money that would be paid as salary or wages to a disabled person, had he been employed.

6.2.15   Workers' Children(Education) Ordinance 1972

This Ordinance calls for the levy of an education cess on every establishment which employs ten or more workmen. The rate of cess is Rs. 100 per worker per annum. It requires the provincial government to provide free education up to any level of education to two children of every worker employed in an establishment.

6. 2. 16   Maternity Benefit Ordinance 1958

The Ordinance is applicable to all industrial and commercial establishments employing women and provides for leave and maternity benefits for three months, six weeks before and six weeks after the delivery of a child. The maternity benefit is equal to the wages she was entitled to during the three months. It also places restrictions on the dismissal of a woman employee during maternity leave. The Mines Maternity Benefit Act 1941 provides similar benefits to women employed in mines.

6. 2. 17   Protection Against Harassment of Women at the Workplace Act 2010

This law provides for establishment of systems and procedures at both private sector and public sector organisations for prevention of sexual harassment of women at the workplace. It requires every organisation to constitute an enquiry committee which is responsible for hearing any complaint. Under the Act, sexual harassment means any unwelcome sexual advance, request for sexual favours or other verbal or written communication or physical conduct of a sexual nature or sexually demeaning attitudes, causing interference with work performance or creating an intimidating, hostile or offensive work environment, or the attempt to punish the complainant for refusal to comply to such a request or is made a condition for employment. It also provides for the major and minor penalties to be given to an accused after holding of a proper enquiry and giving an opportunity to the accused person to make a defence.

6. 2. 18   Mines Act 1923

Apart from providing generally for mine operations, the Act also provides for certain health and safety requirements for the benefit of mine workers. It requires the provision of mine latrine and urinal systems at every mine. It requires the provision of safe drinking water, canteen facilities and proper medical facilities. It provides that a mine worker may be required to work for a maximum of six days a week and for a period not exceeding eight hours a day below ground in the mine. The law prohibits the engagement of children in mine work. It grants extensive powers of enforcement to inspectors appointed under the Act.

6. 2. 19   Dock Labourers Act 1934

This Act was enacted to give effect to the convention concerning the protection against accidents of workers employed in loading and unloading ships. It empowers the Federal Government to make regulations for the safety of working places on shore and of any regular approaches over a dock, wharf, quay or similar premises which workers have to use for going to or from a working place. It also enables the government to make regulations concerning various matters for the protection of dock labourers such as the efficient lighting of the means of access to ships.

6. 2. 20   Employment of Children Act 1991

This law prohibits the employment of a child(i. e. a person below the age of 14) from any occupation or processes set out in the Schedule, such as working in a railway canteen, carpet weaving, cement manufacture or building and construction industry.

6. 2. 21   Provident Funds Act 1925

Provident fund is an investment fund contributed to by employees, employers, out of which a lump sum is provided to each employee on retirement. The term "provident fund" has been defined in the Provident Funds Act 1925 as "a fund in which subscriptions or deposits of any class or classes of employees are received and held on their individual accounts, and includes any contributions and interest or increment accruing on such subscriptions, deposits or contribution under the rules of the fund". Establishment of a provident fund for the benefit of the employees is purely discretionary in the private sector, but as a matter of practice, many large private sector companies in Pakistan have established a provident fund for their employees.

Chapter 7 Environmental Laws in Pakistan

7.1 Introduction

Pakistan has an elaborate environmental law regime at the federal and provincial government level. The 18th Amendment of the Constitution in 2010 devolved legislative power in the subject of environment to provincial governments, and soon thereafter all the four provincial legislatures passed provincial environmental legislation. They coexist with legislation that had already been passed by the federal government. Environmental protection laws are enforced by federal and provincial environmental protection agencies. The courts in Pakistan have been very active and conscious in relation to environmental issues and, even where no specific legislative provisions exist, they have given a very expansive meaning to Article 9 of the Constitution of Pakistan (which provides for the fundamental right of life) and held that the right to life includes a life free from hazards of pollution and other environmental risks affecting life. [1]

7.2 Environmental protection laws in pakistan

7.2.1 Pakistan Environmental Protection Act 1997 (PEPA Act 1997)

The PEPA Act 1997 was enacted for the protection, conservation, rehabilitation and improvement of the environment as well as the prevention and control of pollution and promotion of sustainable development. It provides for the establishment of a Pakistan Environmental Protection Council which is responsible for the coordination and supervision of the enforcement of the provisions of The PEPA Act 1997. It is also responsible for developing comprehensive environmental policies and the approval of National Environmental Quality Standards. The PEPA Act 1997 also provides for the establishment of a Pakistan Environmental Protection Agency

---

[1] See generally *Ms. Shehla Zia and Others v WAPDA* (PLD 1994 Supreme Court 693).

(PEPA). The functions of PEPA are as follows[1]:

- administer and implement the PEPA Act and rules and regulations made thereunder;
- prepare national environmental policies for the approval of Pakistan Environmental Protection Council;
- take necessary measures for the implementation of national environmental policies approved by the Council;
- prepare and publish an annual National Environmental Report;
- establish standards for the quality of the ambient air, water and land, by notification in the official Gazette.
- establish systems and procedures for service, surveillance, monitoring, management, examination, investigation, research and inspection and audit to prevent and control pollution and to estimate the cost of cleaning up pollution;
- certify one or more laboratories as approved laboratories for conducting tests and analysis and one or more research institute as environmental research institute for conducting research and investigation;
- initiate enquiries and investigations into environmental issues, either of its own accord or upon complaint from any person or organisation.

According to Section 11 of PEPA Act 1997, "no person shall discharge or emit or allow the discharge or emission of any effluent or waste or air pollutant or noise in an amount, concentration or level which is in excess of the National Environmental Quality Standards". According to Section 12, a proponent of a project before commencing construction or operation must file with a government agency nominated by PEPA or a provincial environmental protection agency and environmental impact assessment (EIA) when the proposed project is likely to cause adverse environmental effect. Where an initial environmental examination has been submitted, the government agency must, subject to standards fixed by PEPA, review and approve it or require the submission of an EIA. If an EIA is submitted PEPA may approve it unconditionally or subject to conditions or reject it as being contrary to environmental laws.

An EIA must be carried out with public participation for the facilitation of which

---

[1]   Section 5 of PEPA Act 1997.

detailed information regarding the project has to be made available to the public. The government agency must communicate its approval or otherwise within the period of four months from the date of the initial environmental examination or the EIA, failing which the initial environmental examination or the EIA as the case may be deemed to have been approved to the extent it does not contravene the provisions of the PEPA Act 1997, and the rules and regulations made under it. [1]

There is a general prohibition on the import of hazardous waste into Pakistan. [2] No person may generate, collect, consign, transport, treat and dispose of any hazardous substance without a licence issued by the PEPA. [3] Similarly, no person may operate a motor vehicle from which air pollutants are emitted in an amount concentration level of which is an excess of levels prescribed by National Environmental Quality Standards. [4]

According to Section 16, if PEPA or a provincial environmental protection agency is satisfied that discharge or emission of any effluent, waste, air pollution or noise or the disposal of wastes, or the handling of hazardous substances, or any other act or omission is likely to occur or is occurring and is likely to cause or is causing an adverse environmental effect the PEPA or the provincial agency may, after giving the person responsible for such discharge, emission, disposal, handling, act or omission an opportunity of being heard, direct the person to take such measures as maybe specified in the order below. These measures may include:

- immediate stoppage, preventing, lessening or controlling the discharge, emission, disposal, handling, act or omission, or to minimise or remedy the adverse environmental effect;
- installation, replacement or alternation of any equipment or thing to eliminate, control or abate on a permanent or temporary basis, such discharge, emission, disposal, handling, act or omission;
- action to remove or otherwise dispose of the effluent, waste air pollutant, noise, or hazardous substances; and
- action to restore the environment to the condition existing prior to such discharge, disposal, handling, act or omission, or as close to such conditions

---

[1]   Section 12 of PEPA Act 1997.
[2]   Section 13 of PEPA Act 1997.
[3]   Section 14 of PEPA Act 1997.
[4]   Section 15 of PEPA Act 1997.

may be reasonable in the circumstances, to the satisfaction of the federal agency or provincial agency.

Section 17 of the PEPA Act 1997 provides for penalties for contravention of the PEPA Act 1997 and any order passed by the PEPA or a provincial agency. The penalties range from simple fines to imprisonment, closure of a factory or the confiscation of machinery and equipment, vehicle, material or substance or record. It may also involve an order to restore the environment at his own cost. Where a contravention of the PEPA Act 1997 has been committed by a corporate body and it is proved that such offence has been committed with the consent or connivance of, or is attributed to any negligence on the part of any director, partner, manager, secretary or other officer of the corporate body, such director, partner, manager, secretary or other officer may be deemed to be guilty of such contravention along with the corporate body and shall be punished accordingly.

The PEPA Act 1997 provides for the establishment of environmental tribunals which are competent to try offences setout in Section 17(1) of the PEPA Act 1997. Environmental tribunals have powers of a court of session under the Code of Criminal Procedure 1998. An environmental tribunal may also hear appeals against any decision or direction of the PEPA or a provincial agency. ① An appeal against the decision of the environmental tribunal lies to the provincial High Court.

The Federal Government has the power to make rules for carrying out the purposes of the PEPA Act 1997. PEPA has the power to make regulations for carrying out the purposes under the PEPA Act 1997, with the prior approval of Federal Government.

6.2.2　Review of IEE and EIA Regulations 2000

Regulation 3 of these regulations provides that a proponent of project falling within the list of projects requiring an IEE must file an IEE with the federal agency. The following projects have been specified as requiring an IEE:

A. Agriculture, livestock and fisheries, etc.

- Poultry, livestock, stud and fish farms with total cost of more than 10 million rupees.
- Projects involving repacking, formulation or warehousing of agricultural

---

① Sections 20 to 22 of PEPA Act 1997.

produce.

B. Energy

- Hydroelectric power generation less than 50 MW.
- Thermal power generation less than 200 MW.
- Transmission lines less than 11 KV, and large distribution projects.
- Oil and gas transmission systems.
- Oil and gas extraction projects including exploration, production, gathering systems, separation and storage.

C. Manufacturing and processing

- Ceramics and glass units, with total cost of more than 50 million rupees.
- Food processing industries including sugar mills, beverages, milk and dairy products, with total cost of less than 100 million rupees.
- Man-made fibres and resin projects, with total cost of less than 100 million rupees.
- Manufacturing of apparel including dyeing and printing, with total cost of more than 25 million rupees.
- Wood products with total cost of more than 25 million rupees.

D. Mining and mineral processing

- Commercial extraction of sand, gravel, limestone, clay, sulphur and other minerals not included in Schedule II with total cost of less than 100 million rupees.
- Crushing, grinding and separation processes.
- Smelting plants with total cost of less than 50 million rupees.

E. Transport

- Federal or provincial highways (except maintenance rebuilding or reconstruction of existing metalled roads) with total cost of less than 50 million rupees.
- Pots and harbour development for ships less than 500 gross tons.

F. Water management, dams, irrigation and flood protection

- Dams and reservoirs with storage volume less than 50 million cubic meters or surface area less than eight square kilometres.
- Irrigation and drainage projects serving less than 15,000 hectares.
- Small scale irrigation systems with total cost less than 50 million rupees.

G. Water supply and treatment

Water supply schemes and treatment plants with total cost of less than 25 million rupees.

H. Waste disposal

Waste disposal facility for domestic or industrial wastes, with annual capacity less than 10,000 cubic meters.

I. Urban development and tourism

- Housing schemes.

- Public facilities with significant off-site impacts, e. g. hospital wastes.

- Urban development projects.

J. Other projects

Any other project for which filing of an IEE is required by the Federal Agency under sub-regulation(2)of Regulation 5.

Similarly, a separate list of projects requiring EIA is also provided in Schedule Ⅱ of these regulations, many of which include:

A. Energy

- Hydroelectric power generation over 50 MW.

- Thermal power generation over 200 MW.

- Transmission lines(11 KV and above)and grid stations.

- Nuclear power plants.

- Petroleum refineries.

B. Manufacturing and processing

- Cement plants.

- Chemicals projects.

- Fertilizer plants.

- Food processing industries including sugar mills, beverages, milk and dairy products, with total cost of 100 million rupees and above.

- Industrial estates(including export processing zones).

- Man-made fibres and resin projects with total cost of 100 million rupees and above.

- Pesticides(manufacture or formulation).

- Petrochemicals complex.

- Synthetic resins, plastics and man-made fibres, paper and paperboard, paper pulping, plastic products, textiles (except apparel) printing and publishing, paints and dyes, oils and fats and vegetable gee projects, with total cost more than 10 million rupees.

- Tanning and leather finishing project.

C. Mining and mineral processing

- Mining and processing of coal, gold, copper, sulphur and precious stones.
- Mining and processing of major non-ferrous metals, iron and steel rolling.
- Smelting plants with total cost of 50 million rupees and above.

D. Transport

- Airports.
- Federal or provincial highways or major roads (except maintenance, rebuilding or reconstruction of existing roads) with total cost of 50 million rupees and above.
- Ports and harbour development for ships of 500 gross tons and above.
- Railway works.

E. Water management, dams, irrigation and flood protection

- Dams and reservoirs with storage volume of 50 million cubic meters and above or surface area of 8 square kilometres and above.
- Irrigation and drainage projects serving 15,000 hectares and above.

F. Water supply and treatment

Water supply schemes and treatment plants with total cost 25 million rupees and above.

G. Waste disposal

- Waste disposal and storage of hazardous or toxic wastes including landfill sites and incineration of hospital toxic waste.
- Waste disposal facilities for domestic or industrial wastes with annual capacity more than 10,000 cubic meters.

H. Urban development and tourism

- Land use studies and urban plans in large cities.
- Large-scale tourism development projects with total cost more than 50 million rupees.

I. Environmentally sensitive areas

All projects situated in environmentally sensitive areas.

J. Other projects

- Any other project for which filing of an EIA is required by the Federal Agency under sub-regulation(2) of Regulation 5.

• Any other project likely to cause an adverse environmental effect.

In addition to the categories specified above, an EIA is required in case of a project which is likely to cause adverse environmental effects or in respect of which PEPA has issued guidelines for construction and operation. PEPA may issue guidelines for the preparation of an IEE or an EIA, including any specific sectoral guidelines in respect of specific projects. Public participation in examination of EIA is mandatory and PEPA is required to publish a notice in the newspaper specifying the type of project, its exact location, the name and address of the proponent and the places at which the EIA can be accessed. The notice must also specify the date and time of the public hearing. The review of IEE or EIA by PEPA must be based on a quantitative and qualitative assessment of the documents and data furnished by the project proponent. An approval of an IEE or an EIA is, in addition to any conditions imposed by PEPA, subject to the condition that the project must be designed and constructed strictly in accordance with the IEE or the EIA. If at any time PEPA, on information received, is of the opinion that the conditions of an approval have not been complied with or that the information supplied by a proponent in the approved IEE or EIA is incorrect, it may cancel the approval after giving an opportunity to the proponent to explain.

7. 2. 3 Environmental Samples Rules 2001

These rules prescribe for the procedure to be followed in the examination of samples relating to any contravention of the PEPA Act 1997. An authorised person may exercise powers of inspection and related powers of enforcement if he has reasonable grounds to believe that an offence under the PEPA Act 1997 has been committed. An authorised person has the power to enter and inspect any premises, examine any machinery or equipment and take any document or article into possession. He may take into possession any article which he reasonably believes to be involved in or furnishes evidence of the commission of an offence only if he has obtained a special warrant in that behalf. He may not take into possession such article if it affects the production or operation in such place, unless prior permission in writing has been obtained from the environmental tribunal or the environmental magistrate having jurisdiction. An authorised person taking any sample must forthwith divide the sample into three portions in the presence of the person from whom the sample is taken. One portion of the sample duly packed and sealed must be handed over to the person from whom it was taken. The second portion must be duly packed and sealed and delivered within 48 hours to an environmental laboratory for testing and analysis. The third portion must be retained by the authorised person for future testing and analysis. Upon receiving the laboratory report an authorised person may, if the report indicates a contravention of the law or the commission of an environmental offence, file a complaint in the Environmental Tribunal or the Environmental Magistrate having jurisdiction. Only an environmental tribunal may try an offence regarding discharge of effluents or waste or air or noise pollution as provided in Section 11 of the PEPA Act 1997.

7.2.4   National Environmental Quality Standards (Certification of Environmental Laboratories) Regulations 2000 (NEQS 2000)

These regulations provide for the criteria for the certification of environmental laboratories. PEPA is authorised to issue certifications to environmental laboratories provided they fulfil the criteria and conditions of certification as provided in Regulations 5 and 9 of the NEQS 2000.

7.2.5   The National Environmental Quality Standards (Self-Monitoring and Reporting by Industry) Rules 2001

These rules provide that every industrial unit is responsible for the correct and timely submission of Environmental Monitoring Reports to PEPA. The industrial units have been classified under categories A, B and C and depending on which category an industrial unit falls there is a slight difference in the timeline for providing such Environmental Monitoring Reports.

7.2.6   The Pollution Charge for Industry (Calculation and Collection) Rules 2001

These rules provide for the mechanism for the calculation of the pollution charge payable by a person who contravenes any prohibition regarding discharges and emissions as provided in Section 11(2) of the PEPA Act 1997. According to Rule 6, the pollution charge must be calculated by multiplying the pollution level with the actual production during the period for which the charge is to be paid, and with the applicable rate per pollution unit for the year in accordance with the rates and escalation table shown in Schedule Ⅲ of these Rules.

7.2.7   National Environmental Policy 2005

The National Environmental Policy 2005 provides an overarching framework to address environmental problems Pakistan faces. The aim is to protect, conserve and restore Pakistan's environment in order to improve quality of life of the citizens through sustainable development. It provides for sectorial guidelines concerning water supply and management, air and noise pollution controls, waste management, sustainable management of forests, conservation of biodiversity and protected areas, meeting the challenges of climate change and ozone depletion, promoting energy efficiency and renewable sources of energy, and achieving sustainable agricultural and livestock development. It also provides for the formulation of policy instruments for the purpose of achieving the objectives of the National Environmental Policy 2005. Policy instruments are expected to deal with matters such as integrating environmental considerations in policy-making and implementation, capacity development of environmental protection agencies at all levels, promoting environmental fiscal reforms such as reduction of trade barriers for import of clean technologies and fuels, providing incentives for private and public sector to comply with environmental laws and standards, raising public awareness through education regarding environmental issues and encouraging public-private-civil society partnership regarding environmental matters.

7. 2. 8   Pakistan Biosafety Rules 2005

These rules provide for the establishment of a National Biosafety Committee which is responsible for the standards and procedures for risk assessment and labelling of living modified organisms, substances or cells and products thereof. It is also responsible for considering applications for import, export or commercial release of living modified organisms. The rules also provide for the establishment of a technical advisory committee to advise the National Biosafety Committee on biosafety issues. It is an offence for any person to import, export, sell, purchase or trade living modified organisms, substances or cells and products without a licence issued by the PEPA.

7. 2. 9   Environmental protection provisions under the Pakistan Penal Code 1860

According to Section 277 of the Pakistan Penal Code 1860, it is an offence to voluntarily corrupt water of any public spring or reservoir so as to render it less fit for the purposes for which it is ordinarily used. The punishment for this offence is imprisonment for a term which may extend to three months or a fine which may extend to Rs. 1,500, or both. Similarly, under Section 278 it is an offence of anyone to vitiate the atmosphere in any place so as to make it noxious to the health of the population in general dwelling or carrying on business in the neighbourhood or passing along a public highway. The punishment for this offence is a fine which may extend to Rs. 1,500.

7.2.10 Chemical Weapons Convention Implementation Ordinance 2000 (CWCI Ordinance)

The CWCI Ordinance implements the Convention on the Prohibition of the Development, Production, Stockpiling and use of Chemical Weapons and on their Destruction. According to Section 3 of the CWCI Ordinance, no person is permitted to develop, produce or otherwise require, stockpile or retain a chemical weapon, or transfer, directly or indirectly, a chemical weapon to anyone.

7.2.11 Provincial environmental protection regime

Each of the four provinces of Pakistan put in place an environmental protection law after the 2010 constitutional amendment providing for environment to be a provincial subject. They are: Punjab Environmental Protection Act as amended in 2012; Khyber Pakhtunkhwa Environmental Protection Act 2014; Baluchistan Environmental Protection Act 2012; and the Sindh Environmental Protection Act of 2014.

The Punjab Environmental Protection Act, for instance, has the following salient features:

- It provides for the establishment of Punjab Environmental Protection Council which is the body which coordinates and supervises the enforcement of the provincial act;
- It provides for the establishment of a Provincial Environmental Protection Agency which is responsible for the administration and implementation of the provincial law;
- Like the federal PEPA, the Provincial Environmental Protection Agency also has the power to inquire and investigate into environmental issues. It has the power to enter and inspect, with a search warrant issued by an Environmental Tribunal or an Environmental Magistrate; take samples of any materials, products, articles or substances; arrange for testing and analysis of the samples at a certified laboratory; and confiscate any article used in the commission of an offence where the offender is not known or cannot be found;
- It provides for establishment of a provincial Sustainable Development Fund;

- It provides for the prohibition of discharges or emissions of any effluent or waste or air pollutants or noise in an amount in excess of the levels provided under the Punjab Environmental Quality Standards(PEQS);
- Like the federal PEPA Act, it also provides for IEE and EIA;
- It also empowers the Provincial Environmental Protection Agency to pass Environmental Protection Orders to prevent discharges, emissions, disposals, handling or acts or omissions in relation to any adverse environmental effect being caused;
- It also provides for penalties and creation and establishment of environmental tribunals, etc.

The Sindh Environmental Protection Act 2014, the Khyber Pakhtunkhwa Environmental Protection Act 2014 and the Baluchistan Environmental Protection Act 2012 are similar in concept and institutional framework. In Baluchistan Environmental Protection Act 2012 provision has been made in respect of dealing in electronic waste.

7.3 Important court decisions on environmental laws in Pakistan

The most celebrated and perhaps the most important case on the fundamental rights aspect of environmental law is the *Shehla Zia* case[1] where the Supreme Court of Pakistan held that the right to life guaranteed under Article 9 of the Constitution of Pakistan included all facets of human existence. The petitioners had challenged the installation of a grid station in the vicinity of a residential area as being injurious to life of the residents and the Supreme Court held that the right to life includes a right to enjoyment of quality life free from environmental hazards of electromagnetic fields or any other such hazards generated by power generating plants, power grids and similar installations. Critically, the Supreme Court held that where the life of citizens is degraded, the quality of life is adversely affected and health hazards are created affecting a large number of people, Supreme Court may directly intervene and grant relief.

In *General Secretary, West Pakistan Salt Miners Labour Union(CBA) Khewra, Jehlum v The Director, Industries and Mineral Development Punjab, Lahore*,[2] the

① PLD 1994 SC 693.
② 1994 SCMR 2063.

petitioners sought direct intervention of the Supreme Court to enforce the right of the residents to have clear and unpolluted water. The apprehension of the petitioners was that in case the miners were allowed to continue their activities which extended to the water catchment area, the water course, reservoir and the pipelines would get contaminated. It was held that water was necessary for the existence of life and if pollution or contamination would pose a serious threat to human existence, persons exposed to such danger were entitled to claim their fundamental rights to life.

In *suo moto* case No. 10 of 2005,[1] a judge of the Supreme Court issued an injunction to prevent a massive tree cutting exercise to facilitate the New Murree City Project to build a tourist resort in the Patriata Forest, which had been declared a reserve forest as far back as 1886. The government abandoned the project, admitting that the project was an environmental disaster. The Supreme Court recently sought a compliance report from the Punjab environmental officers on receiving complaints that the work had not been halted altogether.[2]

In the case of *Syed Mansoor Ali Shah v Government of Punjab*,[3] Lahore High Court, while dealing with the issue of air pollution caused by vehicular emissions, directed the government to implement the recommendations of the commission appointed by the court. The court issued a writ in terms of the recommendations of the commission and directed the provincial government and the federal PEPA to strictly implement the same. These recommendations involved introduction of CNG or Euro II compliant buses for public transport, phasing out of existing buses in two years, cap age for buses to 10 years strictly enforce the ban registration of two-stroke auto cab rickshaws. It also provided for setting up the Ambient Air Quality Standards, Vehicular Emission Standards and Fuel Standards, etc.

In *suo moto* Case No. 25 of 2009 (dated 15 September 2011)[4] "Cutting of Trees for Canal Widening Project, Lahore", the court declared the green belt around the Lahore Canal as a public trust resource which could not be converted into private or

[1]　A *suo moto* case refers to a judicial inquiry conducted by a judge of his own motion, without there being an application made to the court seeking judicial assistance. In Pakistan the judiciary has liberally resorted to *suo moto* actions.

[2]　See "Ban on New Murree City Project: Supreme Court seeks compliance report from Punjab environment officers", *The Express Tribune*, 12 April 2016. http://tribune.com.pk/story/989727/ban-on-new-murree-city-project-supreme-court-seeks-compliance-report-from-punjab-environment-officials/.

[3]　PLD 2007 Lahore 403.

[4]　Available at http://www.supremecourt.gov.pk/web/page.asp? id=798.

any other use other than public purpose. It allowed the widening of the canal bank road to a limited extent and subject to the recommendations set out in the Mediation Committee which was formed to look into the canal widening project. The court referred to several cases from other jurisdictions and scholarly articles, in particular to Professor David Takacs regarding public trust doctrine in American Jurisprudence and its three elements, which are: (i) the sovereign holds certain resources in trust for the common good; (ii) the public has some kind of right to protection of these resources; and (iii) while democracy may seem subverted when a court overrules the acts of elected officials, such judicial acts in fact serve democracy by preserving rights invested in all the people.

Chapter 8   Laws Relating
to Dispute Resolution

8. 1   Introduction

The Constitution provides for an independent judicial system, separate from the influence and control of the executive branch of the government. Pakistan's legal system combines features of an Islamic legal system based on *sharia* (Islamic Law) with a Western system based on English common law. [1]Foreign and domestic entities in Pakistan are treated without any discrimination and on an equal footing at all levels of courts in Pakistan. Pakistan has an elaborate arbitration law regime which provides in detail the procedural steps involved in a domestic arbitration. Pakistan has recently promulgated national statutes implementing the United Nations Convention on the Recognition and Enforcement of Foreign Arbitral Awards 1958 (New York Convention) and the International Convention on the Settlement of Investment Dispute between States and Nationals of other States(ICSID Convention). Courts in Pakistan have generally upheld the validity of arbitration agreements, with a few exceptions, including arbitration agreements where a foreign arbitration forum has been agreed by the parties.

8. 2   Court system in Pakistan

8. 2. 1   Supreme Court of Pakistan

The Supreme Court of Pakistan is the highest court of the country and has original jurisdiction, to the exclusion of every other court, in disputes between provincial governments. Under Article 184(3) of the Constitution, it has jurisdiction if there is a question of public importance with reference to the enforcement of any of the fundamental rights set out in chapter 1 of Part 2 of the Constitution of Pakistan.

---

[1]   Herber M. Kritzer, *Legal Systems of the World, A Political, Social and Cultural Encyclopedia*, Vol. III, ABC – CLIO, 2002.

The Supreme Court has appellate jurisdiction to hear and determine appeals from judgements, decrees, final orders or sentences of a High Court. It also has appellate jurisdiction in matters arising out of an appeal from a decision of a Services Tribunal (that is, the tribunal which has exclusive jurisdiction in matters relating to terms and conditions of service of civil servants and employees of authorities, public corporations and similar bodies created by federal law) and the Election Tribunals. The permanent seat of the Supreme Court is in Islamabad, while it has Branch Registries in all four provincial capitals, i. e. Lahore, Karachi, Peshawar and Quetta. All decisions of the Supreme Court are binding on all courts below it.

The Supreme Court is made up of a Chief Justice and 16 senior judges who are appointed by the President in accordance with the recommendations of the Judicial Commission of Pakistan and subsequent confirmation by the Parliamentary Committee as provided in Article 175(A) of the Constitution of Pakistan. Judges retire at the age of 65, and may only be removed from office by the Supreme Judicial Council on account of being incapable of performing the duties of his office by reason of physical or mental incapacity or misconduct. The Supreme Judicial Council consists of Chief Justice of Pakistan, the next two senior most judges of the Supreme Court of pakistan and the two most senior Chief Justices of the Provincial High Courts.

8. 2. 2   Provincial High Courts in Pakistan

Each province in Pakistan has a provincial High Court which has original and appellate jurisdiction. Apart from the provinces, Islamabad Capital Territory also has a separate High Court. A Chief Justice presides in each High Court and the number of judges of the High Court varies from province to province. The High Court has benches in various cities in a province in order to bring justice nearer to people. Although the jurisdiction of the court is not strictly compartmentalised, there are specialised benches for civil cases, criminal cases, company matters and tax disputes. Under Article 199 of the Constitution of Pakistan a provincial High Court has extensive powers of judicial review of executive action. It can issue writs of *quo warranto*, *mandamus*, *prohibition*, *certiorari* and *habeas corpus*. It is also responsible for the enforcement of fundamental rights in Chapter 1 of the Constitution of Pakistan.

8. 2. 3   Federal Shariat Court

There is a Federal Shariat Court in Pakistan which has the power to determine whether or not any law or provision of law is repugnant to the injunction of Islam as laid down in Holy Quran and Sunnah. It also has revisionary jurisdiction in respect of the enforcement of any Islamic punishment given by a criminal court in Pakistan. Appeals against the decision of the Federal Shariat Court lie in the Supreme Court of Pakistan.

8.2.4　Judicial Commission of Pakistan

Judicial Commission of Pakistan is a constitutional forum established under Article 175 (A) of the Constitution of Pakistan consisting of the Chief Justice of Pakistan, four senior most judges of the Supreme Court of Pakistan, a Former Chief Justice or a Former Judge of the Supreme Court of Pakistan, Federal Minister for Law and Justice, Attorney General for Pakistan, a Senior Advocate of Supreme Court of Pakistan. For appointment of the judges of High Court, the Judicial Commission also includes the Chief Justice of the High Court to which the appointment is being made, the most senior judge of that High Court, Provincial Minister for Law and an advocate of not less than 15 years' practice in High Court to be nominated by the concerned Bar Council. For appointment of judges of the Federal Shariat Court, the Judicial Commission also includes the Chief Justice of the Federal Shariat Court and the most senior judge of that court as its member. The judges so nominated by the Judicial Commission of Pakistan must be referred to a Parliamentary Committee consisting of members of the Senate of Pakistan and the National Assembly of Pakistan for confirmation.

8.2.5　District courts

There is a subordinate judiciary at the district and Tehsil (Tehsil is an administrative area) level comprising of Civil Judges and District and Sessions Judges. The Civil Judges constitute the court of first instance in respect of all civil matters. The civil matters include rent, probate, specific relief, contract, family matters, guardian ship cases. For criminal cases, there is a Court of Magistrate and separate Court of Sessions.

District court judges are appointed by the Chief Justice of the High Court of the province in which they are located. There is a District Judge for each district in the province. Additional District Judges are also appointed by the Chief Justice of the High Court and they perform such functions of the District Judge as the District Judge may assign. The procedure of civil justice system in Pakistan is governed and regulated by the Code of Civil Procedure 1908. This law is enforced through the civil courts. Civil courts in Pakistan are established by each province under the Civil Courts Ordinance 1962.

The criminal procedure system in Pakistan is laid down in the Code of Criminal Procedure 1898, whereas the substantive law regarding crimes and their punishments is provided in the Pakistan Penal Code 1860. The main criminal courts in Pakistan are the High Courts, the Sessions Court, and the Courts of Magistrate.

Where any person is sentenced to death by a Sessions Court, the sentence of death may not be carried out unless and until the High Court of the province in which the Sessions Court is located confirms the sentence. A Sessions Court is established for every geographical division. It is a trial court for heinous offences such as murder, rape, and causing hurt cases. Magistrates are of three different categories, i. e. Magistrate of the 1st Class, Magistrate of the 2nd Class, and Magistrate of the 3rd Class. All magistrates are subordinate to the Sessions Judge of their respective division.

8. 2. 6 Specialised courts and tribunals

There are special courts and tribunals for specialised matters. There are Banking Courts which exclusively deal with disputes between the banks and the customers. Similarly, there are tribunals which deal with income tax, customs, sales tax and excise matters. There are separate courts for drugs and narcotics offences. Similarly, there are also specialised courts for terrorism related offences. Each district also has separate Anti-Corruption and Accountability Courts which try corruption offences and offences relating to misuse of authority. These courts and tribunals are governed by special law. The procedure applicable to them is either laid down in the special law or in absence of such procedures, the Code of Civil Procedure 1908 and the Code of Criminal Procedure 1898 are applicable. There are also labour courts which govern disputes between employers and "workers".

8. 3 Arbitration law in Pakistan

8. 3. 1 Arbitration Act 1940

The principal legislation in Pakistan governing the conduct of arbitration proceedings is the Arbitration Act 1940. It governs local arbitration where the parties have specifically provided that the arbitration proceedings under the agreement are to be governed by Pakistani law or where the arbitration agreement has been executed in Pakistan by local parties and the arbitration agreement is silent as to the procedural law applicable to the arbitration. It defines an arbitration agreement as a written agreement to submit present or future differences to arbitration. In other words, an arbitration agreement in order to be enforceable must be reduced to writing by the parties. Any challenge to the existence or validity of an arbitration agreement or an award is determined by the court[1]. Where parties to an arbitration agreement are unable to agree on the appointment of an arbitrator, any one of them may file an application to the court for appointment of an arbitrator. [2]The court has the power to stay any legal proceedings instituted by a party to an arbitration agreement in respect of any matter which was agreed to be referred to arbitration. [3]

The courts in Pakistan have by and large upheld arbitration agreements and stayed legal proceedings instituted by parties in courts where the dispute in question has been previously agreed to be referred to arbitration. Similarly, courts have also upheld arbitration agreements which envisage arbitration at a foreign venue or where the procedural law applicable to the arbitration agreement provides for a foreign institutional arbitration arrangement. The important exception of this general rule is that courts will not enforce such arbitration agreements where there are questions of criminality (corruption, fraud and violation of mandatory law). The courts have held that where the validity of the arbitration agreement itself in question, it may refuse to stay legal proceedings in courts in Pakistan despite the fact that the agreement is governed by a foreign arbitration agreement. [4]

According to Section 11 of the Arbitration Act, the court may on an application of a party remove an arbitrator or umpire who fails to use all reasonable dispatch, i. e. fails to perform expeditiously or has misconducted himself or the proceedings. Where the court removes an umpire or an arbitrator, it may, on an application filed on behalf of a party, appoint a replacement arbitrator or umpire as the case may require.

The arbitrator or umpire has the power (unless a contrary intention is expressed) to:

---

[1]   Section 33 of the Arbitration Act.

[2]   See generally Sections 8 and 20 of the Arbitration Act.

[3]   See Section 34 of the Arbitration Act.

[4]   See *Maulana Abdul Haque Baloch v Government of Balochistan* (PLD 2013 Supreme Court 641) and *HUBCO Power Company v WAPD* PLD (2000 SC 841).

i . administer an oath to the parties and witnesses appearing before it;

ii. state a special case for the opinion of the court on any question of law involved;

iii. make the award conditional or in the alternative;

iv. correct in an award any clerical mistake or error arising from any accidental slip or omission;

v . administer to any party to arbitration such interrogatories as may, in the opinion of the arbitrators or umpire, be necessary.

vi. make an interim award.

Once an award has been made, it must be signed by the arbitrator and notice in writing has to be given to the parties regarding the award. The award and any dispositions and documents are then required to be filed in the court. The court then gives notice to the parties about the filing of the award. [1] The court is empowered by order, to modify or correct an award if part of it seems to be on a matter that had not been referred to arbitration, where it is in imperfect form or contains any obvious error which can be modified without affecting such decision, or where the award contains a clerical mistake or an error arising from an accidental slip or omission. A court may also remit an award to the arbitrator or the umpire where the award has left undetermined any of the matters referred to it for arbitration or where it has determined any matter not referred to it for arbitration or where the award is indefinite as to be incapable of execution; or where an objection to the legality of the award is apparent upon the face of it. [2] Where the court sees no reason to remit the award or has refused an application for setting aside the award, it must pronounce judgement according to the award, and upon judgment so pronounced, a decree follows and no appeal lies from such decree.

The court has the power to pass such interim orders after the filing of award, as it deems necessary, if it considers that a party has taken or is about to take steps to defeat, delay or obstruct the execution of any decree that may be passed upon the award, or that speedy execution of the award is just and necessary. [3] Under Section 30, an award can be set aside on one or more of the following grounds, (a) that an

---

[1]   Section 14 of the Arbitration Act.

[2]   Section 16 of the Arbitration Act.

[3]   Section 18 of the Arbitration Act.

arbitrator or umpire has misconducted himself or the proceedings; (b) that an award has been made after the court has issued an order superseding the arbitration or after the arbitration proceedings have become invalid under Section 35 of the Arbitration Act; or that an award has been improperly procured or is otherwise invalid.

In respect of an arbitration, the court has all the powers of a civil court under Code of Civil Procedure 1908 such as the power to order interim measures and issue temporary injunctions.

8.3.2   Recognition and Enforcement (Arbitration Agreements & Foreign Arbitral Awards) Act 2011

This Act implements the New York Convention in Pakistan's domestic law. The New York Convention is reproduced in the Schedule of the law. It repeals the earlier Arbitration(Protocol and Convention) Act 1937. The court for the purposes of this law is the High Court. This is a welcome change as the initiation of enforcement proceedings in the High Court would reduce one level of court proceedings, making the enforcement much quicker as opposed to domestic arbitrations under the Arbitration Act 1940. Under this law, a foreign arbitral award is recognised and enforceable in the same manner as a judgement or order of a court in Pakistan. A challenge to the recognition and enforcement of a foreign arbitral award may only be made under grounds provided in Article 5 of the New York Convention.

8.3.3   Arbitration(International Investment Disputes) Act 2011

This law provides for the implementation of the ICSID Convention. Under this law, the recognition and enforcement of an award rendered pursuant to ICSID Convention must be registered in the High Court. The Act reproduces the ICSID Convention as a Schedule.

8.4   Mediation

Section 89(A) of the Civil Procedure Code 1908 read with Order X Rule 1(A) provides for alternative dispute resolution mechanisms. It provides that the court may, where it considers necessary with regards to the facts and circumstances of the case, with the object of securing expeditious disposal of a case, adopt, with the consent of the parties, alternative dispute resolution methods including mediation and conciliation. It must be noted that in Pakistan, mediations are mostly consent-based and are usually provided for in an agreement between the parties.

Sri Lanka

Professor Austin Pullé

About the Author

Austin Pullé is an Associate Professor of Law in the Department of Law in the Singapore Management University Business School. He obtained his LLB degree from the University of Colombo, and his LLM and SJD degrees from the Harvard Law School. He is admitted as an attorney in the District of Columbia and Massachusetts, and is a solicitor of the Supreme Court of New South Wales.

He is a Senior Fellow of the Australian Institute of Foreign and Comparative Law at the University of Queensland, a member of the International Law section of the American Bar Association and a member of the Center for International Legal Studies, Salzburg, Austria. Prior to assuming teaching appointments, Austin Pullé practiced as an expatriate counsel engaged in negotiating and documenting a range of cross-border commercial transactions including foreign direct investment joint venture agreements, oil and gas transactions, offshore lending and security, and infrastructure projects.

He was the first expatriate counsel in a leading law firm in Jakarta, and has worked as a lawyer in law firms in Boston, Washington, D. C. and Sydney. He was an international consultant on commercial law reform in Pakistan, in a project funded by the Asian Development Bank.

Austin Pullé's teaching experience includes teaching part-time at the La Salle Business School in Manila, The Philippines, and full-time teaching at the Nanyang Business School in Singapore. Austin Pullé's research interests are cross-border commercial dispute resolution and commercial law reform in ASEAN and South Asia.

Introduction

Geography and history

"Sri Lanka" means resplendent or beautiful land. It features in the Indian epic, the *Valmiki Ramayana* which, in a version of the Helen of Troy story, is a tale about the abduction of an Indian princess, Sita, to Lanka and the epic war that ensued to rescue her. Legend also has it that Sri Lanka was the original Garden of Eden, referred to in the Book of Genesis, from which Adam and his consort were expelled. Indeed, even today maps of the area show a chain of islets named as "Adam's Bridge". Sri Lanka has been known by other names, the Greeks called it Taprobane, the Arabs Serendib, the Dutch Zeiland, and the British "Ceylon". It was only in 1972, when a new constitution was adopted that the country reverted to its indigenous name "Sri Lanka". It is now known as the "Democratic Socialist Republic of Sri Lanka".

Sri Lanka is situated between 79°42′ and 81°52′ east longitude and 5°55′ to 9°50′ north latitude, 650 km north of the equator. It is separated from the South of India by the thirty two or so kilometres wide Palk Strait. The island is 65,610 square kilometres in area (with land area of 62,705 sq. km),430 kilometres in length (north to south) and 225 kilometres in width (east to west). It has no territorial disputes with third states although the fishing areas around the island of Katchatheevu located in the Palk Strait have been poached on by Indian fishermen and have led to nationalistic demands in the Indian state of Tamil Nadu to "take back" the island. The central government of India and the Indian Supreme Court have not entertained such requests.

The former administrative capital, Colombo, which remains the commercial capital is a port city located in the Western coast of the country. Sri Jayawardenapura, a suburb of Colombo, hosts the Parliament of Sri Lanka and is the new administrative capital of the country.

Sri Lanka is a multi-religious and multi-ethnic country with a population that exceeds 20 million. The majority community consists of the Sinhala people who comprise about 73. 8 percent of the population. Although a system of castes prevails among the Sinhala people, its main significance is in the system of arranged marriages and there is no caste based discrimination. The caste system among the Tamils is somewhat more rigid. The minority ethnic groups comprise the Tamils, Moors who are descendants of Arab traders who settled down, Malays, Burghers who are descendants of Dutch settlers, and others. The Tamil population includes descendants from indentured Tamil labour who were brought by the British during colonial rule to work on the tea plantations. They are mainly based in the central highlands of the country. The majority religion is Theravada Buddhism. Many Tamils profess the Hindu faith. The Moors are Muslims. The Christian faith is professed by Sinhalese and Tamils as well as Burghers.

Sri Lanka has a recorded history of over twenty-five centuries. Before the Portuguese, Dutch and the British arrived, parts of the country were ruled by the Sinhala Kings and at times by the Tamil Kings who were from South India. In the early 1500s, the Portuguese arrived and, taking advantage of the civil strife and internal dissensions among the locals, entrenched themselves in the maritime areas. Christianity was introduced during their rule. They named the island "Ceilao". In the 17th century, the Dutch expelled the Portuguese with the assistance of local chieftains and renamed it "Ceilan". They built churches, canals, fortresses, and courts and introduced their system of Roman-Dutch Law, which still forms an integral part of the laws of the Sri Lanka. In 1796, by the Treaty of Amiens, the Dutch ceded all their possessions in the maritime areas of the country to the British, who renamed the country "Ceylon". After the Kandyan Convention of 2 March 1815 was signed between the British and the Kandyan chieftains, the entire country came under the British rule. The British captured and exiled the King of Kandy who was of South Indian descent and had feuded with the Kandyan aristocrats.

Independence movements in South Asia gathered momentum in the first half of the twentieth century and the British granted independence to Sri Lanka on 4 February 1948.

Politics and constitutions

For several decades, Sri Lanka was the only country in Asia that saw regular and peaceful changes of power as a result of elections. Even in 2015 after the shock defeat of the then president, Mr. Mahinda Rajapaksa, the transition of power was handed peacefully even though many feared widespread violence. The main parties are the United National Party which is a centre-right party and is market friendly and the Sri Lanka Freedom Party which is less market friendly, favoured import substitution, and brands itself as a nationalist party. There are also parties organised along ethnic and religious lines but the two main parties with coalition allies from smaller parties have governed Sri Lanka since independence.

Until 1972, Sri Lanka was a British dominion. The British monarch was the nominal head of government and was represented by a governor-general. There were four governors-general after Sri Lanka received independence. In 1972, a constituent assembly declared the country a republic and formally changed its name from Ceylon to Sri Lanka. The post of governor general representing the British monarch was replaced by a similar ceremonial head of state, the President, who exercised the same powers regulated by unwritten constitutional conventions of the Westminster Parliament. The legislature ceased to be bi-cameral and become unicameral. It was in 1978 that Sri Lanka's constitutional system underwent a tectonic change by means of two important changes.

In 1978, a landslide election victory resulted in the defeat of Mrs. Bandaranaike's government and the new government was formed by the United National Party. The new prime minister was Mr JR Jayawardene who proposed a new constitution which had several unique features. First, the system of cabinet government that had hitherto prevailed and was modelled under the Westminster system where the prime minister was merely *primus inter pares* was replaced with a Gaullist type executive presidency that conferred vast and almost unchecked powers on the presidency. Mr Jayawardene became the first executive president of the country. Second, the electoral system was re-organised and the first-past-the-post system inherited from the British was replaced by a system of proportional representation. This was done in order to abate political upheavals that resulted from minor swings in voting resulting in lop-sided victories in the Sri Lankan Parliament to the victorious party.

The 1978 Constitution has been amended nineteen times. Parliament passed unanimously the Seventeenth Amendment in order to dilute the vast powers exercised by the president over appointments but for various reasons this Amendment did not become operative. The Eighteenth Amendment was far more controversial in that it removed the then existing two-term limit of the executive presidency. The Supreme Court held that the electorate did not need to approve this radical change contained in the Eighteenth Amendment by means of a referendum on the simplistic ground that by allowing a sitting president to run for a third term, the franchise of the people was enlarged because the people had one more candidate to vote for! Pursuant to the removal of the two term limit, the then president, Mahinda Rajapakse, who had been elected twice ran for the post of the president a third time and was defeated in 2015. The Nineteenth Amendment, passed in 2015, restored the two term limit and imposed a disability on dual nationals from seeking election to Parliament. Other changes in the proposed amendment that shifted executive powers to the prime minister and his cabinet were ruled by the Supreme Court as requiring approval in a referendum and were dropped. The Government has announced that it proposes to submit a draft for an entirely new constitution in 2017 and the Parliament has converted itself to a constitutional assembly to achieve this aim.

Legal system and laws

Sri Lanka's legal system consists of a mixture of the civil law and common law system supplemented by personal laws. Under the English law principle enunciated in *Campbell v Hall* that the laws of a conquered colony continue in force until amended or abrogated, the English courts held that the Roman-Dutch law continued in effect after Sri Lanka became a British colony. English law supplanted the existing law in commercial matters such as the sale of goods, agency, and partnership. The main personal laws that applied were the Thesawalamai, a personal law that applied to those styled as a "Malabar inhabitant of the Province of Jaffna", the Muslim law which applied to the Muslims of the country, and the Kandyan law. These personal laws are of little commercial significance because they deal with matters like family law, succession, and the distribution of matrimonial assets.

The legal system of Sri Lanka shares features typical of mixed legal systems such as South Africa, Zimbabwe and the American state of Louisiana.

Contract law and the law of property

Roman-Dutch Law is the foundation of the law of property, contract, persons and successions but legislation has amended or modified principles of the Roman-

Dutch law.

The general law of contract is the Roman-Dutch Law except in commercial matters. The commercial law of Sri Lanka is the English Law or statutes based on the English Statutes. Capacity to contract of persons governed by special laws such as the Kandyan Law, Thesavalamai and the Muslim Law are governed by the special system applicable to the parties to the contract. A contract may be defined as "a promise or a set of promises for the breach of which the law gives a remedy or the performance of which the law in some way recognises as a duty". A contract must be distinguished from other obligations such as those arising out of delicts, quasi-contracts and trusts. To constitute a valid contract the following elements should be present: Agreement between the parties; actual or presumed intention to create a legal obligation; due observance of the prescribed forms or modes of agreement, if any; consideration in contracts to which English law applies or causa where the Roman-Dutch law applies; capacity of parties to contract; and reality of consent (viz. the agreement should not be impeachable on the ground of fraud, fear, misrepresentation, undue influence or such other reason).

Section 2 of the Prevention of Frauds Ordinance states that the following classes of contracts are of no force or avail in law unless they are reduced to writing and signed in Sri Lanka in the presence of a licensed notary public and two or more witnesses and attested: Any sale purchase transfer assignment or mortgage of land or other immovable property; any promise bargain contract or agreement for effecting any such object and for establishing any security interest or encumbrance affecting the land or other immovable property; and any contract or agreement for the future sale or purchase of land or other immovable property.

A foreigner may not purchase landed property but may take long term leases and purchase condominium apartments. It is expected that this restriction may be removed in the near future.

Contract law comprises Roman-Dutch law which applies to non-mercantile contracts while sale of goods is governed by English law principles. The law of partnership and agency are governed by English law. The Trusts Ordinance embodying English law principles of trust provides for the creation of express trusts and introduces the concepts of constructive and resulting trusts into Sri Lanka. The law of fidei-commissum which allowed the tying up of landed property for generations was abolished in the seventies. The principal features of the Roman-Dutch

law of contract which are different from English law as it obtains in Sri Lanka are:
(a) consideration is not required in order to form a contract; (b) contracts can be
made to benefit a third party and the latter may sue on such contracts unlike the
English law where the doctrine of privacy is a part of the common law and where the
law must be amended by legislation in order to allow third parties to enforce contracts
to which they were not a party; and (c) the remedy of specific performance is not a
discretionary remedy unlike in the English law of contract where the default remedy
is damages. This means that a party who sues for a breach of contract can request the
remedy of specific performance and does not have to show special circumstances for
this remedy to be provided as in English law.

Roman-Dutch law governs the law of property. Sri Lanka does not have a
system of registration of title, although it is moving towards this system of a
registration of title. Two consequences flow from this system of registration of
documents. First, lawyers would check through a chain of title to ensure that the
transferor had valid title. Second, once a transfer of land is concluded, the transferee
who registers the transfer first in the land registry obtains priority of title over a
subsequent registrant. This system is economically burdensome as it needlessly
increases transaction costs. Exclusive occupation of land for a period of ten years in
an adverse position and not as a licensee gives the adverse possessor the right to
claim ownership of such land.

The law of business organisations

Sri Lankan law recognises three types of business, which are: proprietorships;
partnerships and companies.

A single individual can carry on business under his personal name or under a
business name registered in terms of the provisions of the Business Names
Ordinance. Although the Legislature enacted in 1988 a new statute titled the Business
Names Act No. 58 of 1988 to replace the Business Names Ordinance, it has not yet
come into operation. With the establishment of Provincial Councils, all businesses in
the provinces should be registered with the Provincial Registrar of Companies.
Provincial Councils have enacted suitable statutes to give effect thereto, almost
adopting the Business Names Ordinance.

Two or more persons may carry on business in partnership under a business
name registered in terms of the provisions of the Business Names Ordinance. If a sole

proprietor or partners carry on business under a business name without registering the business name or without furnishing the particulars required by the Ordinance, he or they will not be able to enforce any contract entered into in the name of that business without the approval of court for valid reasons for the default.

English law governs partnership in Sri Lanka, subject to certain provisions contained in the Partnership Ordinance which enumerates certain situations where a partnership shall be deemed not to exist. Under the English law definition, a partnership is a relationship which subsists between two or more persons carrying on business in common with a view to profit. Although partnerships are usually the result of an express contract it need not be so, and if the persons in question are carrying on a business with a view to profit, the law would deem that a partnership exists. In terms of the Prevention of Frauds Ordinance, any agreement for establishing a Partnership should be in writing if the capital of the partnership exceeds Rs. 1,000. A Partnership stands dissolved on the death of a partner unless provided otherwise by a written partnership agreement. In any action instituted in a court of law each and every partner should join as plaintiff in his personal name. Similarly in the case of an action against a partnership each partner should be made a defendant. Partners are jointly and severally liable in tort but in the case of contracts their liability is only several unless otherwise agreed to. A partner is regarded as the agent for the other partners in most of the matters.

The institution of action in the name of the business was permitted under the procedure set out in the Administration of Justice Law which was in operation from 1975 to 1978 but it is not permissible under the Civil Procedure Code which has taken its place.

Companies are now regulated by the Companies Act No. 7 of 2007. Three types of companies may be established: Limited company; unlimited company; and company limited by guarantee.

The doctrine of "ultra vires" is no longer a rule of Sri Lankan company law. A company is not required to have a memorandum. However, it has the option of including the objects as a part of the Articles of Association more particularly, if the rule of the Exchange Commission or Stock Exchange or a Board of Investment agreement requires the objects to be included. However, the new law contains limitations in respect of major transactions:

• Contracts on behalf of the company: One of the important deviations made by the new Act is dispensing with the mandatory requirements of the common seal. A contract or other enforceable obligation may be entered into by a company by its authorised persons as provided for in Sections 19 and 20 of the Act. However, the new Act recognises that a company may have a common seal.

• Authority to contract: Section 19(1) of the Companies Act provides the rules which must be followed by a company to enter into a valid contract. Two directors of the company may bind the company. Where a contract is required to be in writing, it may be signed on behalf of the company by any person acting under the express or implied authority of the company. Where a contract is not required to be in writing, a company is bound by a written or oral contract entered into by a person acting under the company's express or implied authority.

Common law principles on agency, specifically the doctrine of ostensible authority, will apply in order to determine whether a person purporting to act on behalf of the company had implied authority.

The common law principle of the indoor management rule is enshrined in Section 21. A company or a guarantor of the company is precluded from pleading non-compliance with formalities prescribed in the articles of association. In particular the company or a guarantor of the company may not plead that the person who purported to act on behalf of the company did "not have authority to exercise the powers and perform the duties that are customary in the business of the company or are normal for a director, officer or agent of a company carrying on business of the kind carried on by that company; or directors, officers and agents".

The directors of a company owe the following duties imposed by the Act: to act in good faith and in the best interests of the company; to comply with the Act and the company's articles of association; not to act in a manner which is reckless or grossly negligent but to exercise the degree of skill and care that may reasonably be expected of a person of his knowledge and experience; to rely on and use information and advice received from others only if he knows that such reliance is not unwarranted and if he is not put on notice after making adequate inquiries to make disclosure of interests; not to use company information; to disclose share dealings; to approve remuneration and other benefits for directors only as provided for the Act; not to give a loan or provide a guarantee or security to a director unless permitted under the Act to act as provided for in Section 219 in the event of a situation of insolvency to call an extraordinary general meeting as provided for in Section 220 if it appears that there will be serious loss of capital.

The duties specified in the Act are not exhaustive. Section 190 of the Act states that "the provisions contained in this Act are in addition to and not in derogation of any provisions contained in any other law relating to the duty or liability of directors or officers of a company". In effect the familiar principles common law principles regarding the fiduciary duties of the director and the proper purpose rule familiar to company lawyers would apply in to supplement the duties imposed by the Act.

Every company should maintain an Interests Register. However, in the case of a private company, such register can be dispensed with. A director of a company should disclose his interests and have the same entered in the Interests Register. Furthermore, remuneration and other benefits to directors should also be entered in the Interests Register.

A company can indemnify or directly or indirectly effect insurance for a director or employee of the company or of a related company only in the manner set out in Section 218.

A company need not have authorised capital or par value for shares under the new Act. The Act has introduced the concept of "Stated Capital". Provisions are included in the Act to protect minority shareholders. Minority Buy-Out Rights are also recognised in the new Law.

A company incorporated outside Sri Lanka can establish a place of business in Sri Lanka and register its branch in Sri Lanka under the provisions of Part XVIII of the Act. Although the Companies (Special Provisions) Law No. 19 of 1974 and the Foreign Companies (Special Provisions) Law No. 9 of 1975 have been repealed by Section 533 (2) of the Act, Section 489 (7) of the Act provides that a company incorporated outside Sri Lanka should not establish a place of business within Sri Lanka or be registered as an overseas company, where the business being carried on by that company does not conform to the stipulations made by or under the Exchange Controller.

Chapter 1 Customs Law and Telecommunications Law

1.1 Customs law

Sri Lanka Customs is a non-ministerial government department which performs the duties of collecting customs duties and other taxes and levies in Sri Lanka. It comes under the purview of the Ministry of Finance. The Minister of Finance oversees the administrative supervision of Customs through the Secretary of the Treasury. Customs functions are distributed among several directorates: Administration, Imports, Exports, Valuation, Baggage, Air Cargo, Automated Data Processing, Policy Planning & Research, and Human Resources Development.

Customs law and practice is important for two reasons. First, the sweep of the customs laws and regulations is immense. Evasion of customs duties by undervaluation is common and so is customs fraud. The penalties for these are severe. Second, reports of extortion of bribes by customs officers have become increasingly common and care must be taken in dealing with such persons.

The department exercises the powers vested in it under the Customs Ordinance (Chapter 235). In addition several other related enactments are applicable. The major functions of the department include the collection of government revenue as customs duty and other levies on behalf of several other government authorities and safeguarding the country at the entry point. It has limited policing powers, such as arresting suspects and confiscating contraband.

Section 10(1) of the Customs Ordinance states that the customs duties set forth in Schedule A to the Ordinance, which may be revised from time to time, "shall be levied and paid upon all goods, wares, and merchandise imported or exported from Sri Lanka". The Customs Tariff provides for two forms of duties: (a) *ad valorem*, or the face value of an article. Customs duties and other levies on most articles are based on *ad valorem* rates. Schedule E of the Customs Ordinance stipulates how the transaction value is to be determined; and (b) specific rates which are based on units of quantity. Both ad valorem and specific rates of customs duties fall into two categories, "general" and "referential" rates of duty.

Section 52 of the Ordinance provides that where "it shall appear to the officers of the customs that the value declared in respect of any goods in according to Section 51 is a false declaration, the goods in respect on which such declaration has been made shall be forfeited together with the package in which they are contained". In *Perera v Hatton National Bank* the Supreme Court analysed the duty payable on software in light of Paragraph 1 of Schedule E of the Customs Ordinance. This paragraph which was the umbrella provision of the Schedule read that "the value of any imported goods shall be the normal price, that is to say, the price which they would fetch at the time of importation on a sale in the open market between a buyer and a seller independent of each other". The Court of Appeal had wrongly assumed that in order to levy customs duty there must have been a sale, and since the software was on licence, no duty could be levied. The Supreme Court disagreed and held that the value of the intangible component could be taken into account. The software in question was customised for the bank. The court observed that there is no legal basis for the proposition that customised software packages imported as intangible property on a licence fee should be valued on the basis of carrier medium only, while "off the shelf sold outright to a user are liable to customs duty on their full value".

1.2   Export procedure

The Sri Lanka Customs Export Procedure has been simplified to a great extent in recent past. Rules and regulations have been relaxed and duty exemptions and concessionary duty rates are given to exporters as an encouragement. Export promotional schemes have been implemented with collaboration with other state agencies as part of state endeavours to develop Sri Lanka as a country with an export oriented economy. Sri Lanka Customs is required in its supervision of export related activities to safeguard national wealth such as archaeological treasure and fauna and flora by implementing related laws.

1.3   Rules on origin of goods

In order to give effect to concepts such as most favoured nation, national treatment, tariffs, and eligibility under various Generalised System of Preference schemes, it is essential that there be rules by which the origin of goods could be determined. Apart from determining eligibility, rules of origin which state how the country of origin of the goods in question will be determined provide predictability and certainty which are essential in an international system of trading goods. In a globalised environment where a supply chain that runs halfway across the globe results in the production and manufacture of goods in more than one country, comprehensive rules of origin are necessary to avoid minimal processing, trade diversion and similar circumvention methods that frustrate trade arrangements.

There are two types of rules of origin: Non-preferential rules of origin and preferential rules of origin.

Non-preferential rules of origin are the default set of rules that are vital for determining tariffs, quotas, dumping and subsidies, and marketing of goods under national treatment obligations.

Preferential rules of origin are used to determine goods which may enter a country under preferential treatment. That is, they are used to establish whether the goods are eligible for special treatment under a trading arrangement between two or more economies. Preferential (or reduced) rates of duty are applied to goods which are found to be the products or manufacture of a country defined as a preference country. The principal objective of preferential rules of origin is to ensure that benefits are restricted to those goods which originate and are traded within the particular preference area. Sri Lanka has concluded treaties with Pakistan and India that provide for preferential rules of origin. For example, in the agreement with Pakistan, there are two sets of criteria for determining rules of origin.

Article 7 deals with "wholly obtained or produced" goods which are enumerated as follows:

Within the meaning of rule 6(a), the following shall be considered as wholly produced or obtained in the territory of the exporting Contracting Party:

(a) raw or mineral products extracted from its soil, its water or its seabed, (raw, or mineral products include mineral fuels, lubricants and related materials as well as mineral or metal ores);

(b) vegetable products harvested there, ("vegetable products" include agricultural and forest products);

(c) animals born and raised there;

(d) products obtained from animals referred to in clause (c) above;

(e) products obtained by hunting or fishing conducted there;

(f) products of sea fishing and other marine products from the high seas by its vessels, (in respect of vessels or factory ships operated by Government agencies, the requirements of flying the flag of the Contracting Party does not apply);

(g) products processed and/or made on board its factory ships exclusively from products, referred to in clause (f) above, (in respect of vessels or factory ships operated by Government agencies, the requirements of flying the flag of the Contracting Party does not apply);

(h) used articles collected there, fit only for the recovery of raw materials;

(i) waste and scrap resulting from manufacturing operations conducted there;

(j) products extracted from the seabed or below seabed which is situated outside its territorial waters, provided that it has exclusive exploitation rights, and

(k) goods produced there exclusively from the products referred to in clause(a) to (j) above.

Where the goods in question are not wholly produced in Sri Lanka as stated above, they are eligible for preferential treatment on the following criterion: "Not wholly produced or obtained: (a) Within the meaning of rule 6(b): products worked on or processed as a result of which the total value of the material, parts or produce originating from countries other than the Contracting Parties or of undetermined origin used does not exceed 65 percent of the F. O. B. value of the products produced or obtained and the final process of manufacture is performed within the territory of the exporting Contracting Party shall be eligible for preferential treatment, subject to the provisions of clauses(b), (c), (d)and(e)of rule 8 and rule 9".

Article 8(d)of the FTA with Pakistan states that the following shall in any event be considered as insufficient working or processing to confer the status of originating products, whether or not there is a change of heading:

(a) operations to ensure the preservation of products in good condition during transport and storage(ventilation, spreading out, drying, chilling, placing in salt, sulphur dioxide or other aqueous solutions, removal of damaged parts, and like operations);

(b) simple operations consisting of removal of dust, sifting or screening, sorting, classifying, matching(including the making-up of sets or articles), washing painting, cutting up;

(c) changes of packing and breaking up and assembly of consignments, simple slicing, cutting and repacking or placing in bottles, flasks, bags, boxes, fixing on cards or boards etc. , and all other simple packing operations;

(d) the affixing of marks, labels or other like distinguishing signs on products or their packaging; simple mixing of products, whether or not of different kinds, where one or more components of the mixture do not meet the conditions laid down in these Rules to enable them to be considered as originating products;

(e) simple mixing of products, whether or not of different kinds, where one or more components of the mixture do not meet the conditions laid down in these Rules to enable them to be considered as originating products; simple assembly of parts of products to constitute a complete product;

(f) simple assembly of parts of products to constitute a complete product,

(g) a combination of two or more operations specified in (1) to (6); and

(h) slaughter of animals.

1. 4   Anti-dumping and countervailing duties law

An Anti-Dumping and Countervailing Duties Bill was introduced in Parliament in February 2006, but not enacted, to give effect to the agreement on implementation of Article Ⅵ of the General Agreement on Tariffs and Trade 1994 and the agreement on Subsidies and Countervailing Measures. This regulation was meant for the investigation and imposition of anti-dumping duties and countervailing duties with regard to products imported to Sri Lanka. The Director General of the Department of Commerce was named as the authority for investigating the said regulations with the supervision of an inter-ministerial committee, which assures the process of application to higher level of involvement. The US has recently initiated an anti-dumping investigation against tyres from Sri Lanka and India. The ceramic industry has called upon the government to introduce as urgent matter anti-dumping laws to protect the domestic ceramics industry from dumped products.

1. 5   Sri Lanka Telecommunications Act(No. 25 of 1991)

Section 4 of the Act defines the objectives and job functions of the Authority as follows: to ensure the provision of a reliable and efficient national and international telecommunication service in Sri Lanka (save in so far as the provision thereof is impracticable) such DM will satisfy alt reasonable demands for such service intruding emergency services, public call box services, directory information services, maritime services and rural services as may be considered essential for the national well-being; without prejudice to use generality of Paragraph(a) , to secure that every operator: shall have and employ the necessary technical, financial and managerial resources to ensure the provision of the services specified in his licence; to protect and promote the interests of consumers, purchasers and other users and the public interest with respect to the charges for, and the quality and variety of telecommunication services provided and telecommunication apparatus supplied; to maintain and; to promote effective competition between persons engaged in commercial activities connected with telecommunication and promote efficiency and economy on the part of such persons to promote the rapid and sustained development of telecommunication facilities both domestic and international; to ensure that operators are able to carry out their obligations for providing a reliable and efficient service free of undue delay, hindrance or impediment; to promote research into and the development and use of new techniques in telecommunications and related fields; to encourage the major users of telecommunication services whose places of business are outside Sri Lanka to establish places of business within Sri Lanka; and to promote the use of Sri Lanka for international transit services.

Section 5 of the Act enumerates the various powers and duties of the Authority as follows; to ensure that the telecommunication services in the country are operated in a manner which will best serve and contribute to its overall economic and social development and advancement; to advise the Minister in the granting of licenses to operate telecommunication systems under this Act; to advise the government on matters relating to telecommunication including policies on tariffs, pricing and subsidies and legislative measures required for the provision of public telecommunication services; to pay due regard to the public interest and the convenience and wishes of the general public as regards the telecommunication services provided by an operator; to comply with such general policy directions as may be given from time to time by the Minister regarding the performance of the duties and exercise of the powers of the Authority, and furnish such information as may be required by him in accordance with the provisions of Section 67; to take such regulatory measures as may be prescribed to comply with any general or special directions that may be given to him from time to time by the Government of Sri Lanka in the interest of national security, public order and the defence of the country; to direct any operator to comply with requirements laid down by the

International Telecommunications Union and other relevant international organisations in respect of both equipment and technical standards; to ensure compliance by operators with international or other obligations entered into by the Government of Sri Lanka in relation to telecommunication; to assist where requested, the relevant ministries in the conduct of negotiations to establish agreements with the International Telecommunications Union, other international bodies and foreign telecommunication operators, regarding standards and procedures for the establishment of a telecommunication system; where so required at the request of the minister or of any other relevant ministry, to represent the Government in international conferences or international and foreign bodies concerned with telecommunication; to specify by rules in consultation with the minister and the minister in charge of finance, the tariffs or methods for determining such tariffs, taking into account government policy and the requirements of the operators in respect of the telecommunication services provided by the operators: provided that the tariff rates, call charges and other charges in force immediately prior to the transfer date shall continue in force and shall be deemed to be the tariffs specified under this Act, until revised or amended under the provisions of this Act; to approve interconnection charges and charges for calls between licensed interconnected telecommunication systems where operators of those systems are able to agree on such charges, and to determine such charges where operators are unable to agree; to require operators of telecommunication systems to adopt such accounting systems as may be approved by the authority; to require any operator to submit to him transmission plans, signalling plans, switching and numbering plans and to approve or modify such plans as well as to publish and ensure compliance with such plans; to specify technical standards and procedures for the provision of telecommunication services; to specify standards for the education and training of technical manpower in telecommunication; to approve types of telecommunication apparatus which may be connected to a telecommunication system; to take such regulatory measures including the issue of directives as may be deemed necessary to monitor the quality of services provided by operators and to ensure that these services conform to standards relating to quality of service specified by rules made under this Act; to promote, in cooperation with the operators or otherwise, research and development in telecommunication at universities and research, institutes in Sri Lanka; to establish such advisory bodies as he may deem necessary for the purpose of advising him on any matter pertaining to the exercise, performance and discharge of the powers, functions and duties of the authority under this Act; to negotiate with any public corporation or other person, for the prevention of any obstruction or interference with a radio beam or any communication facility or for the removal of any such obstruction or interference; to ensure the conservation and proper utilisation of the radio frequency spectrum by operators and other organisations and individuals who need to use radio frequencies; to make and enforce compliance with rules to minimise electro-magnetic disturbances produced by electrical apparatus and all unauthorised radio frequency emissions; and to do all such other acts which may be incidental or conducive to, the attainment of the objects of the Authority or the exercise or discharge of his powers and duties under this Act.

Section 17 of the Act states that no person to operate telecommunication system in Sri Lanka without a licence. The minister may grant a license on the recommendation of the authority but he has the power to reject such a recommendation for reasons and is also allowed to grant a license at his own discretion.

The terms and conditions of a license may include: such conditions (whether relating to the operating of the telecommunication system to which the license relates or otherwise) as appear to the minister to be requisite or expedient having regard to the provisions of Section 4 of the Act; conditions requiring the payment to the Authority on the grant of the license or during the currency of the license or both on the grant and during the currency of the license such sum or sums of money as may be determined by the authority to defray any expenses incurred by him in granting the license and requiring the payment of an annual cess calculated at a rate on the annual turnover of the operator to be used by the authority for prescribed purposes; conditions requiring an operator to furnish to the authority, in such manner and at such times as may be reasonably required by the authority, such documents, accounts, estimates, returns or other information as the authority may require for the performance of his duties under this Act; conditions prohibiting an operator from showing preference to, or from exercising discrimination against a particular person or persons of any class or description as respects any service provided, connection made or permission given; conditions requiring an operator to publish in such manner and at such times as are specified in the license, a notice specifying the charges and other terms and conditions that are to be applicable to the services provided, connection made or permission given; conditions requiring an operator to ensure that an adequate and satisfactory information system which may include billing information, tariff information, directory services and directory inquiry services be made available to users: conditions requiring an operator to keep the authority informed of the practices followed by him in the routing of national and international traffic and ensure that compensation is paid to persons affected by the running of underground cables or overhead lines; conditions requiring an operator (a) to comply with any direction as to such matters as are specified in the license (b) except with the consent of the authority to do or refrain from doing such things as are required to be done or required not to be done under the license (c) to refer for determination by the authority such questions arising under the license as are specified in the license; conditions requiring the connection to any telecommunication system to which the licence relates or permit the connection to any such system, of such other telecommunication systems and such apparatus as are specified in the licence; conditions requiring an operator to develop and publish a plan to restore service during emergencies; conditions specifying acceptable economic criteria in accordance with which the authority shall approve tariff adjustments proposed by an operator.

Chapter 2 Foreign Investment Law

2.1 Introduction

The British who ruled the whole of Sri Lanka from 1815 until 1948 introduced tea and rubber as commercial crops to Sri Lanka. After independence, tea, coconut and rubber were the main agricultural exports. During the centre-left administrations of the late Mrs. Bandaranaike, the focus was on import substitution and the nationalization of the key industries. The government nationalized foreign petroleum distributors and attracted the sanctions of the Hickenlooper Amendment which required the American government to cut off assistance to countries that nationalized American owned property without compensation. A subsequent UNP government resolved this matter by paying compensation to foreign petroleum distributors. However, the ownership of tea estates that were formerly owned by foreigners remained with the government. In 1978, there was a change in government and the Government of Mr JR Jayawardene embarked on several market liberalization measures. He welcomed foreign investment and declared: "Let the robber barons come". However, festering racial animosities erupted into massive civil conflict. Caught in the conflict was a company that had its investment destroyed in the East Coast of Sri Lanka, leading to the first investment dispute filed with the International Centre for Settlement of Investment Disputes(ICSID). In *Asian Agricultural Products Limited v Republic of Sri Lanka*, the ICSID tribunal examined the scope and application of the host country's full protection and security obligation under the UK-Sri Lanka bilateral investment treaty. In 2009, the conflict was brought to a close. The Sri Lankan government led by President Mahinda Rajapakse actively courted foreign investment from China leading to the construction of the controversial Port City project. In an election called in 2015, Mr Rajapakse was defeated and a new coalition between the two principal parties with Mr Sirisena representing the centre-left parties was elected president and Mr Wickremasinghe, representing the market friendly UNP was appointed as the Prime Minister. The future of the Port City project was uncertain in view of the opposition voiced to the project by government ministers who were then in the opposition. However, it appears that an agreement has been reached and the project will be allowed to continue.

The US-based global information company IHS Inc. has ranked Sri Lanka among Asia-Pacific's top ten foreign direct investment hotspots. The company stated that Asia Pacific is forecast to be the fastest growing region of the global economy and offers the biggest potential gains for foreign direct investment. It also observed that Sri Lanka is expected to show rapid growth in the next decade. Whether Sri Lanka will be able to transform this potential into reality would depend on the government streamlining the investment process, reducing if not eliminating capital controls, reform its legal system so as to make it more transparent and the courts more efficient, and reducing bureaucratic corruption.

2.2   Legal status of approved foreign investments in Sri Lanka

Article 157 of Sri Lanka's Constitution provides that where Parliament approves with a two thirds majority that an international treaty or agreement that Sri Lanka has entered into with a foreign government is essential for the development of the national economy, such treaty or agreement has the force of law in Sri Lanka. No legislation or executive action may be taken in contravention of such treaty except in the " interests of national security ". This provision confirms the customary international law requirement that expropriation of property must be lawful and on payment of prompt and adequate compensation; extends the most favoured nation treatment to approved investments; enables free remittance of earnings, capital and business fees; and provides for settlement of disputes regarding compensation by international arbitration including settlement under the International Centre for Settlement of Investment Disputes.

Sri Lanka has signed bilateral Investment Protection Agreements (IPA) with 28 countries and other types of investment agreements.

The countries with which Sri Lanka has concluded bilateral investment treaties are: Australia, Belgium-Luxembourg, China, Czech Republic, Denmark, Egypt, France, Finland, Germany, India, Indonesia, Italy, Netherlands, Norway, Pakistan, Republic of Korea, Romania, Kuwait, Malaysia, Sweden, Thailand, United Kingdom, Vietnam.

2. 3   The Sri Lanka Board of Investment

The Board of Investment Law No. 4 of 1978 (BOI Law) has set up a Board of Investment (BOI) which is the Sri Lankan regulatory body tasked with approving and regulating foreign investments as well as local investment. The BOI has its origins in the Greater Colombo Economic Commission (GCEC) established in 1978. In 1992 the Commission was reconstituted as the Board of Investment of Sri Lanka. Foreigners may invest in any permitted business activity either under Section 16 or Section 17 of the BOI Law. Most sectors of the Sri Lankan economy are now open for foreign direct investment.

The BOI functions as a central point or quasi-one stop shop for investors. It operates as an autonomous statutory body that is directly responsible to the President of Sri Lanka. The Board of Directors of BOI is drawn from the private sector, public sector and several departments that are geared to facilitating the investment process. Salient features in the BOI agreement are that the specific incentive granted to an eligible company as tax holidays or preferential tax rates, exemption from custom duty and foreign exchange controls remain valid for the life of the enterprise. The provisions and the spirit of the agreement cannot be changed by the government.

The predecessor institution to the BOI, the GCEC was initially established with the objective of encouraging Foreign Direct Investment in export-oriented activities. In pursuance of this objective, Export Processing Zones (EPZs) were developed as industrial estates with the necessary infrastructure and other needs of GCEC enterprises. These Export Processing Zones come under the sole authority of the GCEC. The first to be established in 1978 was the Katunayake EPZ. It is located in dose proximity to the International Airport. This was developed in three phases and covers an area of approximately 200 hectares. The second EPZ at Biyagama is situated between the Colombo Port and the Katunayake International Airport, 24 kilometers from Colombo, and covers an area of 180 hectares. A third zone, the Koggala EPZ, covering an area of 80 hectares, was opened in mid-1991, close to the southern seaport at Galle, which is 115 kilometers south of Colombo.

2. 4   Laws applicable to foreign investment

The main law governing foreign investment is found in the Law No. 4 of 1978 as amended in 1980, 1983, 1992 and 2002 and regulations made under the Act. The Board of Investment Law was amended by : Greater Colombo Economic Commission (Amendment) Act No. 43 of 1980; Greater Colombo Economic Commission (Amendment) Act No. 21 of 1983; Greater Colombo Economic Commission (Amendment) Act No. 49 of 1992 whereby the title of the Law was changed to the Board of Investment of Sri Lanka Law; and Board of Investment of Sri Lanka (Amendment) Act No. 10 of 2002.

The most relevant BOI Regulations are: 1 of 1978 8/2 of 31. 10. 1978;1 of 1978 (Amendment) 111/4 of 24. 10. 1980;1 of 1978(Amendment) 127/9 of 11. 02. 1981; 1 of 1978 (Amendment) 171/16 of 18. 12. 1981; 1of1978 (Amendment) 329/7 of 27. 12. 198;1 of 1978(Amendment) 522/18 of 08. 09. 1998; 1 of 1978 (Amendment) 685/14 of 25. 10. 1991 ;1 of 1991 690/9 of 28. 11. 1991 ;1 of 1978(Amendment)697/ 4 of 13. 01. 1992 ;1 of 1978 (Amendment) 780/12 of 16. 08. 1993 ;1 of 1994 813/21 of 08. 04. 19942 of 1994 813/21 of 08. 04. 1994; 1 of 1978 (Amendment) 813/21 of 08. 04. 1994 ; 1of 1995 896/17 of 10. 11. 1995 ; 1 of 1994 (Amendment) 941/13 of 19. 09. 1996 ;1 of 1995(Amendment)941/13 of 19. 09. 1996 ;1 of 1995 (Amendment) 969/10 of 01. 04. 1997 ; 1 of 2002 ; 1242/29 of 28. 06. 2002 ; 1 of 2006 1447/15 of 31. 05. 2006 ;1 of 2006 1469/35 of 02. 11. 2006.

The Exchange Control and the Inland Revenue Act are the other two important laws which affect foreign investors.

2.5   Reserved (negative list) and regulated activities

Fields of business that are totally reserved for Sri Lankans or the negative list items are money lending; pawn brokering; retail trade with a capital investment of less than USD 1 million; personal services other than for exports or for tourism; coastal fishing; education of students who are citizens of Sri Lanka and not over 14 years of age; and award of local educational degrees.

Foreign investment in the regulated areas will be allowed by the relevant authorities on a case by case basis. The BOI will direct potential foreign investors to the appropriate authorities who regulate these activities and evaluate foreign investment proposals. The regulated areas are: air transportation; coastal shipping; industrial undertaking in the second schedule of the Industrial Promotion Act No. 46 of 1990 namely any industry manufacturing arms, ammunitions, explosives, military vehicles and equipment aircraft and other military hardware, any industry manufacturing poisons, narcotics, alcohols, dangerous drugs and toxic, hazardous, or carcinogenic materials, any industry producing currency, coins or security documents; lotteries and large-scale mechanised mining of gems.

2.6   Approval of investment applications

The approval of the BOI for foreign investment is automatic in most instances unless the same is in respect of foreign investment of more than 40 percent in an activity in the non-automatic list or if that involves provision of fiscal and financial incentives. The non-automatic list given by the BOI is as follows: export production of goods subject to international quotas; growing and primary processing of tea rubber coconut rice cocoa sugar and spices; timber-based industries using local timber; fishing; deep sea fishing mass communications; education; freight forwarding; travel agencies; shipping agencies.

Foreign investment exceeding 40 percent will be subject to case by case evaluation and approval by the BOI in consultation with the relevant authorities. This non-automatic list is stated to be under review with the aim of further simplification.

2.7   Incentive packages

As an impetus to the development effort, the BOI provides a wide range of incentives and concessions. These incentives and concessions depend on the type of project proposed. The incentives offered belong to two classes or "regimes" and the enterprise may become eligible for incentives offered by either of these two regimes. Reproduced below are the investment incentives as announced by the BOI.

(a) General Incentives: Section 16 of the BOI Law.

The incentives offered under this regime are also available to both local and foreign investors. Firms that do not qualify for concessions under Section 17 of the BOI Law may seek incentives available under the normal laws of the country such as Inland Revenue Act, Turnover Tax Act, Excise (Special Provisions) Act and Customs Ordinance. Foreign investment entry to operate under the normal laws is conferred under Section 16 of the BOI Law which entities the enterprise to repatriate profits and dividends attributable to foreign shareholders.

(b) BOI Incentives under Section 17 of the BOI Law.

Special incentives, outside identified laws of the country, are available to enterprises approved by the BOI, under Section 17 of the BOI Law, if they meet certain criteria. Section 17 (1) of the Board of Investment of Sri Lanka Law (BOI Law) reads as follows: "The Board shall have the power to enter into agreements with any enterprise in or outside the Area of Authority and to grant exemptions from any law referred to in Schedule B hereto, or to modify or vary the application of any such laws, to such enterprises in accordance with such regulations as may be made by the Minister". The laws referred to in the Schedule B of the BOI Law are the following: The Inland Revenue Act No. 4 of 1963; The Inland Revenue Act No. 28 of 1979; The Inland Revenue Act No. 38 of 2000; The Customs Ordinance; The Exchange Control Act; The Companies Act; The Merchant Shipping Act; The Finance Act No. 65 of 1961, Parts I, II, V, VI, VII & VIII; The Air Navigation Act.

"Enterprise" has been defined by section 35 of the BOI Law and it means and includes only the enterprise, which is established with BOI approval for the purpose of carrying on the envisaged business.

Section 17 (2) reads as follows: "every such agreement shall be reduced to writing and shall upon registration with the Board, constitute a valid and binding contract between the Board and the enterprise". Enterprises which satisfy specific eligibility criteria qualify for incentives under Section 17 of the BOI Law. The incentives offered by the BOI were expanded in November 1995. The new incentives represent a two pronged strategy: diversification of exports towards advanced technology and value addition and investments in large scale projects including infrastructure.

For the purpose of granting the new incentives, "advanced technology" has been defined as follows by the Ministry of Finance.

Technology which introduces a new design, formula or process for the manufacture of an article or in the provision of a service, resulting in one or more of the following: higher productivity resulting in lower cost of production; quality improvement of product/service; better utilisation of raw materials; upgrading of technical skills; minimising/controlling environmental pollution and/or wastage; manufacture of products using a technology hitherto not applied in Sri Lanka (excluding technology involving only simple processing) ; technology for the local processing of raw materials, which are currently imported in processed form, excluding simple types of processing; technology hitherto unutilised in Sri Lanka that would make use of local resources to provide public utilities and infrastructure services.

Investments in non-traditional export-oriented manufacturing, advanced technology electronics sector information technology and Services, regional operating headquarters and direct and indirect exporters are the main types of investment that qualify for incentives under Section 17 of the BOI Law, with applicable conditions.

2.8   Immigration for investors: Resident Visas

The BOI is responsible for the approval of all foreign direct investment. Foreign investors need to invest at least USD 50, 000 in the equity of the enterprise in order to qualify for approval under Sections 16 or 17 of the BOI Law and to be eligible for a Resident Visa.

2.9   Establishing a BOI company

Option 1: Section 17 projects

Both foreign and local investors can request to set up a Section 17 project if the applicant can meet the eligibility criteria stipulated by the BOI regulations with respect to the Investment Sector(Sector) the applicant has chosen to invest in. Section 17 projects are eligible for certain concessions including: corporate tax concessions granted under the Inland Revenue Act of Sri Lanka; customs duty-free Import of capital goods and raw materials(granted under the BOI Law) ; and exemption from Exchange Control Act(Part I-VI) (granted under the BOI Law).

Selected projects approved under Section 17 may additionally qualify for approval as a Strategic Development Project (SDP). SDPs are considered to be of strategic importance, and likely to bring substantial economic and social benefit to the country. SDPs may also qualify for tax exemptions of up to a maximum duration of 25 years and will require approval by the Cabinet of Ministers as well as by a resolution of Parliament. For more details, please see Strategic Development Projects later in this guide.

Option 2: Section 16 projects(foreign investment or joint ventures only)

Foreign investors may obtain BOI approval to set up a Section 16 project(for foreign investment entry only) if the project does not fulfil the approval criteria required under Section 17 of the BOI Law or the applicant is transferring shares of a non-BOI enterprise to foreign investors. Projects set up under Section 16 of the BOI Law will operate under the normal laws of Sri Lanka and are not eligible for any of the special concessions provided under Section 17 of the BOI Law. Section 16 projects may also be set up as a joint venture with a local partner.

2.10   Foreign investment in equities

Foreign investment in the local equity market is open to approved country funds and regional funds. Ministry of Finance approval is required but this is a mere formality. Citizens of foreign states (whether resident in Sri Lanka or outside Sri Lanka) and Sri Lankans resident outside Sri Lanka may also invest in the local equity market. Foreign investors may invest in up to 100 percent of the issued capital of a limited company, subject to certain exclusions, limitations and conditions. Prior approval from the relevant authorities for investments in an unlisted company. Foreign investment is permitted in all sectors of the economy except in the following activities which are reserved for citizens of Sri Lanka: money lending; pawn broking; retail Trade with a capital investment of less than USD 1 million; personal services other than for exports or for tourism; coastal fishing; education of students who are citizens of Sri Lanka and not over 14 years of age; award of local educational degrees.

The BOI now permits 100 percent foreign ownership in a number of areas of investments. Foreigners are permitted to acquire shares up to 100 percent in public quoted companies subject to the limitations set out in the notification of the Controller of Exchange in the Government Gazette No. 721/4 of the 29 June 1992, 1122/12 of 7 March 2000 and 1232/14 of 19 April 2002. The monies for such investment should be received through a SIERA (Share Investment External Rupee Account). Prior to 1992 the Finance Act No. 11 of 1963 imposed a transfer tax of 100 percent on the transfer of shares in Companies to non-citizens of Sri Lanka but that tax was abolished in 1992.

The "SIERA" Account

Foreign investors are permitted to invest in shares of (a) companies listed at the Colombo Stock Exchange and (b) unlisted companies in which foreign investment has been approved by the Board of Investment of Sri Lanka or the Government of Sri Lanka or by any legal or administrative authority set up for approval of any such investment.

To facilitate investment by foreign investors, authorised dealers are permitted to open and maintain Share Investment External Rupee Account for (a) country funds and regional funds as may be approved from time to time by the Minister of Finance, corporate bodies incorporated outside Sri Lanka and (b) citizen of foreign states, and citizen of Sri Lanka resident outside Sri Lanka.

SIERA shall only be credited with inward remittances or transfers form a non-resident foreign currency Account or from and off shore unit of a bank and converted into Sri Lanka Rupees. The credits to this account will comprise inward remittances, proceeds of share sales, dividend and commission on such transactions. Funds in this account may be utilised for all payments related to share transactions such as broker's fees, bank charges, etc. , expenses in Sri Lanka of the account holder subject to certain limits. For remittance of dividends abroad, tax clearance has to be obtained, confirming that withholding tax has been paid. Sale proceeds of shares of listed companies may be remitted without delay. Such remittances are made by banks without the need for prior exchange control approval. Although remittances are subject to the production of a tax clearances certificate, the procedure for the issuance of this certificate has been streamlined.

2. 11   China-Sri Lanka Investment Treaty on the Reciprocal Promotion and Protection of Investments (the BIT)

The BIT does not provide a right of establishment to investors of the states. Article 2 of the BIT states that the BIT would apply only to "all investments made by nationals and companies (of the other country) which are approved in writing by the competent authority designated by the Government of the (host country) and upon such conditions, if any, as it shall deem fit". Applying the rules of interpretation of the Vienna Convention of the Law of Treaties, the privilege given to the approving investment authority to approve the investment "upon such conditions, if any, as it deems fit" cannot be taken to mean that such conditions could erode into the substantive protections accorded to the investor under the BIT.

Article 3 of the BIT requires that investments admitted under Article 2 are entitled to fair and equitable treatment and protection in accordance with the BIT. It is unclear whether this standard refers to the minimum standard required by customary international law or the more expansive standard developed in the investment dispute arbitral jurisprudence. While there is an obligation to provide "most favoured nation" treatment to foreign investors, there is no obligation to extend national treatment to the foreign investors.

Article 6 of the BIT deals with expropriation. Article 6. 2 permits the investor to challenge the legality of any measure of expropriation before a competent court in the host country. However, under Article 13. 2 of the BIT, if an investor chooses to do this, he is precluded from seeking the establishment of an international arbitral tribunal to settle a dispute over compensation resulting from expropriation. It would appear that only disputes over the amount of compensation due can be submitted to an international arbitral tribunal and that too, only if local remedies have not been sought. For all other breaches of the BIT including complaints over denial of the most favoured treatment obligation and the fair and equitable obligation, the only reliefs that can be sought are in the courts of the host country. Whether local courts can evaluate investment disputes claims with the same thoroughness of international investment tribunals with arbitrators specialised in foreign investment law is an open question.

2. 12   Membership in international foreign investment institutions

Sri Lanka is a member of ICSID and has not submitted any reservations pursuant to Article 25 (2) of the ICSID Convention requiring that local remedies be first exhausted prior to a dispute being submitted to ICSID.

Sri Lanka is also a member of the Multilateral Investment Guarantee Agency (MIGA) of the World Bank which provides guarantees against non-commercial risks, such as those arising out of political changes or political instability and insecurity. MIGA issues guarantees including co-insurance and re-insurance of investments, against non-commercial risks such as losses resulting from expropriation, breach of contract, war and civil disturbances.

2. 13   Double taxation treaties

Sri Lanka has concluded treaties for the avoidance of double taxation with the following countries and regions:

Australia, Bangladesh, Belgium, Canada, China, Denmark, Finland, France, Germany, Italy, Japan, Republic of Korea, Kuwait, Malaysia, Nepal, Netherlands, Norway, Qatar, Romania, Russia, Saudi Arabia, Singapore, Sweden, Switzerland, Thailand, UAE, India, Indonesia, Iran, Oman, Pakistan, Philippines, Poland, UK, USA, Vietnam, and Hong Kong Special Administrative Region of China.

Chapter 3   Monetary and Banking Law

3. 1   Banking legislation

Section 2 of the Banking Act No. 30 of 1988 provides for the licensing of institutions that carry on banking business in Sri Lanka. Section 2(1) states that "no banking business shall be carried on except by a company under the authority of a licence issued by the Monetary Board with the approval" of the Minister of Finance. A "licensed commercial bank" is a bank that has been duly approved under Section 2. Section 2(5) makes it an offence for any entity that has not obtained a license to carry on the business of banking. However, in the recent past Sri Lanka has been plagued by Ponzi scheme scandals where companies have crashed leaving depositors who were promised handsome rates of interest bereft, the most prominent of which was the Golden Key scandal. The Central Bank regularly publishes notifications of "licensed commercial banks" with the accompanying statement that the Central Bank supervises the operations of these banks and thereby implies that those institutions not included in the list are risky. However, the lure of quick returns has proven irresistible to large numbers of Sri Lankan citizens.

3. 2   Asset securitisation and enforcement

The law of property in Sri Lanka is governed by the Roman-Dutch law. Unlike in English law, in the Roman-Dutch law when a property is mortgaged the mortgagor remains the owner of the property. In English law, the title to the property is conveyed to the mortgagee. This factor combined with the slowness of the pace of litigation in the Sri Lankan courts contributed to banking inefficiencies. A major problem that banks faced was the delay they encountered in the courts when attempting to enforce after an event of default. Years would drag by in the original courts and more years in the appeal courts before effective recovery could be made. The attempt by the legislature to make it more efficient for banks to execute against defaulting borrowers has encountered limited success.

Until the enactment of the Recovery of Loans by Banks(Special Provisions) Act of 1990, the Civil Procedure Code of Sri Lanka regulated actions by creditors in loan recovery actions against debtors. The Civil Procedure Code provided for an expedited procedure known as "summary procedure" for claims relating to recovery of moneys due on checks, promissory notes, and similar instruments. The Mortgage Act No. 6 of 1946 governed the recovery of money granted on the security of a mortgage. Much dissatisfaction was expressed by banks and other creditors about the problems they faced in debt recovery. A dysfunctional banking system can be a massive break on the development of an economy. Under prodding by donor institutions, important stakeholders, and the legal profession, legislation was enacted in 1990 that allowed parate execution. "Parate", which means immediate or instant, allows the creditor to bypass the lengthy trial proceedings on the merits in the courts and enforce against the collateral provided by the debtor.

Parate execution as regulated by the Recovery of Loans Act is a procedure permitted only to banks and not to other creditors such as non-bank financial institutions or moneylenders and allows the resale of property mortgaged to the bank. The mortgage is enforced without going through court proceedings. The bank itself is given the power to hold an auction for the sale of the property by the appointed auctioneer. The procedure is relatively quick. The customer-debtor is given the right to pay off the loan during the interim period.

Parate execution originated with state mortgage banks, then was adopted by the Bank of Ceylon and People's Bank and has now been taken up by private commercial banks. The Recovery of Loans by Banks (Special provisions) Act No. 4 of 1990, empowers all commercial banks while the Bank of Ceylon and the People's Bank has their own Acts. Anecdotal evidence suggests that parate execution has resulted in a loan recovery rate of 90 percent. The scope of the facility is best demonstrated by the language of critical provisions of the statute itself.

Section 3: Whenever default is made in the payment of any sum due on any loan, whether on account of principal or of interest or of both, default shall be deemed to have been made in respect of the whole of the unpaid portion of the loan and the interest due thereon up to date; and the Board may in its discretion take action as specified either in Section 5 or in Section 4, provided, however, that where the Board has in any case taken action, or commenced to take action, in accordance with

Section 5, nothing shall be deemed to prevent the Board at any time from subsequently taking action in that case by resolution and Section 4 if the Board deems it advisable or necessary to do so.

Section 4: Subject to the-provisions of Section 7 the Board may by resolution to be recorded in writing grant authority person specified in the resolution to sell by public auction any property mortgaged to the bank as security for any loan in respect of which default has been made in order to recover the whole of the unpaid portion of such loan, together with the money and costs recoverable under Section 13.

Section 15: (1) If the mortgaged property is sold, the Board shall issue a certificate of sale and thereupon all the right, title, and interest of the borrower to, and in, the property shall vest in the purchaser; and thereafter it shall not be competent for any person claiming through or under any disposition whatsoever of the right, title or interest of the borrower to, and in, the property made or registered subsequent to the date of the mortgage of die property to the bank, in any court to move or invalidate the sale for any cause whatsoever, or to maintain any right title or interest to, or in, the property as against the purchaser.

(2) A certificate signed by the Board under subsection (1) shall be conclusive proof with respect to the sale of any property that all the provisions of this Act relating to the sale of that property have been complied with.

(3) If the purchaser is some person other than the bank, the certificate shall be substantially in the prescribed form and, if the purchaser is the bank, the certificate shall be substantially in such other form as may be prescribed.

(4) Every certificate of sale shall be liable to stamp duty and charges as if it were a conveyance of property and to any registration and other charges authorised by law, all of which shall be payable by the purchaser.

(5) Where the property sold consists of the interest of a lessee under a lease from the State, then, if the purchaser of the property is some person other than the bank, the certificate of sale shall not be signed by the Board unless the Land Commissioner, in the exercise of his discretion, has approved the purchaser.

While it cannot be said that the parate execution scheme has created more problems than it has solved, its implementation has not come without practical problems. Gaps in the law have proved difficult to remedy. For instance, a developer of a condominium may mortgage the property and when the units are sold to buyers, there could be substantial injustice when the entire development is subject to parate execution.

The second and more pressing problem is the reach of the remedy against guarantors who have mortgaged their property to the bank to collateralise the guaranty. Usually, non-public companies are undercapitalised and have no significant assets. It is the shareholders of the companies who are possessed of assets which they offer as security. Upon a default can a bank levy a parate execution against the assets of the guarantor? Denial of a right to proceed against the assets of the guarantor would appear to stymie the purpose of the legislation which is to unblock the flow of credit. However, there has been judicial resistance to this and hostility to the concept of piercing the corporate veil in order to attach liability directly on the shareholder.

It would appear that the best course of actions for the banks would be to provide the loans jointly and severally to the company and the shareholder or provide the loan to the shareholder with the stipulation that the loan moneys be transferred to the company as equity. The only problem with the latter approach is that the bulk of the loan may be tied up as a corporate asset enforcement against which will encounter the same problems.

In *Ramachandran and Others v Hatton National Bank*, the Supreme Court held that only property owned by the borrower and provided to the bank as security will be subject to parate execution. This meant that a guarantor of the debt who has mortgaged his property to securitize the guaranty would not be subject to parate execution. Silva CJ who delivered the opinion for the majority reasoned that it is only against a person belonging to a class confined to borrower that the Board of Directors of a bank may pass a resolution authorising sale by public auction any property mortgaged to the bank by him as security for any loan in respect of which default has been made in order to recover the whole of the unpaid portion of such loan, together with the money and costs recoverable under Section 13 of the said Act. In coming to this conclusion, Silva CJ pointed out that the class of persons subject to parate execution is clearly identified in the provisions of the Act commencing from Section 2 itself. Section 2(1)(a) requires "every person to whom any loan is granted by a bank on the mortgage of property" to register with the bank the address to which a notice to him may be sent. A resolution of the Board to sell by public auction, as empowered by Section 4, has to be dispatched to this address in terms of Section 8. Similarly, the notice of sale in terms of Section 9 should be dispatched to that address. The judge states that there is a clear link in the provisions between the taking of a loan and the mortgage. The law will apply where a mortgage is given by the person to whom the loan is granted. In Sections 7, 14, 15, 16 and 17 this person is identified as the "borrower". The borrower is none other than the person to whom a loan is granted and who is required in terms of Section 2 to register his address with the bank. In terms of Section 14 where the mortgaged property is sold and an amount in excess of what is due to the bank is recovered, such amount has to be paid by the bank to the borrower. This clearly established that it is only the property mortgaged by a borrower that could be sold by a bank to recover a loan granted to him. If the provisions are extended by a process of interpretation to cover a mortgage given by a guarantor, Section 14 will bring about a preposterous result in which the guarantor's property is sold and the excess recovered is paid by the bank to the borrower, Silva CJ stated. The majority of the judges thus favoured a strict interpretation of the provisions of the Act which Silva CJ stated was in keeping with the rule of law and the existing legal position. Accordingly, parate execution was only available against those who had borrowed money by mortgaging property owned by them. The language of the Act excluded from this category mere "guarantors" who were not party to the loan agreement with the bank.

However, Shirani Bandaranayake J (as she then was), in her dissent, favoured a broader interpretation to include "third party mortgagors" who were not party to the loan provided by the bank. The dissenting judge pointed out that the loan in question had been given to both the borrower and the guarantor jointly and severally. Arguably, this was an error on the part of the bank because a borrower cannot also be simultaneously a guarantor of the same loan. It is submitted that the dissent of Bandaranayake J represents a better understanding of the law. If the majority opinion had taken into account the Roman-Dutch law rule on guarantees that the guarantor who has paid the debts of the guaranteed has rights of recourse against the latter and the law of unjust enrichment together with the law on resulting and constructive trusts, the so-called "preposterous" result could have been avoided. In *People's Bank v Yashoda Holdings Ltd*, principles of English law relating to piercing of the corporate veil were invoked to justify parate executions.

3.3   Anti-money laundering legislation

The Panama Papers has refocused the attention of the world on money laundering and tax evasion strategies of many wealthy persons. Joining the group of countries that have established reporting funds of dubious origin, Sri Lanka has enacted the Financial Transactions Reporting Act of 2006(FTRA). The following are the highlights of the FTRA: (i) FTRA require the establishment of a Financial Intelligence Unit (FIU) as a national central agency to receive, analyse and disseminate information in relation to money laundering and the financing of terrorism. The FIU is set up in the Central Bank of Sri Lanka; (ii) The FTRA obliges institutions to report to the FIU cash transactions above a value prescribed (Rs. 1 million). The term "institutions" covers a wide array of persons and entities; (iii) The FTRA requires institutions to report to the FIU all electronic fund transfers above such sum as prescribed by the regulations; (iv) All suspicious transactions also have to be reported to the FIU regardless of the amount involved; (v) The FTRA also requires an institution covered by the Act to appoint a Compliance Officer who would be responsible for the institution's compliance with the Act; (vi) The FTRA makes the opening and operating of accounts under a fictitious name, an offence; (vii) The FTRA makes "tipping-off", i. e. warning a suspect of an impending investigation, an offence; (viii) The FTRA provides for whistle-blower protection so that persons making reports under the Act are protected from civil or criminal liability and the banker's duty of confidentiality will not apply in such cases.

3.4   Foreign exchange law and regulations

Like all countries in South Asia, Sri Lanka has from the time of independence imposed controls on the outflows of currency. It is expected that the present government with its free market policies would substantially liberalise the exchange control regime that has prevailed since independence and replace existing legislation with an Exchange Control Act.

The Exchange Control Act restricts some dealings in gold, foreign currency and other properties unless such dealings have obtained the prior required permission of the Controller of Exchange. Persons in or resident in Sri Lanka may not open bank accounts abroad or acquire any foreign assets without permission. Likewise no payments in or outside Sri Lanka to a person outside Sri Lanka or to his credit can be made without the permission of the Controller of Exchange. The Exchange Control Act contains provisions in respect of securities, import and export, duty to collect debts, tourist services, shipping agencies, airline agencies, other agencies, and blocked accounts. Accordingly prudence demands that when transactions, payments and receipts involving non-residents and foreign currencies take place, a check should be made that there is compliance with the Exchange Control Act. NRFC and RFC accounts can also be opened and operated as permitted by the regulations of the Controller of Exchange. The present government expects to completely lift exchange controls in the future. However, until then one should expect strict enforcement of exchange control laws, and in doubt, clarification should be sought from the relevant department at the Central Bank. For the purpose of the Exchange Control Act the following are considered non-residents:

i. All persons whose permanent abode is outside Sri Lanka including citizens of Sri Lanka who have made their permanent abode abroad.

ii. Citizens of Sri Lanka who have emigrated from Sri Lanka or who have proceeded outside Sri Lanka for taking up employment or setting up in business or profession.

iii. (a) The Diplomatic Representative, Consul or Trade Commissioner in Sri Lanka(by whatever name or title designated) of the Government of any foreign country.

(b) Any member of the staff of any person referred to in sub-paragraph (a) who is a citizen of the country represented by such Diplomatic Representative, Consul or Trade Commissioner, and is not a person who carries on or exercises in Sri Lanka any other employment, trade, business, profession or vocation.

(c) Any expert, adviser, technician or official whose salary or principal emolument is not payable by the Government of Sri Lanka and who is brought to Sri Lanka through any specialised agency of the United Nations Organisation or any organisation approved by the minister.

(d) Any official of the United Nations Organisation, IMF, World Bank, IBRD, ADB, or other similar organisation, who is in Sri Lanka, excluding citizens of Sri Lanka who have been recruited locally.

iv. Any member of the family of any person treated as being resident outside Sri Lanka under sub-paragraphs(a), (b), (c)or (d)or paragraph(ii).

v. Any trainee from abroad who is sent to Sri Lanka under any of the Technical Cooperation Programmes of the United Nations Organisation and its Specialised Agencies or of the Colombo Plan Organisation or of any other organisation approved by the minister.

vi. Personal representatives, including attorneys, administrators, when acting solely in that capacity for a deceased person, who at the date of death was resident, for exchange control purposes, in a country outside Sri Lanka.

vii. Sri Lanka trustees of will trusts or inter vivo settlements when acting solely in that capacity where the deceased at the time of death, or the settler at the time the settlement was made resident, for Exchange Control purposes, outside Sri Lanka.

The following shall be treated as "resident in Ceylon/Sri Lanka":

(i.) Citizens of Ceylon or citizens of foreign countries married to citizens of Ceylon, if the permanent place of abode of such person is Ceylon.

(ii.) Citizens of Ceylon referred to in paragraph 1(i) above, who have preceded outside Ceylon, temporarily on holiday, business or medical treatment, or for any other similar reason.

(iii.) (a) The Diplomatic Representative, Consul or Trade Commissioner of the Government of Ceylon resident outside Ceylon (by whatever name or title designated) ;

(b) Any person who is a citizen of Ceylon, if he is a member of the staff of any person referred to in sub-paragraph (a) above, or a member of the staff of a Government Corporation, Institution or a Statutory Board incorporated in Ceylon , serving abroad, except those recruited abroad ;

(c) Any member of the family of any person treated as being resident in Ceylon under sub-paragraph (a) or (b) of paragraph 1 (iii).

(iv.) Citizens of foreign countries who are in Ceylon, except passengers in transit to other countries or visitors touring the country for pleasure or business ;

(v.) Offices and branches in Ceylon of companies, firms, banks or any other organisations whether owned by citizens of Ceylon or foreigners.

3. 5   Bank accounts

NRFC (Non-Resident Foreign Currency) account

An NRFC may be opened for (a) a citizen of Sri Lanka who is or has been employed outside Sri Lanka ; or (b) a national of a foreign country who prior to the acquisition of such nationality was a citizen of Sri Lanka ; or (c) with the prior written approval of the Controller of Exchange, a foreign employment agency licensed by the Sri Lanka Bureau of Foreign Employment. An NRFC may be opened for a person referred to in (a) and (b) above while such person is resident outside Sri Lanka or within ninety days after the return of such person to Sri Lanka.

Funds in a NRFC may be utilised for: (a) Making any payment in foreign currency to or for the credit of a person resident outside Sri Lanka; or (b) Transfer of funds from one NRFC to another NRFC; or (c) Making any payment in Sri Lankan rupees converted at the prevailing rate of exchange; or (d) Issue of traveller's cheques and, of foreign currency notes for travel outside Sri Lanka to the account holder where such holder is a person referred to in clauses (a) and (b) of paragraph 6. 2. 1 above or a proprietor, partner or a director of the account holder where such holder is a foreign employment agency, on production of an unutilised travel ticket; (e) An investment in a BOI Enterprise; (f) Subject to such restrictions as may be imposed under the Banking Act No. 30 of 1988, as security for the grant of rupee loan facilities for third parties.

RFC (Resident Foreign Currency) account

An RFC account may be opened for (a) an individual resident in Sri Lanka, whether a citizen of Sri Lanka or not, who could satisfy the authorised dealer that the individual owns or holds foreign exchange of an amount not less than five hundred United States Dollars or its equivalent in other foreign currency on inward remittances in favour of the individual or brought to Sri Lanka on arrival therein by the individual; or (b) a citizen of Sri Lanka resident in Sri Lanka who owns or holds foreign exchange of an amount not less than five hundred United States Dollars or its equivalent in other foreign currency.

Funds in an RFC may be utilised for: (a) Making any payment in foreign currency to or for the credit of a person resident outside Sri Lanka; (b) Transfer of funds from one RFC to another RFC; and (c) Making any payment in Sri Lanka in Sri Lankan rupees converted at the prevailing rate of exchange. Any documents for making any of the above payments shall be endorsed as being issued in Sri Lanka against the funds in the RFC.

3. 6   Buying and selling of gold in Sri Lanka

Extraordinary Gazette No. 1263/10 of November 22, 2002 has been issued regarding transactions for the purpose of: (i) Buying gold in Sri Lanka; (ii) Selling gold in Sri Lanka by any person who is resident in Sri Lanka; (iii) Importing into Sri

Lanka or exporting from Sri Lanka of gold by any person subject to the conditions specified in the paragraphs (2) and (3) thereto.

However gold is not allowed to be imported into Sri Lanka on consignment account basis by any person other than a licensed commercial bank or a limited liability company approved by the Controller of Exchange, which is primarily engaged in trading of gold or manufacturing gold jewellery or other gold products for exports, which has a paid up capital of not less than Rs. 10 million, which has a good financial track record for not less than three years and which has experience in gold trading for not less than three years.

3. 7   Sale of shares: Issue and transfer of company shares to non-residents

The Exchange Control Act does not permit the issuance of shares or their transfer to a non-resident without the permission of the Controller of Exchange. General permission has now been granted by the Controller of Exchange for the issue of transfer of shares in a company up to 100 percent of the issued capital of such company to non-residents, subject to certain exclusions and limitations. The payment for shares in any issue or transaction so permitted should be made out of or into a Share Investment External Rupee Account (SIERA) opened in a commercial bank in accordance with the directions given by the Controller of Exchange. All transfers, remittances of dividends and sale proceeds of securities should be through the SIERA accounts and could be permitted by an Authorised Dealer subject to the production of the following: a certificate of balance in the SIERA account at the date of application, contract notes in proof of sale price and number of shares sold and income tax clearance covering the amount to be repatriated.

References

1. Weerasooria, W. S. , The Financial System, Banking and Cheque Law in Sri Lanka, The Institute of Bankers of Sri Lanka, 1998.

2. Weerasooria, W. S. , The Law Relating to Banking and Inter-Related Services, The Institute of Bankers of Sri Lanka, 1997.

3. Weerasooria, W. S. , Is Sri Lanka's legal System Secure Enough for the Successful Operation of Banks and Banking Business? Annual Convention-Association of Professional Bankers-Sri Lanka, 2001.

4. Karunaratne, P. , How to Recover Large State Bank Default Loans?, *The Daily Mirror*, 21 July 2006.

5. Presidential Commission on Finance and Banking—First Interim Report—31 March 1991.

6. Presidential Commission on Finance and Banking—Second Interim Report—31 July 1991.

7. Presidential Commission on Finance and Banking—Third Interim Report—21 July 1992.

Chapter 4   Infrastructure Laws and Regulations

4.1   BOO, BOT and BOOT projects

Private sector participation in the construction of infrastructure projects first began to be popular in East Asia and is now common in many parts of the developing world. These projects given acronyms according to the nature of the involvement in and duration of the private sector party's involvement are commonly referred to as Build-Own-Operate (BOO), Build-Own-Transfer (BOT) or Build-Own-Operate-Transfer (BOOT). The Sri Lankan Board of Investment has been established a Bureau of Infrastructure Investment (BII) to oversee private sector participation in infrastructure projects. The BII is directly responsible for all transactions pertaining to BOO projects and BOT infrastructure projects in Sri Lanka. The BII functions as the promoting, facilitating and co-ordinating agency for servicing the Line Ministries/ Line Agencies in this regard under the overall supervision of the Ministry of Finance. However, the final responsibility and authority of selection and approval will lie with the relevant line Ministry and the Cabinet of Ministers respectively.

These projects typically take the form of privately owned and managed ventures or public-private partnerships whereby the resources, risk and profits connected with the venture are shared. Projects are usually structured on the basis of BOO, BOT or BOOT. The Government of Sri Lanka has sought the collaboration of the private sector, local and foreign, on mutually beneficial terms in the development of such infrastructure.

In determining the terms of the BOO/BOT/BOOT projects, the Government is tasked to negotiate with the objective of providing satisfactory services to the public at reasonable cost, while providing the private sector owner/operator with a risk-adjusted return. In the case of projects initiated by the Government, a tendering process must be conducted to secure such services at reasonable cost to the consumer by encouraging competition among potential private sector participants, while ensuring that their return on investment is reasonable but not excessive.

Private investors are already active in telecommunications services such as cellular services, wireless local loop systems and pay phone networks. Investments into the power sector, ranging from mini-hydro systems to large-scale generation plants, and the port sector are now being implemented. Other opportunities in infrastructure investments are wide ranging highways; public transport and environment are a few examples. Foreign ownership up to 100 percent is allowed in these ventures.

In 1996, the Government issued new guidelines on the Government Tender Procedure. Part II of these guidelines deals with private sector finance projects. These guidelines require a Government agency which decides that certain infrastructure projects are to be implemented by or with the participation of the private sector to follow the procedure laid down in those guidelines. According to those guidelines, the BII is the coordinating agency of all activities in relation to such projects.

In terms of the guidelines set down by the Government, the procurement process relating to infrastructure projects commences with the issue of a request for proposals. The proposals will be evaluated by a Project Committee which functions under a Cabinet Appointed Negotiating Committee (CANC).

In the alternative, in terms of the guidelines it is also possible for an investor to submit an unsolicited proposal. Where such a proposal is submitted, the relevant Government Agency will examine the need for such an infrastructure project and if the need for such a project is recognised, the Government Agency will thereafter submit the unsolicited proposal to a competitive process. By this method the Government expects to obtain the best terms even from such an unsolicited proposal.

Infrastructure projects which are not identified to be financed under the Consolidated Fund may be identified to be financed/developed by private investors. Projects financed by the private sector will be considered on a BOO/BOT/BOOT and other variants would be built, owned and operated by the investor or transferred or leased to the public sector after a concession period.

Coordination of projects

Preliminary Screening: All priority projects identified by the respective line Ministries will be discussed informally with the BII and a financial and technical viability report to screen such projects has to be prepared jointly by the proposing agency and vetted by the BII for clearance by the Ministry of Finance and Planning. Once the clearance from the Ministry of Finance and Planning is obtained the line

Ministry will present a Cabinet Memorandum including the formal Project Proposal seeking approval of the Cabinet to proceed with the Project. Infrastructure Projects Infrastructure Development Projects managed by the Private Sector on BOO, BOT or other variant basis, which will be wholly or partly implemented by the private sector include, but are not limited to: power plants, highways, ports, airports, telecommunications, railways, transport systems, industrial parks, solid waste management, water supply and drainage, warehouses, housing, markets, etc. , land reclamation and other infrastructure.

Steering the Project Proposals: All matters pertaining to BOO/BOT Projects will be channelled through a CANC assisted by a Project Committee(PC). The approving authority for award of a BOO/BOT project is the Cabinet. Final recommendation of CANC on the award as well as recommendations at various important stages would also be submitted to the Cabinet for approval.

Procedure for Processing Proposals: Formal approval for the Project: Priority projects considered by the Government of Sri Lanka(GOSL) for development through the private sector, once identified and screened by the relevant line Ministry with the assistance of the BII (in regard to the economic and financial viability of the project), will then be submitted to the Ministry of Finance and Planning for preliminary clearance. On the determination of the Ministry of Finance and Planning that the project should be proceeded with, the relevant line Ministry would then have to submit a Cabinet Memorandum including the outline of the project proposal seeking: (i) The formal approval for the project in principle; (ii) The appointment of a Negotiating Committee by the Cabinet with authority to develop the proposal. The relevant line Ministry would thereafter, request the Ministry of Finance and Planning to appoint a Project Committee.

Cabinet Appointed Negotiating Committee: The Cabinet will appoint a Negotiating Committee to handle all matters pertaining to BOO/BOT projects and make recommendations on the selection of a proponent. The composition of Cabinet Negotiating Committee will be determined by the Cabinet. Generally the Chairman of CANC would be the Secretary to the Treasury or Deputy Secretary to the Treasury. The Secretary of the relevant line Ministry/Ministries and Chairman/BOI may be the other members.

Project Committee: The PC will be constituted once the Cabinet in principle approves the project. The Secretary to the Treasury at the request of the Secretary of the line Ministry in liaison with BII will appoint the members of the PC. Its members will include representatives of the following Ministries/Departments: the Line Ministry, Ministry of Finance & Planning, BOI/BII, Relevant State Agencies, members from the Attorney-General's Department, any other Ministry/Department/ Agency as appropriate, and the Central Environmental Authority. The PC may co-opt consultants/experts from time to time to obtain expert advice. A representative of BII will function as the Secretary/Convener to the Project Committee. The Committee will service project development and will also be responsible for guiding the project through its various stages of implementation.

Terms of Reference of Project Committee(TOR of PC): The PC will be mainly responsible for steering the preparation of the Request for Proposal(RFP) documents and submit them for the approval of the CANC. The RFP would include the following: (i) criteria of assessment of technical and financial viability of the project; (ii) details of specifications; (iii) models of relevant agreements as decided on a case by case basis; (iv) environmental data and information; and (v) any other relevant information. The other responsibilities of the PC are as follows: schedule bids and evaluate same for consideration of the CANC; monitor the progress during project development phase and report to CANC periodically; co-ordinate all activities including scheduling meetings, correspondence, etc. , relating to the project.

Legal Obligations: Because negotiations on project proposals may result in legal obligations on the part of the Government, recommendation for any contractual commitments and Government guarantees, if any would be made by the relevant line Ministry/BII in consultation with the Treasury and Attorney-General and be approved by the Cabinet prior to entering into any formal contractual commitment.

Time Frame: The period of time from invitation to conclusion viz. , the issuing of a Request for Proposals(RFP) to signing of an Implementation Agreement (IA) should be limited to one year (12 months). However, the time frame may be extended with Cabinet approval depending on the complexities of the project proposal on a case by case basis.

Unsolicited Proposals: Line Ministries, Agencies and BOI/BII receiving unsolicited proposals are required to have them processed according to the procedures applicable to solicited proposals. An unsolicited proposal may contain all basic information required by the GOSL/Line Ministry/BII to ascertain the economic and financial viability of the project, including the following: (i) outline technical details of the project. (ii) Financial details to demonstrate the justification of the total cost/ premium requested. (iii) Letters from financial institutions and consortium members agreeing to commit funds if the project is accepted by GOSL and to proceed with construction. Once the need is determined the relevant line Ministry should, by advertisement, call for proposals on the same generalised lines, incorporating the actual goals sought to be achieved. The party which made the original offer should be given a chance to improve on it in the invitation for bids/offers where the proposal has been significantly changed to suit the needs and objectives of the agency involved. This would apply in the case of all BOO/BOT proposals, sale of public assets or for the grant of exclusive rights for any State sponsored venture. No decision will be taken solely on the basis of unsolicited offers without inviting proposals/bids through public advertisement. When owing to urgent and exceptional circumstances, it becomes necessary to deviate from the above-prescribed procedure, specific Cabinet approval is required.

Procedures for issuing RFP and Assisting Bidders

Once the approval of the Cabinet of the Ministers is obtained to proceed with the project, the Line Ministry will solicit proposals from the private sector on the basis of International Competitive Bidding (ICB) for the award of the project through a RFP.

Method for calling of Proposals: The CANC must ensure that the RFP carries sufficient information to solicit a complete proposal from potential bidders. The method for issuing of RFP would be by advertisement and solicitation of responses from interested bidders on the basis of International Competitive Bidding.

Pre-qualification of Proponents: The CANC may decide whether the pre-qualification of proponents should be done. However all large scale projects (estimated cost USD 100 million or more), and/or in the case of technically complex projects, the solicitation of bids should be preceded by a pre-qualification of proponents.

Invitation for Expression of Interest (EOI): If CANC decides to follow the process of pre-qualification of proponents, it would be initiated by the issue of an invitation for Expression of Interest. This invitation of EOI will be given the widest publicity in the international media.

Evaluation of EOI: The EOI will be evaluated by the Project Committee and will make its recommendations to the CANC for approval. Only the pre-qualified firms will be eligible for the issuance of the RFP.

Publication of RFP: The RFP will be given wide publicity, through foreign and local newspapers and electronic media and through Sri Lanka missions abroad.

Contents of RFP: A RFP will contain: (a) all relevant information on the project;(b) specific information required from the bidders to evaluate the proposal; (c) a defined format for the bidders to follow in submitting their proposals. The RFP would consist of the following components: (a) Introduction: This part will outline the Government's policy on private sector investment in infrastructure projects. (b) Summary of the Project: This part will provide a summary of the project and the main responsibilities of the project bidders during the construction and operation phases.

Technical and financial proposals: This part will provide information for the bidders on preparation of technical and financial proposals.

Evaluation and Selection Process: This part will provide the main information required from the bidders, including the technical parameters of the project, the basis for screening and scheme of evaluation of the proposals, and subsequent steps. The information provided in this section will be set out in sufficient detail so that the selection is unambiguous and the process is clearly understood by the potential investors or bidders.

Contractual, financial and legal framework: This part will describe: (a) drafts of the contracts and agreements which will need to be entered into between the private and public sector agencies involved; (b) financial requirements; (c) fiscal and regulatory issues and the relevant laws; and (d) The Bid/Performance Bonds required to be entered into.

Private Sector Infrastructure Development Company (PSIDC): Financing could be obtained from the PSIDC. This organisation has been set up with the support from the World Bank and other multilateral Agencies for the purpose of disbursing long term subordinated debt to qualifying Private Sector Infrastructure Projects. If these funds are to be used for projects, WB procurement regulations for the portion of the procurement to be financed by the Fund have to be followed.

Schedules and Appendices: In addition to the above components, the RFP will be supported by "Schedules and Appendices" containing supplementary descriptive information relating to the project and the procedures and formats for the submission of proposals, as follows:

Schedule 1: Further Information for Bidders. This schedule will give detailed supporting information on aspects of the project which is not fully covered by the

RFP;

Schedule 2: Proposal Contents. This schedule will provide detailed formats and structures for the submission of proposals by the bidders. The structures will be designed to meet the particular needs of the various parties involved in the screening and evaluation of the proposals. The information to be provided by bidders would cover: (a) general information on the consortium of parties to the proposal; (b) technical and environmental information; (c) implementation schedule; (d) cost and pricing structure; (e) financing the project and related issues.

Responsibility for Preparation of the RFP: The Project Committee, which includes representatives from the relevant Ministry or Agency, supported by technical consultants, if necessary, will bear the responsibility for the preparation of the RFP documents.

Clarifications: The RFP will have instructions inviting bidders to seek clarifications or supplementary information in writing, within the time stipulated but not exceeding two months following the date of issue of the RFP. The Project Committee in consultation with the relevant Ministry, will supply written answers to all questions, and send copies of these to all parties which have purchased the RFP, provided such answers will not amend or add to the RFP in any way. If the answer will materially affect the RFP then the Project Committee should obtain approval from the CANC. CANC may convene a bidder's conference on their own or if requested by at least two bidders within a specified period of time not exceeding two months from the date of publication of the RFP.

Amendments to the RFP: If necessary and up to thirty days before the date of submission of proposals, the Project Committee may, with the approval of the CANC amend or add to the RFP through issuing formal addenda to all who have purchased copies of the RFP. If a major change is made, the time given for submission of proposals should be extended accordingly.

Announcement of Proposal: The Secretary, Ministry of Finance and Planning will invite proposals in the international and national press and give publicity through local diplomatic representatives as well as through Sri Lankan Missions abroad and the electronic media. The press notice may also be sent to all potentially interested firms that have been in contact with the line Ministry/line Agency/BO/BII or otherwise expressed an interest. The announcement will provide a brief description of the project, and indicate: (a) the company profile and experience of the bidders, if required; (b) The address at which the RFP can be obtained; (c) Any payment required for purchasing the documents; (d)Closing date for collection of documents.

Issuing of RFP: The RFP will be issued by the Executing Agency or by the relevant line Ministry after collecting the required non-refundable form fee.

Proposal Guarantee: The proposal must be accompanied by a Proposal Guarantee for a sum as requested in the RFP. Guarantees issued by the following institutions are acceptable guarantees: (i) A bank operating in Sri Lanka approved by the Central Bank of Sri Lanka; (ii) A bank based in another country but the security or guarantee "confirmed" by a bank operating in Sri Lanka; (iii) A reputed insurance company operating in Sri Lanka accepted by the Treasury for acceptance of guarantees. (iv) A letter of credit issued by a foreign bank, but "confirmed" by a bank operating in Sri Lanka. (V) A fixed deposit or a pass book of a bank operating in Sri Lanka, deposits made in the name of the executing agency. (vi) Any other Agency approved by the Treasury from time to time. Time for submission of proposals;The period for submitting proposals will normally be three months. This may be increased to six months depending on the nature of the project. Proposals received after the stipulated closing date and time or due to the reasons of critically non-conformity with the RFP(e. g. non submission of a proposal guarantee)should be rejected by the CANC.

Opening of Proposals: The proposals received including Technical and Financial Proposals would be opened by the CANC or Proposal Opening Committee (POC) authorised by the CANC, immediately after the closing of bids. All project proponents are eligible to be present at the opening of proposals. The membership of the POC includes representatives nominated by the following Ministries/ Departments/Agencies: (i) Line Ministry/Ministries; (ii) Ministry of Finance & Planning; (iii) BOI/BII; (iv) Relevant State Agencies.

Announcement at the Proposal Opening: The following details should be recorded in a book meant for the purpose and announced immediately after the opening of proposals; (a) The names of the proponents; (b) Value of the proposal guarantee and the name of the issuing agency; (c) Whether both technical and financial proposals are submitted.

Revival of Project: If any proposal for which RFP has been issued previously is revived after the lapse of one year from the closing date for proposals, the RFP should be revised accordingly and new approvals should be obtained from the Cabinet before proceeding with the proposal.

Preliminary Evaluation of Proposals

Responsibilities of PC in relation to Evaluation of Proposals: Proposals received by the deadline specified in the RFP will be evaluated by the PC in three stages: (a) Assessment of the adequacy of the proposal—whether all the identified key requirements, such as the bid bond, etc., have been met in the stipulated; (b) Assessment of the responsiveness to the requirements of the RFP and disqualification of non-responsive RFP documents; (c) Evaluation of proposals in order to rank the competing bids, on a clear and objectively verifiable criterion and in all cases where possible based on the tariff structure adjusted for any costs to be borne by the Government. The members of the Project Committee must, where possible, be assigned the evaluation responsibility on a full time basis. The PC will assign Sectoral and Sectional responsibilities to the experienced members for evaluating the various components of the proposal with reference to the feasibility studies, where available. During the evaluation process extreme confidentiality shall be maintained.

Screening of Proposals: All proposals received by the closing date will be included in the screening process and the final evaluation will be confined to the proposals, which pass the screening tests. The PC will ensure that all proposals selected for consideration are: (a) Technically sound in terms of meeting the functional requirements of the project within the necessary time scale, (b) environmentally acceptable, subject to Environmental Impact Assessment EIA) clearance, and (c) financially viable. Evaluation of the proposals will strictly adhere to the criteria specified in the RFP. The evaluation will be completed within three months from the date of receipt of proposals.

Information Screening: When copies of the proposals are provided to the PC, it will assess whether the information provided is sufficient to enable them to complete the evaluation. Bidders shall be notified of all cases of inadequate, unclear or inconsistent information within a specified period. Following closing of the proposal and clarifications should be obtained in writing.

Report of Responsiveness: The Project Committee will assess the general qualifications and experience of the bidders, contractors and suppliers if they have been nominated. If they have not been nominated, the successful bidders should be required to submit the names of the associated companies to the PC for submission to the CANC.

Non-responsive proposals will be rejected by the CANC: Following receipt of all the requested additional information from the bidders, the PC will prepare a report on the completeness of the information supplied for each proposal. This report will include recommendations on any proposal which should be rejected for being incomplete or unresponsive. The decision to reject on the basis of non-responsiveness should be made by the CANC.

Technical Screening: Only the proposals determined to be responsive as above should be examined through a technical screening to ensure whether the given proposals: (a) are capable of meeting the key technical performance criteria as required in the RFP; (b) will perform within the key environmental standards set out in the RFP; (c) comply with health and safety standards in force in Sri Lanka.

Financial Screening: Financial screening is required to establish that: (a) the proposal is financially acceptable; (b) the bidders and their financial partners have a high financial standing and reputation and are capable of raising the required financial resources; and (c) the outline of the financing plan prepared in response to the RFP is fundamentally sound and meets the requirements of project investments bridging any period of negative cash flow. The financial screening carried out by the PC will assess whether the financing plan is realistic, focusing on the credit-worthiness and the financial strength of the bidders and also their bankers' and financial managers' experience.

Cost Screening: Cost screening should be carried out by the PC to ensure that: (a) the bidders have included in their estimates all relevant capital and operating costs of the project; (b) the cost estimates have been clearly set out on the basis of current prices of equipment and other inputs; (c) the cost estimates which form the basis for the tariff, are reasonable.

Basis for Cost Screening: In preparation for the cost screening, the Project Committee shall develop their own capital and operating cost estimates for the project, drawing on the experience gained elsewhere in Government for like projects, with possible inputs from the World Bank and Asian Development Bank. These estimates should have been prepared before the bidders finalised their proposals, so that they are available when proposals are opened. The estimates should be produced on a basis comparable with the cost estimate structure specified in the RFP. The Project Committee will identify relevant capital or operating costs which have been omitted or cost estimates which are significantly out of line with what the Committee considers to be reasonable estimates.

Clarifications and Modifications to Cost Structure: All apparent discrepancies in relation to cost structure will be raised with the bidders during the clarification process and explanations obtained. However during this process, no modifications that will alter the amounts of the estimate so as to materially affect the outcome of the evaluation could be introduced. Cost estimates, which are considered to be completed and clearly set out, should be screened for their reasonableness and judged against the estimate of the costs compiled by the Project Committee. For this comparison, suitable adjustments will be made to place all competing cost estimates on a uniform basis. All the estimates should be exclusive of financing costs. The original estimates of the Project Committee may be suitably adjusted if so indicated by the clarification process with the bidders, where all bidders had adopted costing patterns significantly similar and deviating from the estimate of the PC.

Financial Evaluation of Competing Proposals: The RFP would include a financial template or a "critical factor test" (100 or more in number) which the project proponent is expected to meet on a self-assessment basis. The table will enable the proponent to assess himself by answering "Yes/No". He should be able to answer up to a minimum of 80 percent "Yes" to qualify for the final round, i. e. the Financial Evaluation. At this stage the price per unit will be determined. After all proposals have been screened fully, the proposals would be ranked on the basis of points system specified in the RFP. The weight age would be higher for principal considerations relevant to the project.

Evaluation Criteria

Key Factors of Evaluation: The key factor in the comparative evaluation of different proposals will be: (a) the price offered, e. g. the cost per KWh for power, the proposed toll for a toll road, the rent for a facility, sale price per unit etc. The "base price" includes the fixed and variable components of the unit costs to the public sector entity purchasing the product on the basic assumptions stated in the RFP with regard to inflation, exchange rate, fuel prices for power, etc. Where the project envisages Government participation, the relative costs of such participation will be factored into the evaluation; (b) Duration of operation period; (c) The tariff structure- the most favourable tariff structure adjusted for any costs to be borne by the Government. The Project Committee would have prepared a financial model of the project, which will enable the necessary comparisons and analyses to be made. The evaluation will also have to allow for differences between proposals such as type and size of equipment, construction period and operating life of the project. The calculations should initially be based on the general assumptions in the RFP. This is the base price component of the price evaluation.

Indexation Risk: Indexation risk should be assessed using the criteria in the RFP by testing each proposal by the sensitivity assumptions. The sensitivity of the bidder's prices to the changes in the basic assumptions, given the individual profiles of cost and indexation arrangements, should be analysed. The indexation risk will vary from one proposal to another due to different financing plans, cost structures or price profiles over the time.

Evaluation of Price Escalations (Escalation Formula): The RFP will have an indication of the cost items for price negotiation which might be considered reasonable, but bidders will probably have some of their own cost items, which will have to be recognised. The factors taken into account in assessing price negotiation risk and allocating points will be noted in the evaluation report. If possible, the assessment of the risk will be combined with the comparison of the base prices to yield the expected base prices after the price negotiations have been closed.

Evaluation of Technical Aspects: The main criteria applied to the technical evaluation are: (a) the technical capability and organisation of the sponsor, and their experience with similar projects in similar environments; (b) for power plants, an assessment of operational flexibility and the reliability of plant performance; (c) the sponsor's implementation plan, including the length of the construction period and the planned commissioning/opening date, (d) the extent to which the proposal gives regard to the environmental impact of the project; (e) the procedures to be adopted for matters such as quality assurance, testing, commissioning and training of personnel. The relative importance of these factors should be, will have to be identified at the time of the preparation of documents.

Evaluation of Financing Plan: This is the primary responsibility of the financial experts. The main criteria are: (a) the financial standing and resources of the sponsor and its bankers in relation to the size of the project; (b) the soundness and flexibility of the financing plan in terms of the Project Company's liquidity position throughout the life of the project, and its ability to survive adverse events which could result in a loss or reduction of cash flow; (c) the quality and clarity of the financial model.

General Responsiveness: The Project Committee is required to point out any major deviations from RFP and the overall obligations of Government in supporting the project and any legal, financial and fiscal implications.

Final report of the Project Committee

The Project Committee will issue a final report to the CANC, which will consist of the interim reports issued during the evaluation phase (Pricing, Technical, Financing Plan and General). A comprehensive executive summary will be prepared to include the following: (1) Introduction: Summary of the process from the issuance of the RFP to the selection of Finalists and clarifications with Finalists; (2) Technical: Summary of the technical review compared to the RFP requirements and comparing each proposal; (3) Commercial: Summary of Bid Bond and proposed Letters of Association from prospective project company members; (4) Financial: Summary of capital cost and price of product(power, water, tolls, etc.) presented in detail comparing each proposal; (5) Price Negotiations: Summary of each sponsor's price negotiations and an evaluation of the impact of each price negotiation on the cost of the product; (6) Conclusions: Summary of PC's overall ranking and recommendations.

Negotiations and Award of Contract

Negotiations: The CANC will conduct the final negotiations with the selected bidder. If necessary, the assistance of PC may be obtained for negotiations. In BOO/BOT projects price negotiation and risk-allocation will be the crucial factors.

Letter of Intent (LOI): After the negotiations are successfully completed, the PC with the relevant Line Ministry will prepare a draft LOI for approval by the CANC and finally by the Cabinet. Attorney-General's concurrence for draft LOI should be obtained before the approval by the CANC and the Cabinet.

The Purpose of the LOI: It is to grant to the bidder exclusivity in relation to the project for an agreed period to enable the sponsor to complete all activities and preparations leading up to signing of the final contracts and agreements. The LOI is signed by the Secretary of the line Ministry and the Head of the Line Agency involved and is countersigned by the bidder accepting the LOI.

The LOI will typically be a letter with necessary annexes and will contain the following information: (a) a statement of the period for which project exclusivity is conferred; (b) a summary of the sponsor's Bank Guarantee as required on acceptance of the LOI; (c) a completion of all amendments to the proposal as agreed with the

PC/CANC;(d)a statement setting out all the price negotiations agreed upon;(e)a statement of the project sponsor's obligations during the period of exclusivity;(f)a summary of the relevant guaranteed technical performance criteria upon which the LOI is based;(g)requirements of the EIA;(h)any extensions to the LOI may be granted only after receipt of approval from CANC.

Sponsor's Obligations: The project sponsor will:(a) conduct detailed investigations sufficient to confirm the accuracy of the RFPs information, and undertake other studies necessary to close the price negotiations set out in the LOI;(b)agree to negotiate with PC and the line Ministry on any adjustment in tariff permitted by the price negotiations;(c)establish the project company;(d)apply for and obtain all required permissions and consents;(e)conclude negotiations on all relevant contracts and agreements including financing.

Performance Guarantee: Within two weeks of the receipt of the LOI, the sponsor shall furnish a Performance Guarantee for fulfilling his obligations, valid for an agreed period and encashable without recourse to the sponsor in the form of an irrevocable Bank Guarantee to the value of five percent of the project cost. If the Guarantee is not furnished within six weeks, the LOI will automatically lapse and neither the sponsor nor the Project Company shall have any claim for compensation or damages against the Government of Sri Lanka or any other Governmental agency on any grounds. The period of six weeks may be extended under exceptional circumstances by the CANC upon a maximum period of eight weeks. The Period of Exclusivity:The period of exclusivity granted in the LOI should be sufficient to allow the sponsor to complete the tasks required by the LOI. The period should not usually extend beyond six months, but a longer period may be allowed for complicated projects by the CANC on the recommendation of the PC. Extension to Exclusivity: The agreed extensions to the proposal's exclusivity not exceeding one year may be authorised by the CANC. Extensions for longer periods than one year, where absolutely necessary should be granted with the approval of the Cabinet.

Price Negotiations Leading to a Final Fixing of Prices: Major subject for final negotiations should be the price. Price negotiations should:(a)take into account the allocation of risks between GOSL and the Bidder;(b)be restricted to a minimum in terms of both number and cost;(c)give the reasons for the particular costs clearly;(d)establish clearly the relationships between the results of further investigations and the consequent price changes;and(e)define the limits on the price changes which will be permitted.

Finalising the project (solicited and unsolicited)

Period covered: At the finalisation stage common procedures would be adopted for both solicited and unsolicited proposals. This would cover the period from the issuance and acceptance of the LOI for solicited proposals and approval of pre-feasibility and feasibility studies for unsolicited proposals, up to the signing of agreements and the contracts. Unsolicited proposals will have to follow from the stage of the approval of feasibility studies the same procedure as solicited proposals.

Major Activities: The major activities, which will take place during the finalisation stage, include: (a) the establishment of a Project Company; (b) preparation of an implementation plan by the project bidders (or GOSL appointed consultants) and its appraisal by the Project Committee; (c) finalization of the price negotiations, (d) application for, and where possible, obtaining of consents and approval by the project sponsor; (e) negotiation and completion of all other agreements and contracts, (f) finalization of the financing plan.

Agreements: A typical list of agreements would be: (a) the Implementation Agreement between the Government and the Project Company; (b) the Service or Product Purchase Agreement authorising the sponsor to charge and collect reasonable tolls, fees and rentals for use of the project facility. These will not exceed those incorporated in the relevant contracts based on a pre-determined formula using official price indices and as agreed by contract for unsolicited proposals; (c) for thermal power plants or similar projects, a Fuel Supply, Sale/Purchase Agreement with price; (e) if applicable, a Turnkey Contract; (f) an Operation and Maintenance Contract; (g) the Shareholders Agreement or Joint Venture Agreement between project Bidders; (h) Loan Agreement and other documents necessary for the financial obligations of the Project Company; (i) Escrow Agreements; (j) Land Lease or Purchase Agreements; (k) Insurance policies; (l) Trust Deeds; and (m) All approvals and licenses required.

The Product Purchase Agreement (PPA): The RFP and the LOI will include a draft PPA which will include: (a) the date of commencement and duration of the PPA; (b) the obligations of the Project Company to design, construct, operate and maintain the project; (c) the arrangement for commissioning and testing the project at completion; (d) the target performance levels and the procedure for meeting them during the life of the project; (e) payment obligations to the project company by the

Government or other Agency purchasing the product, including all details of charges and arrangements for indexation; (f) the respective obligations of the Government entity and the Project Company to install any facilities required to put the project into operation, i. e. inter-connection facilities for power, feeder roads for highways, etc. (g) the Project Company's obligations to operate the project to meet minimum accepted international standards, (h) the Project Company's obligations to maintain the project and the arrangements for advance scheduling of planned maintenance; (i) the arrangements for establishing an Operating Committee to deal with technical and operational issues; (j) the arrangement for dealing with disputes, arbitration and force majeure events; (k) bonus and penalty clauses.

Fuel Supply Agreement(FSA): In the case of projects such as gas-fired and oil-fired power plants there may be usually a FSA between the Project Company and a public sector body such as the Ceylon Petroleum Corporation. This is a straightforward document, which sets forth the fuel supplier's obligations to supply and the Project Company's obligation to receive fuel over the life of the project or any other specified period.

The Implementation Agreement(IA): The contents of the IA will be negotiated by the BII, the line Ministry or Agency involved and the Project Company who may be assisted by their legal advisors and will be submitted to the CANC for ap Cabinet Approval: Before signature of the IA, the final proposal with the agreed draft agreements would be submitted to the Cabinet for approval. The line Ministry submits the Cabinet Memorandum and the CANC recommendations along with a report compiled by the BII, which will include: (a) the results of the appraisal of the PC summarized by BII, its consultants and the relevant State Agency involved; (b) the final price and other major features negotiated; (c) the major features of the negotiated IA.

Signing of Agreement: After approval is granted by the Cabinet of Ministers and when all agreements and contracts have been finalised, the Ministry of Finance and Planning, Line Ministry and the Project Company will sign the IA. All agreements have to be signed at the same time.

Chapter 5   Employment Law

5.1   Introduction

Sri Lankans are employed in various fields, such as the resource extraction sector, or tea, rubber, and coconut plantations. Fisheries and mining sectors have thousands of employees. The government and state owned enterprises also account for hundreds of thousands of jobs. Persons also work as domestics and care-givers. Thousands of Sri Lankans constitute a part of the migrant labour workforce and account for a substantial part of Sri Lanka's revenue in hard currency. Except in the case of domestic labour, Sri Lankan employment law does not recognise the American labour law doctrine of employment at will. Law and regulations address almost all facets of the employment relationship and thus it is no surprise that there are a plethora of laws on the subject.

Sri Lankan tort law recognises the doctrine of vicarious responsibility whereby the employer is liable for the wrongs of the employee committed in the course of employment. The principle may be enunciated as follows: "An employer will be liable not only for a wrongful act of an employee that he has authorised but also for a wrongful and unauthorised mode of doing some act authorised by the master. But a master(as opposed to an employer of an independent contractor) is liable even for acts which he has not authorised, provided they are so closely connected with the acts which he has authorised that they rightly may be regarded as modes, (although improper modes) of doing them". The Sri Lankan courts have held that the Roman-Dutch law principles (applicable in Sri Lanka) and the English principles are the same.

5.2   Overview of Sri Lankan labour legislation

Legislation in Sri Lanka relating to industrial, employment and labour relations can be divided into seven categories as follows:

Laws on social security

Employees provident Fund Act, Employees Provident Fund (Special Provisions) Act, Employees Trust Fund Act, Employees Trust Fund (Special Provisions) Act, Payment of Gratuity Act.

Laws on welfare and wellbeing of employees

Employment of Women, Young Persons and Children Act, Maternity Benefits Ordinance, Employment of Females in Mines Ordinance.

Occupational safety and health and workmen's compensation

Factories Ordinance and Workmen's Compensation Ordinance.

Laws relating to terms and conditions of employment

Wages Board Ordinance, Shop and Office Employees (Regulation of Employment and Remuneration) Act, Employment of Trainees (Private Sector) Act.

Labour relations

Trade Union Ordinance Employees Councils Act, Industrial Disputes Act, Termination of Employment of Workers (Special Provisions) Act.

Laws relating to plantations and estate labour

Estate Labour (Indian) Ordinance, Medical Wants Ordinance, Indian Immigrant Labour Ordinance, Minimum Wages (Indian Labour) Ordinance, Trade Union Representatives (Entry in Estates) Act, Estate Quarters (Special Provisions) Act, Allowances to Plantation Workers Act, Services Contracts Ordinance.

Foreign employment

Sri Lanka Bureau of Foreign Employment Act.

5. 3 Summary of key labour legislation

5. 3. 1 Laws relating to Social Security

Social Security of employees is addressed by three main mechanisms. They are the Employees' Provident Fund, Employees' Trust Fund and the Gratuity Fund. By them employees are granted financial benefits upon completion of a statutory period of service, change of employment or reaching the retirement age.

Employees Provident Fund (EPF): The Employees Provident Fund was established by Act No. 15 of 1958. Since then there have been nine amending Acts on the subject. Employers have to remit every month to the Central Bank, an amount equivalent to 20 percent of the employee's total earnings to the Fund. The employee's contribution is eight percent and the employer has to contribute an amount equivalent to 12 percent of the employee's total earnings. "Earnings" include wages, cost of living allowances and similar allowances, payment in respect of holidays and leave, cash value of food provided by the employer and meal allowance but exclude overtime payments. Payments for work done during normal working hours on weekly holidays, Poya (full moon) days or public holidays should also be considered as earnings for the computation of EPF contributions. Failure to remit EPF results in surcharges ranging from five to 50 percent.

Employees Trust Fund (ETF): The Employees' Trust Fund Act No. 46 of 1980 (as amended) obliges the employer only to contribute monthly three percent of the employee's total wages to the Trust Fund created under it.

Gratuity: A "Gratuity" to an employee is over and above the EPF and ETF payments discussed above and is governed by the Payment of Gratuity Act No. 12 of 1983. A gratuity is a lump sum payment made in recognition for services at the end of a period of employment. Under the Act any employer who has employed more than 15 workmen in any industry during the 12 months preceding the termination of the workman in question, is required to pay a gratuity to that workman if he has completed five years of service under him. The amount for monthly paid employee is calculated at the rate of half a month's salary for each completed year of service. A gratuity is also payable to workmen who are paid weekly or daily, at the rate of 14 days salary for each completed year of service. A gratuity is payable whether termination was by the employer of employee, except if the termination was for reasons of fraud, misappropriation of the employer's money or wilful damage to the employer's property, the amount of the loss or damage may be deducted from the amount of gratuity due under the Act. If the workman dies while employed, any gratuity due to him must be paid to his legal heirs.

5.3.2 Laws relating to welfare/well-being of the employees

Employment of Females in Mines Ordinance: No female of any age at any time, who has not been exempted by regulation, shall perform or be employed on any underground work in a mine or enter a mine for the performance of any work.

Maternity Benefits Ordinance: This is a law that was first enacted as far back as 1939. Subsequently, there were seven other amending Acts passed in this regard from

1952 to 1985.

An employee is restricted from knowingly employing any women during the period of four weeks immediately following her confinement. "Maternity benefits" mean the amount payable under the provisions of this Ordinance to a woman worker. A woman worker who has no children or has only one child is entitled to a period of 12 weeks for which maternity benefits must be paid by the employer. However, in the event the woman has two or more children, she will be entitled for a six-week period of maternity benefits.

Employment of Women, Young Persons and Children Act: There are three Acts on this subject. They are in relation to employment of women, young persons and children at (a) industrial undertakings and at sea; (b) other than industrial undertakings night; and (c) at sea.

Employment of women and young persons at night: The legislation prohibits employment of any person under the age of 18 at night whether in a public or private industrial undertaking or branch. Women can be employed at night subject to certain basic requirements. It must be voluntary and written authority must be got from the Labour authorities for working after 10:00 pm; for night work she must get 1.5 times the normal pay; female wardens must ensure the worker's welfare; there must be availability of rest rooms and refreshments and not more than ten days of night work can be allocated per month. Exemptions are granted to women holding a management or technical nature position, or those who are employed in health and welfare services and in an industrial undertaking in which only members of the family are employed.

Employment in industrial undertakings and at sea: No employer can employ a child of age 15 or below unless otherwise the undertaking or the ship is one which only members of the same family are employed or children from a technical school with the approval and under the supervision by an authority of the technical school.

Employment other than in industrial undertakings and at sea: This part applies in relation to employment other than employment in industrial undertakings and at sea. Children under 14 cannot be employed during school hours and in the night(8:00 pm to 6:00 am)and must not be made to lift or move heavy items which can injure the child. Nor can such children be given work in any occupation injurious to their health, education or wellbeing as spelt out in the relevant provisions. Importantly, no such child can be employed in work commonly referred to as the "street industry".

Occupational Safety and Health, Factories Ordinance and workmen's compensation: Occupational health is regulated by the Factories Ordinance of 1942 and all persons operating factories are conversant with the comprehensive provisions of this legislation first enacted in 1942. There have been over seven amendments to the law. Three main areas covered are health, safety and welfare as follows:

Health: Every factory must be kept clean with a conducive work environment. It must not be overcrowded; there must be proper temperature, fresh air and ventilation. Floors must not be wet and there must be suitable and sufficient hygiene and sanitary convenience recognizing the different sexes.

Safety: English legislation has influenced Sri Lankan law in the area of safety. It is required that there must be proper fencing of machinery, protection against dangerous substances, stairways, gangways to the property to be fenced, proper training before an employee is asked to work on machines and preventive measures in handling items like hoists, lifts, cranes, boilers and explosives etc. Provisions are also made against accidents by fire.

Welfare: The employer must supply safe drinking water, clothing for factory work, washing facilities, proper restrooms and seating facilities.

Workmen's compensation: The Workmen's Compensation Ordinance, first enacted in 1934, provides for the payment of compensation to workmen who are injured in the course of their employment. Since its enactment it has been amended several times especially by Act No. 15 of 1990. The Ordinance specifies and regulates the employer's liability to pay compensation and specifies the instances in which the compensation should be paid. The compensation has to be paid for an injury to a workman by accident arising out of and in the course of his employment and an occupational disease contracted by an employee whose service is not less than six months in any process which is directly attributable to the nature of his employment. The amount of compensation is to be determined by the Commissioner of Labour or his Authorised Officers depending on the nature of injury to the workman. Most employees take out insurance policies with insurers to cover this risk. An issue that normally arises is whether the accident to the workman arose "in the course of his employment". An accident that occurred when the workman was at his own home or at a time after or before work will not be covered. Also, the workman will not be covered for accidents caused when he was under the influence of liquor or drugs or was guilty of wilful disregard of the safety equipment and procedures provided at the workplace. A claim for workmen's compensation must also be made within two years of the accident. If an employer fails to pay, the workman or his dependant can apply to the Commissioner of Labour within one year of the accident. An employer who fails to pay within thirty days is liable to a surcharge, while wrongful refusal to pay can also result in a fine. A claim under the Workman's Compensation Ordinance does not prejudice the right of a workman or his dependants to institute proceedings in a District Court of the area where the accident occurred for the recovery of damages. However, in such a case he will be bound by the general principles of tort liability that usually require proof of negligence unless the employer was in breach of some duty imposed on him by statute. Any award for damages by the court will normally take into account any sum already paid to the workman under legislation.

Wages Boards: Wages Boards are bodies set up under the Wages boards Ordinance of 1941 (as amended) to ensure minimum wages and a few other conditions such as holidays, leave and overtime rates in respect of specified trades. As of 2013, Wages Boards had been set up for 55 trades such as Banking, beedi manufacturing, the brick and tile trade, cinema, coconut and rubber, garments, hotel and catering, janitorial services, metal quarrying, security services, textile, tobacco, etc. These Wages boards comprise an equal number of representatives of employers and employees in a given trade and up to three persons appointed by the Minister of Labour. Their principal function is to determine the minimum wage payable to workers in a particular trade. Many employees pay more than the minimum wage.

The minimum wage may be prescribed as a basic rate plus a special living allowance based on the cost of living index or a consolidated amount. Failure to pay at least the minimum wage is an offence. Employees can, however, receive a higher wage by agreement with the employer. They often do.

Shop and office employees: One of the most important and relevant statues in Sri Lankan Labour law is the Shop and Office Employees (Regulation of Employment and Remuneration) Act No. 19 of 1954. This legislation was the result of a report of a Committee of Inquiry appointed in the 1940s to examine the employment conditions of the country's mercantile employees. The Act applies to all employees within the definition of a "shop" or "office" and is in five parts as follows: Part I Regulation of hours of employment in shops and offices; health and comfort of employees; Part II Payment of remuneration; Part III Regulation of remuneration; Part IV Closing order for shops; Part V General matters.

Hours of work: The normal day's work is limited to hours and a normal working week is limited to 45 hours, excluding 1 hour for meals. Persons employed in different classes of shops and different classes of offices may have different hours of work, subject however, to several restrictions. Work in excess of the normal hours has to be treated as overtime and paid for at a rate not less than one and one-half times the hourly rate, calculated by dividing the monthly rate by 240. Executives in State Corporations are not entitled to overtime. The maximum amount of overtime is limited to 12 hours per week.

Weekly holidays: On completion of 28 hours of work in a "week", the law provides for the granting of one and half days' holidays with pay. "Week" is defined to mean the period between midnight on any Saturday night and midnight on the succeeding Saturday night.

Annual holidays: The total annual leave entitlement is 14, and provision is made when employment commences between certain specified periods for the granting of the corresponding number of days as leave, in the succeeding year. Public holidays are granted with remuneration. Full Moon Poya days should be observed as holidays. Employment on such days is strictly on an overtime basis.

Casual leave: The entitlement of casual leave for a calendar year is seven days. This is to be utilised on account of private business or ill-health. In the commencing year of employment, one day is granted for every two completed months.

Maternity leave: Female employees are entitled to maternity leave as provided in the statute. These entitlements are now well known. Maternity leave shall be in addition to other leave or holiday entitlements.

Salary payments and deductions: The Act placed time limitations within which employee's salaries should be paid and the deductions that may be made from such payments. Employers must strictly observe these conditions.

Letter of appointment: It is a fundamental requirement under the law that an employer issues a letter of appointment to the employee detailing the conditions of employment. This ensures to the employee certain inalienable rights under the law. The letter of appointment so issued becomes a contract between the parties. The minimum requirements of a letter of appointment are spelt out in the Act. However, most employers have developed terms and conditions over and above what is required by the legislation. It is expected that if the letter of appointment is in English it should be explained to the employee in his language (Sinhalese or Tamil) and he or she acknowledges that its terms and conditions were clearly understood. The employee is entitled to a copy of the letter of appointment.

Records of employees: Employers are obliged to maintain certain specified records in respect of their employees as provided by the legislation. This is normally done by maintaining a Register of staff and also a Personal file in respect of each employee which has a record of all details from date of joining.

5.4   Apprenticeship, probation and training

Many employees begin their career as apprentices, probationers and/or trainees. A contract of apprenticeship is one where the employer agrees to instruct or teach the apprentice in his trade and to pay him an allowance during the existence of the relationship. The apprentice in turn agrees to serve the master and to learn from him.

The case of the probationer is different and the assessment during the period of probation relates to his all-round suitability, which includes both his ability to perform the job and his conduct. In the case of an apprentice, the emphasis is on the learning of a skill and it follows that a person engages in a period of apprenticeship only in respect of a job which requires a certain degree of skill, which has to be acquired to perform the job. A probationer would also require some training but it would not necessarily be for the purpose of making him skilled as such.

Under the common law of employer and employee, an apprentice or trainee does not have a contract of service and is therefore not an employee. Yet, many of our statutes such as the Industrial Disputes Act, the Employees Provident Fund Act, the Termination of Employment of Workmen (Special Provisions) Act and the Gratuity Act define a "workman" to include an apprentice or trainee. Employers must be aware of this.

Probation is a period during which an employer assesses the conduct and suitability of an employee for continued employment and the employee similarly assesses the suitability of the conditions of service from his point of view. The period of probation is a contract of service can therefore be taken as a communication by the employer that in the event of the employee proving himself within the period of probation to the satisfaction of the employer that the probationer is a fit and proper person to perform the duties for which he has been engaged. The probationer would be entitled to be confirmed in employment at the end of the probation period and if not, his services can be terminated without notice.

It should be noted that a probationer is a permanent employee in the sense that he is on a monthly contract of employment and the period of probation is strictly relevant only to the question of termination in the event of the probationer being unsatisfactory.

As regards trainees, a statute that employers currently resort to is the Employment of Trainees (Private Sector) Act No. 8 of 1978. This legislation was enacted to boost training of unemployed persons. Those employing "trainees" under this Act are provided specified monetary incentives to pay such trainees but most employers pay more than what is statutorily provided.

Under it, without any prejudice to any scheme of training of, or to the employment of apprentices in any other law, an employer may enter into a contract of training with a person for a period not exceeding one year for the purpose of providing practical training to the trainee in any of the vocations specified in the Act and on the payment of a specified allowance. The vocations specified include: (a) clerks, stenographers, book-keepers, typists, supervisors, salesmen, shop assistants, storekeepers, telephone operators, cashiers, foremen or any other similar vocations; (b) watchers, caretakers, bicycle orderlies, peons, liftmen, office and shop labourers, outside messengers, tea boys or other similar vocations.

The legislation excludes the application of the following statutes to such trainees: The Shop and Office Employees Act, Industrial Disputed Act, Wages Boards Ordinance, Trade Unions Ordinance, Termination of Employment Act and any collective agreement.

The Act also provides for the employer to terminate such training on disciplinary grounds. After the training is over, the employer is expected to provide the "trainee" with employment in a vocation in which he was trained or in other suitable employment. Neglect or refusal to do so amounts to an offence and the Labour Department can initiate action.

Owing to the special requirements of the above legislation, a distinction should be drawn between contracts of training specifically entered under the provisions of the above law and those which are fixed term contracts of training not governed by the law. In the case of the latter, the provisions of Trainees(Private Sector) Act of 1978 will have no application. Consequently, the requirement of obtaining the approval of the Commissioner of Labour will not arise; as such contracts will be governed by the terms specified in such contracts.

5.5 Sexual harassment

According to Article 12(2) of the Constitution, discriminating against a person based on his or her sex is a violation of such person's fundamental right to equality. Sexual harassment is criminally punishable under Section 345 of the Penal Code (Amendment) Act, No. 22 of 1995. Sexual harassment constitutes "Harassment of a sexual nature using assault, criminal force, or words or actions which causes annoyance to the person being harassed". This includes unwelcome sexual advances by words or action used by a person in authority (e. g. Police, armed service personnel, school officials, medical officials and others) and unwelcome sexual advances in the work place.

Sexual harassment in the Penal Code may cover misuse of internet and emails that are obscene or make allegations of a sexual nature in order to harass, intimidate or embarrass. Encouraging or condoning sexual harassment is also a crime under the law.

Donor institutions have been urging various Sri Lankan governments to streamline labour law. However, the strong opposition of the unions and the many benefits that would be removed has made such rationalization difficult. The difficulty of terminating labour, a common problem in South Asia, encourages investors to look to countries in Southeast Asia which balance more equitably the interests of capital and labour.

Chapter 6   Environmental Law

6.1   Introduction

Despite its relatively small size of 65, 610 square kilometres, Sri Lanka is blessed with an astonishing natural diversity. Its beaches, marine life, and reefs are world famous. Some of the finest sapphires, rubies and other precious and semi-precious stones are mined in Sri Lanka. In the salubrious hill country, tea is grown at high elevations. Sri Lanka is also home to diverse fauna and flora and is a stop for migrating birds. It has many wildlife sanctuaries where elephants roam and leopards hunt. The cultural triangle boasts the ruins of cities and temples that are more than a thousand years old. Under the Roman law principle of *res communise* many of these facilities are open to the public unlike in the US where private beaches are not unusual.

According to Article 27 (14) of the Constitution, "The State shall protect, preserve and improve the environment for the benefit of the community". Article 28 (f) imposes a Fundamental Duty on every person in Sri Lanka "to protect nature and conserve its riches" (Article 28(f)). And yet, the bounty is under threat. Despite the existence of many laws that address environmental concerns, there is uneven enforcement and political patronage leads to outright despoliation of the environment. This uneven enforcement and confusion also has a detrimental effect on trade and investment because of the uncertainty that it generates.

The National Environmental Act (Section 33) defines the environment as "the physical factors of the surroundings of human beings, including the land, soil, water, atmosphere, climate, sound, odours, tastes and the biological factors of animals and plants of every description". However, just like the environment, the laws applicable to the environment are both local and international and have sources both in local legislation, international custom, principles of uncertain legal force such as the precautionary principle, and arbitral jurisprudence stemming from classic cases like the *Trail Smelter Arbitration* that was conducted in 1941. The award held that international environmental law applies not only to activities within a particular state but also to those areas beyond its territorial jurisdictions. Accordingly, although every state has sovereignty over its own natural resources, every state also has a responsibility not to cause trans-boundary environmental damage. Sometimes this duty may be compromised when in the interests of friendly relations do not bring actions against their neighbours for damage caused by forest fires. Sri Lanka is a member in the Convention on the International Trade of Endangered Species (CITES) and pursuant to its obligations under the CITES destroyed a large quantity of illegal ivory.

6.2　Geographic factors and the environment

In Sri Lanka there are 103 river basins in the island with the Mahaweli basin dominating in size (16 percent of the total area of the country) : 17 river basins are larger than 1,000 km^2, while 45 are less than 100 km^2. Most of these small basins have been confined within provincial boundaries and are located near the coastal belt. The overall annual average precipitation is more than 2,000 mm, but the monsoon climate and national geography create substantial variability in the amount of water that is available both locally and temporally.

Economic development, population pressure and growing demands for food production, electric power, and adequate water for domestic, industrial and commercial use and sanitation services place increasing pressure on water resources. In addition, current uses of water also include maintenance of carrying capacities for mitigation of impacts from effluent discharges from domestic and industrial pollutants. It also serves as a medium for maintenance of an environment for aquatic biota and reproduction of aquatic species associated with wetlands. Projections show that expected demand far outstrips supply, particularly in the country's dry zone where most of the irrigation schemes are located. The estimated future annual water deficit in this area is 2, 500 million cubic metres.

The available water resources have been subjected to competing uses without concern to its equitable distribution among users. There is no incentive for conserving water although many are deprived of basic requirements of water in terms of volume and acceptable quality for different purposes. There has been frequent water shortages arising from climatic changes and inefficient systems adopted in water use, in the light of rising economic, social and environmental demands.

6.3   Policy and regulatory framework

The relevant statutes are: Sri Lankan Legal Infrastructure Coast Conservation and Coastal Resource Management Act, No. 57 of 1981, as amended by Acts Nos. 64 of 1988 and 49 of 2011; Fauna and Flora Protection Ordinance (Cap 567 – 1980 Ed), as amended by Acts Nos. 49 of 1993 and 12 of 2005 State Lands Ordinance (Cap 286 – 1980 Ed); Sri Lanka Land Reclamation and Development Corporation Act (Cap 606 – 1981 Ed) as amended by Acts Nos. 52 of 1982 and 35 of 2006; Mines and Mineral Law No. 33 of 1992; Fisheries and Aquatic Resources Act, No. 2 of 1996; and National Environmental Act No. 44 of 1980 as amended by Acts Nos. 56 of 1988 and 53 of 2000.

The courts have invoked the doctrine of public trust in environmental law cases to ensure against environmental abuse by state organs as well as by private individuals. According to this doctrine, public power must not be used for personal gain or favour, but always be used to optimise the benefit of the people. To do otherwise, the courts have held, would be to betray the trust reposed by the people within whom, in terms of the Constitution, the sovereignty reposes.

6.4   The role of the courts and the judges

The Magistrates Court implements the provisions of the Act and tries criminal cases (*Karunaratne v Boteju* 7 NLR 127). The Court of Appeal exercises supervisory jurisdiction over the administrative decisions of the Department of other agencies (*Amarasinghe and Others v The Attorney General and Others* [1993] 1 Sri LR 376, *Public Interest Law Foundation v Central Environmental Authority and Another* [2001] 3 Sri LR 230). The Supreme Court of Sri Lanka deals with appeals from the Court of Appeal and also with Article 126 applications for the redress of violations or imminent violations of fundamental rights (*Bulankulame v Secretary, Ministry of Industrial Development (Eppawela Case)* [2000] 3 SLR 243, *Environmental Foundation Guarantee Ltd and others Mahaweli Authority of Sri Lanka* [2010] 1 SLR 1, *Environmental Foundation Guarantee Ltd and others v The Director General of Wild Life Conservation and others* SC FR Application No. 224/10).

Appendix

National Environmental Act No. 47 of 1980 (as amended by Acts No. 56 of 1988 and 53 of 2000) and the Regulations under the Act establish the Central Environmental Authority (CEA) and define its powers, functions and duties. It provides overall environmental protection legislation, including licensing procedures, environmental standards and project approval procedures.

Fauna and Flora Protection Ordinance No. 2 of 1937(as amended by Act Nos. 49 of 1993, 12 of 2005) and the Regulations under the Ordinance provide for the conservation of plants and animals, which have been declared as protected species. The Act empowers the Minister to declare any area of State land as a National Reserve or Sanctuary.

Forest Ordinance No. 16 of 1907 (as amended) and the Rules and Regulations under the Ordinance consolidate the laws relating to forests and to the felling and transportation of timber. It empowers the Minister to declare an area of State land as a Reserved Forest, Conservation Forest or a Village Forest.

Mahaweli Authority of Sri Lanka Act No. 23 of 1979 (as amended) and the Regulations under the Act established the Mahaweli Authority of Sri Lanka and provide for the conservation and maintenance of the physical environment of Mahaweli Areas, including watershed management, soil erosion and the protection of reservation areas.

State Lands Ordinance No. 8 of 1947 (Parts VI, VIII, IX) provides for how State lands and their resources, including lakes, rivers and streams, should be allocated, used and managed. It also provides for the declaration of State reservations.

Mines and Minerals Act No. 33 of 1992 regulates mining, exploitation processing, trading and export of minerals.

Irrigation Ordinance No. 32 of 1946 (Part VI) deals with environmental aspects of water, irrigation and land use in irrigated agricultural activities.

Water Resources Board Act No. 29 of 1964 establishes the Water Resources Board and sets out its duties, which include promotion of a forestation, preventing the pollution of rivers, streams and other water courses, and formulation of national policies relating to the control and use of water resources of the country.

Coast Conservation Act No. 57 of 1981 identifies coastal zones and regulates activities within such zones.

Marine Pollution Prevention Act No. 35 of 2008 provides for the prevention, reduction, and control and management of marine pollution in the Territorial Waters of Sri Lanka, any other maritime zone, the foreshore and the coastal zone of Sri

Lanka. It also provides for the establishment of the Marine Environment Protection Authority.

Fisheries and Aquatic Resources Act No. 2 of 1996 makes provision to protect and conserve fisheries and aquatic biodiversity in marine and freshwater areas, for the declaration of fisheries reserves and imposes licensing and registration requirements with regard to fishing. It defines the terms "Sri Lankan Waters".

National Heritage Wilderness Areas Act No. 3 of 1988 provides for the declaration, protection and preservation of any area of State land with unique ecosystems, genetic resources or outstanding natural features as National Heritage Wilderness Areas.

Soil Conservation Act No. 25 of 1951 provides for the conservation of soil resources, mitigation of soil erosion and the protection of lands against flood and drought.

Plant Protection Act No. 35 of 1999 provides for the prevention of wild plants, weeds and plant diseases and controls the introduction of new plant species.

Felling of Trees (Control) Act No. 9 of 1951 provides for the prohibition, regulation and control of the felling of specified tree species, including cultivated tree species such as Jak.

Flood Protection Ordinance No. 4 of 1924 provides for the protection of areas from flood damage and empowers the Director of Irrigation to declare any area as a flood area.

Water Hyacinth Ordinance No. 4 of 1909 provides for preventing the importation, introduction into dissemination in Sri Lanka of the plant known as Water Hyacinth.

Control of Pesticides Act No. 33 of 1980 provides for the licensing and regulation of the import, packing, labelling, storage, formulation, transportation, sale and use of pesticides.

Atomic Energy Authority Act No. 19 of 1969 provides for the establishment of the Atomic Energy Authority, which is empowered to control and regulate the importation, exportation, production, acquisition, transportation, treatment, storage and disposal of radioactive materials.

Health Services Act No. 12 of 1952 provides for the regulation of the environmental aspects of human health.

Municipal Councils Ordinance No. 29 of 1947 provides for the establishment of

Municipal Councils and outline their powers, duties and responsibilities in relation to the built environment and matters such as waste disposal and sanitation.

Urban Councils Ordinance No. 61 of 1939 provides for the establishment of Urban Councils and outlines their powers, duties and responsibilities in relation to the built environment and maters such as waste disposal and sanitation.

Pradeshiya Sabha Act No. 15 of 1987 provides for the establishment of PradeshiyaSabhas and outlines their powers, duties and responsibilities in relation to the built environment and maters such as waste disposal and sanitation.

Urban Development Authority Law No. 41 of 1978 empowers the Urban Development Authority to regulate and manage the urban environment.

Sri Lanka Land Reclamation and Development Corporation Act No. 15 of 1968 empowers the Sri Lanka Land Reclamation and Development Corporation to reclaim low-lying lands and wetlands.

Agrarian Development Act No. 46 of 2000 (Part II) provides for the utilisation of agricultural lands in accordance with agricultural policies, having regard to natural resources.

National Aquaculture Development Authority of Sri Lanka Act No. 53 of 1998 establishes the National Aquaculture Development Authority of Sri Lanka and provides for the development of aquatic resources.

Sri Lanka Sustainable Energy Authority Act No. 35 of 2007 establishes the Sri Lanka Sustainable Energy Authority and provides for the development of renewable energy sources and the implementation of energy efficiency measures and conservation programs.

Section 98 and Section 261 of the Penal Code provide for the removal or abatement of public nuisances.

Nuisances Ordinance No. 15 of 1862 provides for the preservation of public health and the suppression of various types of nuisances.

Chapter 7   Courts and Dispute Settlement

7.1   Judicial settlement of disputes

The hierarchy of Courts of first instance in Sri Lanka is set out in Section 2 of the Judicature Act No. 2 of 1978. Primary Courts, Magistrate's Courts, District Courts and High Courts are the courts of first instance. High Courts exercise appellate and review jurisdiction in some matters. The Court of Appeal and the Supreme Court are the Appellate Courts.

7.1.1   Primary Court and Magistrate's Court

The Primary Court is the lowest Court of first instance. It has limited powers to impose a sentence of imprisonment and of fines. This Court has limited jurisdiction both in relation to civil and criminal disputes. One of the most important subjects, which are very frequently invoked in a Primary Court is Section 66 of the Primary Courts Procedure Act which deals with inquiries into disputes affecting land, where a breach of the peace is threatened or is likely. The monetary jurisdiction of a Primary Court does not exceed Rs. 1,500. The Magistrate of the area acts also as a Primary Court Judge. Magistrate's Courts exercise original jurisdiction in criminal cases subject to limitations on their powers to impose punishments. They also conduct non-summary proceedings before indictment to the High Court. There is a right of appeal and revision from a Magistrate's Court to the High Court in the first instance and thereafter to the Court of Appeal or the Supreme Court in the second instance. In some cases where appeal is made to the Court of Appeal an appeal lies from the order of the Court of Appeal to the Supreme Court if leave is obtained. A Magistrate's Court can impose a sentence of imprisonment for a period not exceeding eighteen months and impose a fine not exceeding one thousand five hundred rupees; several offences under various statutes are also tribal by the Magistrate's Courts.

7.1.2   District Court

A District Court has unlimited civil jurisdiction in all civil, revenue, trust, insolvency and testamentary matters. The jurisdiction of the District Courts in relation to family matters was removed and Family Courts were established to deal with such matters. With the enactment of the Judicature (Amendment) Act No. 71 of 1981, the District Courts are deemed to be the Family Courts. The jurisdiction in respect of causes of action arising out of commercial transactions and a few matters under the specified provisions of the Code of Intellectual Property Act and the Companies Act is now vested in the Commercial High Court. There is a right of appeal and revision from orders and judgments of District Courts to the Court of Appeal and an appeal thereafter, with leave obtained, to the Supreme Court.

7.1.3   High Court

The High Court of Sri Lanka established under the Constitution has power and authority to hear, try and determine all prosecutions on indictment. It has criminal and admiralty jurisdiction and also jurisdiction in regard to offences committed aboard aircraft and within the territorial air space. A High Court trial can be either by the High Court Judge alone or with a jury. It also can hold a Trial-At-Bar where three Judges nominated by the Chief Justice sit in judgment. A party aggrieved by a decision of the High Court can appeal to the Court of Appeal and the Appeal is heard by a Bench of not less than two judges. The High Court is empowered to pass death sentence, life imprisonment and impose fines and give other redress as laid down. In addition to the High Court of Sri Lanka originally established, under the Constitution the 13th Amendment to the Constitution also established a High Court for each province designated as the High Court of the relevant Province and such High Court is now vested with (a) original criminal jurisdiction in respect of offences committed within the Province; (b) appellate and revisionary jurisdiction in respect of convictions, sentence and orders made or imposed by Magistrate's or Primary Courts within the Province; (c) such other jurisdiction and power as the Parliament may provide by law; (d) power to issue Orders in the nature of Habeas Corpus in respect of persons illegally detained within the Province; (e) power to issue Orders in the nature of Writs of Certiorari, Prohibition, Procedendo, Mandamus and Quo Warrantor in respect of any matter set out in the Provincial Council List; and (f) power to inspect and report on the administration of any Court of first instance within the Province as may be delegated by the Judicial Service Commission.

7.1.4   Commercial High Court

The High Court for the Western Province is vested with exclusive jurisdiction in respect of some specified commercial matters in terms of the High Court of the Provinces (Special Provisions) Act No. 10 of 1996 and it was ceremonially opened by the Minister of Justice and Constitutional Affairs on 11 October 1996. The Western Provincial Commercial High Court is vested with Provincial jurisdiction in respect of the following matters with effect from 11 October 1996:

All actions where the cause of action has arisen out of commercial transactions including causes of action relating to banking, export or import of merchandise, services, freightment, insurance, mercantile agency, mercantile usage, and the construction of any mercantile document in which the debt, damage or demand is for a sum exceeding Rs. 3 Million;

All applications and proceedings under Sections 31, 51, 131, 210 and 211 of the Companies Act No. 17 of 1982, i. e. actions to relieve a Company of the consequences of non-compliance with the conditions constituting it a private company (s. 31); actions to make irregular allotments void and actions to recover loss, damage or costs incurred as a result of such irregular allotments (s. 51); actions for a Court to order a meeting of a Company to be held as specified where compliance with the Articles of the Company or the provisions of the Companies Act is impracticable (s. 131); applications complaining against oppression in the conduct of the affairs of a company (s. 210); applications complaining of mismanagement (s. 211);

All proceedings under the Code of Intellectual Property Act No. 52 of 1979 other than proceedings required to be taken in terms of this Act in the District Court of Colombo, must be instituted in the Commercial High Court.

The Commercial High Court does not have jurisdiction in respect of actions instituted under the Debt Recovery (Special Provisions) Act No. 2 of 1990.

The Court has jurisdiction in respect of where the defendant/defendants resides/reside or the cause of action has arisen or the contract sought to be enforced was made or the registered office of the Company is situated within the Western Province.

The High Court of the Provinces (Special Provisions) Act No. 10 of 1996 includes provision for the Minister to make an order vesting in the Western Provincial High Court all island jurisdiction in respect of actions seeking an injunction against the Registrar of Companies or the Securities Exchange Commission all proceedings required to be taken in the District Court of Colombo under the Code of Intellectual

Property Act No. 52 of 1979 and all appeals required to be made under Section 17 of the Fair Trading Commission Act No. 1 of 1987. The making of an order for this purpose by the Minister in the Gazette appears to have been deferred as the Ministry wishes to assess the working of the new Court and then decide on that aspect.

An appeal against an order or judgment of the Court may be made directly to the Supreme Court.

7.1.5 The Court of Appeal

The Court of Appeal established by Chapter XV of the Constitution is constituted of not less than six and not more than eleven judges. It has appellate jurisdiction for the correction of all errors of fact or law committed by any Court of first instance and also revisionary powers and powers relating to restitution in integrum. It has the power to issue Writs of Certiorari, Mandamus, Prohibition, Procedendo Quo Warrantor, and Habeas Corpus and to issue injunctions and examination of records of courts of first instance. It tries parliamentary election petitions. There is a right of appeal from this Court to the Supreme Court (subject to the provisions in Article 128 of the Constitution) with leave had and obtained.

7.1.6 The Supreme Court

The Supreme Court is the highest and final appellate court of the Republic of Sri Lanka consisting of the Chief Justice and not less than six and not more than ten other judges. It has jurisdiction in respect of Bills and interpretation of the Constitution; final appellate jurisdiction; fundamental rights jurisdiction; sole jurisdiction in relation to Presidential Election Petitions, validity of referendums and breach of privileges of Parliament; and consultative jurisdiction on matters referred to it by His Excellency the President. Both the Supreme Court and the Court of Appeal have the power to punish for contempt of such courts and the power to punish for contempt of any other court, tribunal or institution.

7.1.7 Administrative Tribunals

Apart from ordinary courts of law there are a number of administrative tribunals such as the Rent Board of Review, Rent Boards, Ceiling on Housing Property Board of Review, Land Acquisition Board of Review, Agricultural Tribunals and Labour Tribunals, which perform functions of a quasi-judicial nature. Their decisions are subject to the revisionary and appellate jurisdiction of the higher courts.

7.1.8   Meditation Boards

The Mediation Boards Act No. 72 of 1988 established Mediation Boards which operate in various areas in Sri Lanka. A Commission appointed under this Act appoints a panel of mediators to mediate on certain criminal and civil matters, where the State, a public officer or the Attorney General is not involved as a party. Mediation Boards have the power to issue certificates of non-settlement without which a Court of first instance may not entertain any action in relation to movable or immovable property, debt, damage or demand which does not exceed Rs. 25,000.00 in value, matters not specified in the third schedule to the said Act or offences falling within those specified in the second schedule to the Act. The main function of Mediation Boards is to settle disputes amicably.

7.2   Arbitration

The Arbitration Act No. 11 of 1995 (the Act) governs arbitration in Sri Lanka. The Act gives effect to the 1958 New York Convention on the Recognition and Enforcement of Foreign Arbitral awards. Sri Lanka ratified the Convention without any reservation. Unlike Singapore and some other countries which have a dual track system of arbitration, the Act applies uniformly to the conduct of domestic arbitrations as well as to international commercial arbitrations with a foreign element where at least one of the parties is a citizen of another country, a company incorporated abroad or a foreign government. Concepts such as party autonomy, minimal judicial intervention, independence and impartiality of the tribunal and effective enforcement of awards are respected by the provisions of the Sri Lankan Act, which recognises that domestic arbitration proceedings are "consensual in nature and private in character". The Act is based on the UNICITRAL Model Law (the Model Law). The Act does not provide for confidentiality either in arbitration proceedings or in respect of the award. However, the parties could include a confidentiality clause in the arbitration agreement that would be enforceable.

The courts are supportive of international arbitration and will not accept jurisdiction where there is a valid arbitration agreement. In *Elgitread Lanka (Pvt) Ltd v Bino Tyres (Pvt)* Ltd, the franchise agreement provided for arbitration where the appointing authority was the "Sri Lanka Chamber of Commerce and Industry". No such institution existed and the lower court held in view of this fact that the agreement to arbitrate was void. The Supreme Court reversed that decision and held that the mere fact that there the named arbitration institution was not in existence did not make the clause in operative, and that the clause was an agreement to arbitrate. The Court referred to Section 7 of the Act which provided for the appointment of arbitrators by the High Court when the parties had not chosen arbitrators. It held that this section applied and that the party seeking arbitration could avail of this section and thus proceeds to submit the dispute to arbitration.

7.2.1   Ad hoc arbitration

In an ad hoc arbitration with a sole arbitrator, the Act requires that the two parties must agree on the arbitrator. If they are unable to do so, an arbitrator can be appointed by the High Court. In an arbitration with three arbitrators, each party must appoint one arbitrator, and the two arbitrators thus appointed must appoint a third. If a party fails to appoint an arbitrator within 60 days of receipt of a request from the other party, or if the two arbitrators fail to agree on the third arbitrator within 60 days of their appointment, the appointment shall be made upon the application of a party, by the High Court.

In the event of a party failing to appoint an arbitrator, the party referring the matter to arbitration must apply to the High Court (Section 7(3)). If a party to a valid arbitration agreement institutes legal proceedings in court, and the other party objects to the court exercising jurisdiction in this respect, the court will refuse to hear and determine the matter (Section 5).

If a party fails to appear before the tribunal without reasonable cause, or fails to comply with an order made by the tribunal, the tribunal may continue the arbitration proceedings and determine the dispute on the basis of the material available (Section 15(3) of the Act). The Act does not provide for a tribunal to proceed *ex parte*.

7.2.2   The role of the courts in arbitration proceedings

Reflecting the approach of the UNCITRAL Model Law, the Sri Lankan courts have no general jurisdiction to hear and determine matters covered by a valid arbitration agreement (Section 5 of the Act). However, the Act does give the High Court limited jurisdiction on matters such as the removal of arbitrators and the setting aside of an arbitral award. For instance, the Act permits the High Court to remove an arbitrator in circumstances that give rise to justifiable doubts as to that individual's impartiality or independence. Either party may request that an arbitrator be removed within 30 days of becoming aware of the relevant circumstances. If, having made such a request, the party is dissatisfied with the tribunal's decision, it may, within 30 days of being informed of it, appeal the matter to the High Court. If an arbitrator unduly delays in discharging their duties, the High Court may, upon the application of either party, remove the arbitrator and appoint another in that person's place.

7.2.3   Challenges to the appointment of an arbitrator

When requested to serve as an arbitrator, a person must disclose any circumstances likely to give rise to justifiable doubts as to his impartiality or independence. This duty continues throughout the arbitral proceedings. A party may challenge an arbitrator whom they have appointed only for reasons of which they became aware after the appointment was made. Unless the parties have agreed otherwise, a party who seeks to challenge an arbitrator must do so before the tribunal, within 30 days of becoming aware of the circumstances that give rise to doubts about the arbitrator's impartiality or independence. Should the tribunal hold against that party, it may appeal to the High Court within 30 days of receipt of the tribunal's decision.

An arbitrator may be challenged if that individual does not have the qualifications required under the agreement; if he or she becomes unable to perform their duties; or if they unduly delay in discharging their duties.

7.2.4   Interim orders

The Act permits an arbitral tribunal to issue interim orders. Section 13(1) of the Act, empowers an arbitral tribunal "at the request of a party, [to] order any other party to take such interim measures as it may consider necessary to protect or secure the claim which forms the subject matter of the dispute. The arbitral tribunal may also order the party making such request to provide the party ordered to take such interim measures, with security for any expense, loss or damage that may be caused in taking such interim measures. Provided however that, other than in exceptional cases no such order shall be made except after hearing the other parties".

Interim relief available covers: Injunctive relief, security for costs, security for the amount in dispute, pre-arbitration disclosure of documents, and the preservation of evidence. The High Court is required to enforce such interim measures if necessary.

7.2.5   Enforcement of awards

Section 31 of the Act requires applications to enforce arbitration awards to be made within one year and 14 days of the award. Section 33 of the Act enumerates the circumstances under which an award rendered in Sri Lanka can be set aside. This section mirrors the grounds for setting aside awards contained in the UNCITRAL Model Law. Section 34 of the Act provides for the enforcement of foreign arbitral awards in accordance with the New York Convention. Enforcement can take between two and four years, depending on whether the enforcement is challenged.

The procedures for enforcement of domestic and foreign arbitration awards are the same. An application must be made within one year after the expiry of 14 days after the making of the award (any correction, modification or interpretation of the award having been made during the 14-day period). The application, supported by an affidavit, must be accompanied by the original award and arbitration agreement, or duly certified copies. Translations of these documents must also be submitted if they are in a language other than English or the official language of the court.

The time taken to enforce an award varies from case to case. If an appeal is made to the Supreme Court from an order of the High Court, it may take up to three to four years from the time the order is filed in the High Court to complete the case. If there is no appeal, a party may be able to complete forcemeat proceedings in the High Court in about two years from the time of filing the award.

7.2.6   Arbitration institutions and arbitration rules in Sri Lanka

There are two main arbitral institutions in Sri Lanka: the Sri Lanka National Arbitration Centre (Sri Lanka Centre) established in 1985 and the Institute for the Development of Commercial Law and Practice Arbitration Centre (ICLP Centre) established in 1996.

The Sri Lanka National Arbitration Centre was the first institution in Sri Lanka to administer arbitrations. It does not have its own set of arbitration rules, nor does it act as an appointing authority.

The ICLP Centre has regular rules and expedited rules. However, even if the arbitration is conducted at the ICLP Centre, the parties may agree to use alternative institutional rules or ad hoc procedures for the arbitration. The ICLP Centre also acts as an appointing authority.

An overview of ICLP Centre rules

The ICLP rules are modelled on the rules of the Arbitration Institute of the Stockholm Chamber of Commerce and only changes have been made where necessary to make the ICLP Centre rules accord with Sri Lankan laws and conditions. The rules provide that the ICLP Centre may conduct arbitration proceedings under rules such as UNCITRAL rules and ICC rules.

The ICLP will appoint arbitrators in the following circumstances (Rule 7): Two party-appointed arbitrators fail to appoint a chair, the parties are unable to agree upon a sole arbitrator; an arbitrator resigns or is removed (if this arbitrator was party appointed, the Board will act in concurrence with that party).

The ICLP rules also provide for instances where arbitrators may be challenged and for the disqualification of arbitrators (Rules 9 and 10).

A party wishing to challenge an arbitrator must set out its reasons in writing for the Board (with copies to the arbitrators and to each of the other parties). The Board can also decide that an arbitrator is disqualified (with effect from the date of its decision).

The Board can remove an arbitrator for failure to perform their duties in an adequate manner. Before a decision on removal is made, the Board must ascertain the views of the parties and the arbitrators. The award has to be made not later than one year after the case has been referred to the arbitral tribunal; however, the Board has discretion to extend this period if appropriate (Rule 25).

The parties are free to determine the number of arbitrators and the procedure for appointing them.

Ad hoc arbitration under the ICLP rules

A request for arbitration must be made by the claimant in writing to the ICLP Centre. The request must contain the names and addresses of the parties and a statement of claim along with a brief description of the dispute, and may also include the appointment of an arbitrator (Rule 1). If the ICLP Board approves the request, the respondent will be required to submit a reply within a fixed time. The reply may contain the appointment of an arbitrator (Rule 5). After receiving the request for arbitration and the reply from the respondent, the chair of the tribunal (or a sole arbitrator) can be appointed.

The ICLP Board will determine the place of arbitration unless the parties have done so and will fix an amount to be paid as security for costs. As soon as this amount has been paid, the ICLP Board will refer the case to the arbitral tribunal.

ICLP Centre rules on refusal of failure by one party to participate

The failure by the respondent to submit a reply does not prevent proceedings from continuing (Rule 5). In the event that a party fails to appoint an arbitrator within the time prescribed by the ICLP Board, the Board must make the appointment (Rule 7). If a party fails to appear at a hearing or to comply with an order of the tribunal without good reason, the tribunal will proceed with the case or render the award(Rule 23). However, if circumstances require an order against a third party— in order to maintain the status quo or protect or secure the claim, a party to the arbitration would have recourse to court to obtain interim relief against the third party. Other than in exceptional cases, an order for interim relief is only granted after the tribunal has heard the other party. If a party refuses to comply with an order for interim relief, the party requesting the relief may apply to the High Court for enforcement.

The Act allows any party to an arbitration agreement(having obtained the prior consent in writing of the tribunal)to apply to the High Court for a summons requiring a person to attend for examination before the tribunal and to produce to the tribunal any document or thing specified in the summons(Section 20(1)). A person cannot be compelled under any summons to answer any question or produce any document or thing which that person could not be compelled to answer or produce at the trial in an action before the court(Section 20(2)).

The High Court is empowered to order a defaulter to appear before the court for examination, or to produce to the court the relevant document or thing, if a party applies to court in that regard (Section 21). A defaulter will be anyone summoned before a tribunal who:(a)refuses or fails to attend examination;(b)when appearing as a witness, refuses or fails to take an oath or make an affirmation or affidavit when required to do so, (c)refuses or fails to answer a question that the witness is required by the tribunal to answer, (d) refuses or fails to produce a requisite document, or (e)refuses or fails to do any other thing which the tribunal may require.

Challenges to an arbitration under the ICLP Centre rules

A party wishing to challenge an arbitrator must set out its reasons in writing and submit them to the ICLP Board, the arbitrators and the other parties(Rule 9). The

Board decides whether an arbitrator may be disqualified and notifies the arbitrator (who is deemed to have been removed with effect from the date of that decision) (Rule 10). The Board may remove an arbitrator for failure to perform their duties in an adequate manner. Before removing an arbitrator, the Board must as certain the view of the parties and the arbitrators.

The costs of arbitration

A senior practitioner, Mr SL Gunasekera in his book *The Lore of the Law and Other Memories* castigates arbitration practice in Sri Lanka on the ground that arbitrators, usually retired judges, unnecessarily prolong arbitration hearings in order to earn more fees.

The costs of arbitration depend on the rules selected by the parties. Generally, each party bears its own legal costs. In arbitration with a sole arbitrator, the two parties share the arbitrator's fees equally. In arbitration with three arbitrators, each party pays for its own nominated arbitrator, and the fees of the third arbitrator are shared equally between the parties. The parties are also required to share equally the administrative charges of the institution at which the arbitration is held. The tribunal may order the parties to pay a security deposit before commencing arbitration proceedings. At the conclusion of the hearing, the tribunal may award costs at its discretion.

The Act allows for interest to be paid at a rate agreed by the parties or at the legal interest prevailing at the time of making the award. This is to be paid on the principal sum awarded, from the date of commencement of proceedings to the date of the award (in addition to any interest awarded on the principal for any period before proceedings were instituted), with further interest at the same rate on the aggregate sum from the date of the award to the date of payment (or any earlier date determined by the tribunal) (Section 28 of the Act).

Under the ICLP rules (32 to 34), the tribunal must decide in the award the amount of fees due to the ICLP Centre and the arbitrators. The parties will be liable jointly and severally for the payment of all such sums. The party against whom the award is made must pay the fees and costs as well as the fees and costs of the other party unless the circumstances call for a different result.

When a case is terminated before it has been referred to the tribunal, the ICLP Centre must decide the amount of compensation due to it. When a case is terminated before an award has been rendered, the tribunal may decide that the parties shall pay compensation to the ICLP Centre and the arbitrators. An award may be rendered even if it deals only with cost.

The fees of arbitrators must be reasonable in amount and based upon the time spent, the complexity of the case, the amount in dispute and other circumstances. The amount of fees due to the ICLP Centre will be based on its own regulations.

Non-signatories and arbitration

The Act does not address the issue of participation by or enforcement of awards against non-signatories. It is likely that the Sri Lankan courts would take a formalistic view that the arbitration agreement only binds the parties to the arbitration agreement and no others. Accordingly, where one of the parties is an under-capitalised special purpose vehicle, it would be prudent to seek corporate guarantees or provide for the involvement of non-signatories in the arbitration agreement.

7.3   Enforcement of foreign judgments

Judgments entered by Courts in some foreign countries can be enforced under the Reciprocal Enforcement of Judgments Ordinance. Those covered by the Reciprocal Enforcement of Judgments Ordinance are United Kingdom of Great Britain, Northern Ireland, Hong Kong of China, Mauritius, New South Wales, Straits Settlements, Tanganyika, Uganda, Victoria, Federation of Malaya, Australian Capital Territory, Northern Territory of Australia, New Zealand(including the Cook and Nicue Islands) and the Trust Territory of Western Samoa, Queensland, Western Australia, South Australia and Tasmania.

Foreign judgments also create a debt against the judgment debtor and this can be sued for in the Sri Lankan courts just as ordinary contractual debts.

Legal rules of interest

Section 192 of the Civil Procedure Code(as amended by the Act No. 6 of 1990) provides that

"When an action instituted for recover of a sum of money due to the plaintiff, in that action the Court may in the decree order interest according to the rate agreed on between the parties by the instrument sued on, or in the absence of any such agreement at the legal rate, to be paid, on the principal sum adjudged from the date of action to the date of the decree, in addition to any interest adjudged on such principal sum for any period prior to the institution of the action, with further interest at such rate on the aggregate sum so adjudged from the date of the decree to the date of payment, or to such earlier date as the Court thinks fit. "

For the purposes of this Section 192, "the legal rate" is defined to mean the rate per centum perannum determined by the Monetary Board established by the Monetary Law Act, by Notification published in the Gazette, having regard to current rates of bank interest.

Where such decree is silent with regard to the payment of further interest on such aggregate sum as aforesaid from the date of the decree to date of payment or other earlier date, the Court shall be deemed to have refused such interest, and a separate action therefore shall not lie.

Table 1 a summary of the changed in the legal rate of interest is provided:

Table 1. Legal Rate of Interest

No.	Legal Rate of Interest	Effective Date	Relevant Act/Gazette
1.	5% p. a.	1944 onwards	Civil Procedure Code
2.	12% p. a.	11. 12. 1980 05. 03. 1990	Civil Procedure Code (Amendment) Act No. 53 of 1980
3.	18% p. a.	06. 03. 1990 31. 12. 1996	Civil Procedure Code (Amendment) Act No. 6 of 1990 and Gazette Extraordinary No. 613 dated 04. 06. 1990
4.	12. 7% p. a.	01. 01. 1997 31. 12. 1997	Gazette Extraordinary No. 954111 dated 20. 12. 1996
5.	11. 5% p. a.	01. 01. 1998 31. 12. 1999	Gazette Extraordinary No. 100518 dated 10. 12. 1997
6.	9. 1% p. a.	01. 01. 2000 31. 12. 2000	Gazette Extraordinary No. 111211 dated 28. 12. 1999
7.	9. 21% p. a.	01. 01. 2001 01. 12. 2001	Gazette Extraordinary No. 116416 dated 29. 12. 2000
8.	11. 11%	01. 01. 2002 31. 12. 2002	Gazette Extraordinary No. 121615 dated 26. 12. 2001
9.	9. 58%	01. 01. 2003 onwards	Gazette Extraordinary No. 126818 dated 26. 12. 2002

The legal rate of interest was five percent up to 11 December 1980 as provided for in the said Section 192, which was amended by the Amendment Act No. 53 of 1980, increasing the rate to 12 percent. On 6 March 1990 Section 192 was amended, enabling the Monetary Board to determine from time to time the current rates of bank interest.